Affects as Process

An Inquiry into the Centrality of
Affect in Psychological Life

Psychoanalytic Inquiry Book Series

Volume 14

Psychoanalytic Inquiry Book Series

Affects as Process

An Inquiry into the Centrality of Affect in Psychological Life

Joseph M. Jones

With a Foreword by Joseph D. Lichtenberg

THE ANALYTIC PRESS

1995   Hillsdale, NJ   London

Published by
The Analytic Press, Inc.
365 Broadway
Hillsdale, New Jersey 07642

Library of Congress Cataloging-in-Publication Data

Jones, Joseph M. (Joseph Morse)
   Affects as process : an inquiry into the centrality of affect in
psychological life / Joseph M. Jones.
      p.   cm. -- (Psychoanalytic inquiry book series ; v. 14)
   Includes bibliographical references and index.
   ISBN 0-88163-125-6
   1. Affect (Psychology)   2. Psychoanalysis.   I. Title.
II. Series.
BF175.5.A35J66   1995
152.4—dc20   94-46492
                                                           CIP

Printed in the United States of America
10 9 8 7 6 5 4 3 2 1

*For Steve, Bob,
and Sylvia*

Interesting philosophy is rarely an examination of the pros and cons of a thesis. Usually it is, implicitly or explicitly, a contest between an entrenched vocabulary which has become a nuisance and a half-formed new vocabulary which vaguely promises great things.

Richard Rorty (1989)

Contents

x   *Contents*

Acknowledgments

Many people have helped me, in one way or another, in the writing of this book and I owe thanks to each of them. During the late 1970s, I had the opportunity to design and then teach the "Basic Freud" course, first at the Graduate Center for Child Development and Psychotherapy and then at the Los Angeles Psychoanalytic Society and Institute. Teaching the course entailed not only a reading and rereading of Freud's basic theoretical papers, but trying to make them understandable to the students. As I immersed myself in Freud's thought, I became more and more convinced that the difficulties in constructing a psychoanalytic theory of affects were the result of Freud's covert philosophic agenda, which stripped affects of their metaphysical sanction (i.e., their process role). Fortunately, I was able to discuss the philosophic problems with Stephen Erickson—a close friend and chairman of the department of philosophy at Pomona—who convinced me that my ideas were worth pursuing. I am deeply grateful for his assistance and encouragement, particularly with the first essay, "Is Primary Process Primary?"

In the early 1980s, I wrote three papers on affects that were presented at the Los Angeles Psychoanalytic Society and Institute. One of these papers, "Affects: A Nonsymbolic Information Processing System," was presented as a precirculated paper at the winter meeting of the American Psychoanalytic Association. After the presentation—which itself was fairly traumatic for me—I was told that the paper was unfit for publication without major revisions! The rejection left me feeling very discouraged, and for several years I quit writing. During those years Henry Krystal was an important source of encouragement. Even more important was Robert Stolorow, without whose support and a working through of some of the resistances to presenting my ideas to the psychoanalytic community, this book would never have been written. Again, I am deeply grateful.

I also want to acknowledge the invaluable assistance of my editor, John Kerr, whose knowledge of psychoanalytic theory and incisive critique helped me achieve a degree of clarity in exposition that—I hope—does justice to the material. At times, I felt as if we were writing the book together. Nothing I can say in this short paragraph would do justice to his assistance and contributions. I would also like to thank Joseph Lichtenberg for his encouragement and for contributing the foreword to the book. In addition, I would like to thank Sue Clamage, who retyped the 20 or more drafts of this book, and Claudia Kohner, who was invaluable in helping me prepare the final draft of the manuscript. I am also indebted to The Analytic Press for their patience and forbearance at the slow gestation of this book and to Eleanor Starke Kobrin (Lenni) and Nancy J. Liguori at The Analytic Press for their help in shepherding this book through the final stages of preparation and into publication.

I also want to acknowledge the help of many members of the psychoanalytic community who read, critiqued, and offered suggestions for improvement of several of the chapters. I owe particular thanks to Mel Lansky, whose chapter on "The Explanation of Impulsive Action" provided the impetus for my chapter on "Thought Dysfunctions"; our discussions helped me clarify my thinking not only on this subject but also on the difficult topic of "internal objects." I would also like to thank Richard Tuch, as well as the Western Self Psychology Study Group, for their valuable critique of the chapter on "Affects and the Self." Joel Kotin provided valuable comments on many of the early chapters. I would also like to thank Jimmy Fisher for his assistance.

Finally, I am indebted to my wife, Sylvia Jones, not only for reading and rereading many of the drafts of the book and offering helpful suggestions, but, more important, for her unflagging emotional support needed to bring this book to a conclusion. I am deeply grateful to her for being who she is. For these reasons, this book is dedicated to the three people who, more than anyone else, helped bring this book to fruition: Stephen Erickson, Robert Stolorow, and Sylvia Jones.

Foreword

Joseph D. Lichtenberg

"Love is a word—a shameless ragged ghost of a word" (O'Neill, 1925, p. 266). In this poetic utterance, O'Neill makes us aware of the dilemma authors face when they write about emotion. Affects, emotions, feelings, sensations are experiences. Words are designators, categorizers, symbolic representations. In metaphoric usage as in poetry, words may almost convey and evoke the experience. More often, in their linear, pedantic, desiccated forms, words about emotion prove to be poor, even deceptive, substitutes. O'Neill's poor, confused adolescent doesn't know if he is having, can have, or will be permitted by his girl friend's response to have the *experience* of love. He does know that saying the word, offering his protestations, is but a word-ghost, a ragged facsimile, the mask of the *actor*, not necessarily the feeling of the inner self.

From this we can appreciate that Joseph Jones is attempting the impossible, but I am happy to report he does very well with it. He strikes a good balance between scientific writing and evoking the experience we associate with words like joy, pride, love, anger, fear, and shame. Nowhere will the reader find a more thorough effort to restate, appreciatively appraise, and critique Freud's theory of affects. Jones's historical reappraisal gains its authenticity from his extensive knowledge of contemporary theories of affect based on infant studies, clinical experience, and psychological and psychoanalytic theories.

Affects as Process is a book that merits study but should be read. By this I mean that the book is packed with information about the organization and processing of information and the nature of symbolization—all in reference to emotion. Its charm, however, does not lie in its didactic qualities but rather in its evocation of thoughts and associations about familiar topics reseen from a different perspective. Not primarily a book for scholarly outline, *Affects as Process* calls for perusal with pauses for reflection. It reflects the author's having spent years of tussling and puzzling with the unresolved conundrums of cognition, affect, and action; of information processing, intercommunication, and motivation; of subjectivity, intersubjectivity, and objectivity.

Jones begins by engaging us with the relationship of human beings to the remainder of the animal kingdom. He asks us to think about many of Freud's philosophical assumptions. He rescues primary process from Freud's misconceptions about infant development: "If primary process means the first information-processing system to come on-line, then affects are our real 'primary process,' " Jones writes. Thus he grabs the reader's interest in big issues. Now the interplay between reader and author becomes challenging. Jones, as any authentically innovative writer must, presents his ideas in a mixture of tongues borrowed from conceptualizations that have captured *his* imagination. The reader is apt to be more familiar with some, say the extensive references to Freud, than with others. Jones lets us see from his viewpoint such diverse authors as Descartes, William James, Plutchik, Piaget, Pribram, Tomkins, Erikson, Stern, Spitz, Emde, MacLean, Helen Keller, Kohut, Vygotsky, Winnicott, Mahler, and M. Klein. Some conceptualizations may be unfamiliar, say the motivational systems I have suggested (Lichtenberg, 1989), which Jones uses to organize the opening sections of the book. Or the reader may have only a limited knowledge of the scattered but fairly extensive literature on information processing in presymbolic and symbolic forms that are key to all of Jones's assumptions about the role of affects (and the unique character of human cognitive-affective capacities). Consequently, when asked to entertain the hypothesis that affects are "the experiential representation of a nonsymbolic information-processing system that can serve as the central control mechanism for all aspects of human behavior," the reader may have an acute attack of terminological shock. I can only advise: Hang on. There is a point to be learned here, and once mastered, a new, more empirically based view of infant development will be your reward.

My reward as reader touches a more personal chord. Jones understands and utilizes the organizing power inherent in conceptualizing the development of self-organizing, self-stabilizing motivational systems subject to constant dialectic tension and hierarchical rearrangement. Hooray! He, like me, places affects in the center of motivational experience. But better yet for me, while accepting four of the five systems I propose, he challenges my concept of an aversive system. Rather than one system expressive of the innate need to react aversively through antagonism and/or withdrawal as I have suggested, Jones posits two systems: one organized in the infant to respond to the need for self-protection triggered by fear, and one organized to respond to competitive/territorial needs triggered by rage, contempt, and shame. Jones makes a good case for the significance of competitive/territorial strivings and regards these motivations as dominant organizing experiences of latency children. He forces me to recognize the diminished role I have given these widespread motivations by lumping them together with issues of agenda choices and demands and with the inevitable clashes of agenda between child and parent (and between patient and therapist). Nonetheless, I am not converted to the division Jones prefers. My infant and clinical observation leads me to prefer a single system in which an experience a person finds to be aversive triggers individual variations and combinations of fear, anger, shame, and sadness with consequent combinations of antagonism and withdrawal (fight or flight). Activities that involve competition need not be aversive at all—arousing neither rage or shame—but fall, I believe, in the area of exploration and assertion, evoking interest, efficacy, and competence. And so it goes in our field—controversies seeking clarity. Jones and I invite readers to test the different conceptions for fit with their experience.

Arguments about theoretical proposals of the sort I described between Jones and me abound in psychoanalytic essays or "thoughtpieces." These disputes may be interesting to the protagonists and to those who enjoy clashes of ideas while to others they may seem boring irrelevancies. The big issues Jones deals with are what recommends the book to a wide audience. For all developmentalists, a crowning challenge is to account for continuities and transformations. Shakespeare intrigued us with the seven ages of man. Freud staked his claim on transformations that accompanied the drive changes of psychosexual stages. In their efforts to delineate the central features of infancy that establish continuity, theoreticians have emphasized cognitive capacities such as fantasy and reality testing (Freud), phantasy and envy (Klein) or forms and permutations of attachments (Bowlby), object relations (Winnicott), and interpersonal relations (Sullivan). A contemporary era can be said to have begun with Spitz and Erikson independently formulating a theory of epigenesis. In this theory continuity is ensured by each stage's continuing into and influencing the subsequent stages; transformation is ensured by maturations that produce new capacities, new hierarchical organizations, new problems to be solved, as well as new conflicts that perturb the system in a variety of ways. On Freud's psychosexual base, Erikson emphasized social forces and Spitz presented the first compelling theory of affects, which he regarded as early organizers of ego transformations.

Jones believes that the Rosetta stone for understanding continuities and transformations lies in affects. Affects present from the beginning of life constitute a nonsymbolic language that provides a signal both to the infant and to the caregivers as to what motivational system is operative. The reexperiencing of affects at every later time provides a similarity that guarantees a sense of sameness, of relative smoothness, in the sense of self-identity. Affective experience itself, however, changes with maturation. Building on the general affective states (moods) of the infant, transformations lead to the complex emotions of the adult. In traversing this territory, Jones offers many novel suggestions. He identifies the neonate's affective experience as comprising four "moods," each with a specific decipherable message: interest (let's learn), surprise (new information coming); distress (something's wrong), and contentment (everything is okay). The neonate processes information by cross-comparing the affective intensity of motivational systems; the loudest signal gains priority for initiating an innate response pattern. At approximately eight weeks a transformation occurs with the sequential coming on-line of affects that convey more specific information about the perceptual world: disgust (bad food), fear (danger! protect yourself), affection (stay close), and rage (mine!). Behavioral shaping leads to stable response patterns that are represented affectively by what Jones calls complex moods, such as a sense of trust or mistrust, safety, or being in a state of empty depression. Jones relates this stage to character formation and character pathology.

I particularly want to call to the attention of the reader a point Jones makes that calls for a good deal of reflective reconsideration. As I have previously proposed, hypothesizing a capacity for symbolic functioning during early infancy is not necessary to explain fantasies that presumably represent such neonatal experiences as good or bad breasts, merger, oceanic feelings, and the like. In Jones's words, one can assume that the prereflective organization of experience becomes embedded in stable behavioral patterns represented affectively by complex moods. The stable patterns are then *retrospectively* encoded into fantasy when the capacity for symbol usage comes on-line. In my words: "The toddler of about 18 to 24 months is in a position similar to Pirandello's six characters in search of an author: The infant has memories, affects, organized states (with transitions between them), preferences, and complex interactional patterns all in search of a form of symbolic representation" (Lichtenberg, 1983, p. 169).

While Jones and I are in complete agreement about the major significance of the transformation and retrospective recoding that occurs with linguistic symbolic processing, we differ about whether to conceptualize a sense of self as beginning only with reflectiveness or earlier, in prereflective forms. Jones makes the thought-provoking suggestion that "a great deal of the difficulties and disputes about 'the self' is the reification of concretized, unconscious phantasies about the process of attention." By this he means that, if we observe that a baby is both focusing and directing her attention purposefully and intentionally, we tend to assume she is aware of those activities. She is the "who" of who is looking or hearing in our mind, and we thereby assume the same would be true in hers; that is, we "give" her a sense of self in an emergent or early core, prereflective form. Jones asks: Stop and think! Is this necessarily so? My own definition of sense of self would work either with a prereflective or postsymbolic conception: the sense of self develops as a sometimes independent, sometimes interdependent source for initiating, organizing, and integrating motivation and experience. The crucial question would be, Can infants under a year or a year and a half experience themselves as a source for initiating, organizing, and integrating the motivations and experiences they undoubtedly have? Along with Stern (1985), I tend to believe so. My view follows that of Sander (1983) that with each repetition of the ordinary patterns of a motivational system, the infant experiences a re-creation of an affect state. Consequently, the ecological niche infants set up with their caregivers enables them to re-create familiar states. The repetition of the states and of themselves as creator enables infants to recognize themselves. The ability to re-create and reexperience affect states thus can be regarded as a fundamental contribution to an emergent sense of a prereflective self. But the reader will want to compare my conception with that of Jones, who conceives of the self as a dialectic between affective and symbolic processes that emerges only after the latter have come on-line.

Now let us return to love. Jones states that with the transition to symbolization, and with it to the capacity for thought found only in humans, a new set of feelings emerges that transcends their origins as affective signals. The new set of feelings incorporates ideas and thus acquires meaning. These new affect-ideations are love, hatred, sadness, envy, and guilt. Whereas love begins with the infant's affection for the mother, this early affect is transformed, through the incorporation of the idea of idealized goodness, into the complex affect we think of as "love." "Thus, the affect of love endows the beloved . . . with the *quality* of goodness," Jones says. Now affection has acquired both ideation in its relation to idealized goodness and a name for the experience, love, and with the name not only significance but meaning. Jones reminds us that for animals affection may be richly present but would not have the same meaning as love does for humans. But while the word gives meaning to the experience, it also gives it a special quality of discursiveness that makes it displaceable. Once "affects acquire meaning (names), they can then be rearranged as easily as words in a sentence," Jones tells us. The poet was right! Love is a word. Sometimes its intensity, authenticity, and target are as easily rearranged as a word in a sentence, rendering it as empty as a shell, as ragged as a ghost. But, happily, sometimes love is an experience of the most powerful complexity of intimacy, affection, idealization, sensuality, and sexuality. When affect is regarded as a process, symbolization, like the Lord, both giveth and taketh away.

Preface

Anger, fear, love, hate, joy, grief, shame, pride. The *"coarser* emotions," as William James (1892) called them (p. 374). They are the stuff and substance of song and story. As man began to reflect upon the Nature of Man, he began to wonder about them. What are emotions, really? They are easy enough to experience but hard to define and even harder to understand. Are they some kind of feeling or sensation, such as hunger or pain? Or are they similar to an idea or cognition? Are they a kind of physiologic condition or process? Perhaps they are some combination of these. A number of philosophers—Hobbes, Hume, Descartes, and Spinoza, to name but a few—have tried to answer these questions but without much success. "Scientific Psychology," once that discipline emerged in the late 1800s, did not fare much better. Almost 100 years ago, William James lamented:

> From Descartes downwards, [emotion] is one of the most tedious parts of psychology. And not only is it tedious, but you feel that its subdivisions are to a great extent either fictitious or unimportant, and that its pretences to accuracy are a sham. . . . But as far as the "scientific psychology" of the emotions goes, I may have been surfeited by too much reading of classic works on the subject, but I should as lief read verbal descriptions of the shapes of the rocks on a New Hampshire farm as toil through them again. They give one

nowhere a central point of view, or a deductive or generative principle. . . . Whereas the beauty of all truly scientific work is to get to
ever deeper levels [pp. 374–375].

In the century since James penned this bleak description, psychologists and psychoanalysts have fared little better than philosophers
in constructing an adequate theory of the emotions. For example,
David Rapaport (1953) said, "We do not possess a systematic statement of the psychoanalytic theory of affects" (p. 476). A quarter of a
century later, André Green (1977) commented, "We would like to
have at our disposal a satisfactory theory of affects, but that is not
the case" (p. 129). Echoing the same sentiments, Jacob Arlow (1977)
noted, "In spite of the rich literature on the subject, there is widespread conviction, reiterated in the journals, that our understanding
of affects is unsatisfactory" (p. 157). Although some progress has
been made in recent years, we are still a long way from the elegance
and "beauty" of the comprehensive theory that William James
longed for, one that would take us "to ever deeper levels."

Why is this? Why has it been so difficult to develop a "satisfactory
theory of affects"? One could assume that this is simply an unusually
refractory scientific problem and that further theorizing, experimen-
tation, and research will yet lead to a solution. The difficulties of
discovering the structure of DNA (which has already been solved) and
of finding a cure for cancer (which undoubtedly will be) are examples
of this type of problem. There is, however, another possibility.
Ludwig Wittgenstein (1945) once said that "Philosophy is a battle
against the bewitchment of our intelligence by means of language"
(Section 109). Insofar as we are "bewitched" by language, we do not
have a scientific problem but a semantic trap or philosophic puzzle.
As Wittgenstein says, this type of conundrum is not solved by the
acquisition of new information, but by rearranging "what we have
already known" (Section 109). I suggest that our difficulty in constructing a "satisfactory theory of affects" is an excellent example of
this type of process.

The premise of the first essay in this book is that the principal
difficulty in arriving at a reasonably satisfactory psychoanalytic
theory of affects arises from the failure to appreciate fully the
philosophic preconceptions that are embedded within the matrix of
our current theories. The questions involved in conceptualizing
affects raise difficult philosophical issues that, literally, date back
hundreds, if not thousands, of years. The single most critical of these
issues centers on the nature of man and how we differ from other
animals. The problem can be stated reasonably simply: are human

beings a smarter animal, or do we possess some faculty or quality that fundamentally distinguishes us from the rest of the animal kingdom? As we become increasingly familiar with computers and recognize that the brain functions like a biocomputer, we can frame the same question in computer language: do humans simply have a faster, more powerful computer, or do we have a different kind of computer program? No matter how this question is answered, it will subtly, but inevitably, influence how the human mind is conceptualized and thus will prejudice, in one way or another, how human emotions are understood.

In the first essay, "Is Primary Process Primary?" we attempt to understand the philosophic underpinning of Freud's fundamental theories (sometimes referred to as his metapsychology). As I will try to show, Freud's theories conceal a philosophical and metaphysical agenda concerning the nature of man in relationship to the rest of the animal kingdom.[1] As Freud worked out the details of his metapsychological theories, one effect was to partially strip affects of their process role. Recognizing that Freud's covert philosophic agenda stripped affects of their process role can be the Rosetta stone for understanding why psychoanalysis does not yet have a satisfactory theory of affects. The first essay ends with the hypothesis that affects are really our "primary process."

The second essay, "Affects as Process," explores the theoretical and clinical implications of the premise that affects are our own primary process. Specifically, affects are conceptualized as the experiential representation of a nonsymbolic information-processing system that can serve as the central control mechanism for all aspects of human behavior, including the control of physical movements, memory, and all interactions with the environment. Five specific types of affective experience are differentiated: 1) impulses that regulate physical movement; 2) sensations (e.g., thirst, hunger), which give us information about our body; 3) moods; 4) core emotions; and 5) complex affects (core emotions plus ideas). What William James called the coarser emotions—anger, fear, love, hate, joy, grief, pride, shame—function as the affective signal that lets us know about specific motivational systems. A cross-comparison of the intensity of the affects representing competing motivational systems provides a simple control mechanism for prioritizing information and then selecting which motivational system to activate. The first

---

[1] Because a substantial part of this book focuses on the differences between human beings and other animals, for ease of exposition the phrase "animal kingdom" is used to describe animals other than *homo sapiens*.

eight chapters of this essay consider six motivational systems and the specific affects that act as their monitors: 1) the regulation of physiologic requirements; 2) attachment/affiliation; 3) sensual/ sexual pleasure; 4) self-preservative; 5) competence/mastery; and 6) competitive/territorial. Chapter 9 reviews how our presymbolic character structure, heavily influenced by behavioral shaping, can be signaled affectively by complex background moods. In addition, this chapter discusses how infants begin to construct a working map of the world. This introduces the complex topic of representation. Thus, the first half of the essay "Affects as Process" describes how affects, and affects alone, serve as the primary control signals for all animals and presymbolic infants.

Chapters 10 through 16 describe the changes in human functioning that are secondary to the acquisition of the ability to think. Specifically, chapter 10 describes how the ability to use symbols (i.e., thought) is superimposed on this presymbolic character structure, thus laying the substrate for the "divided mind." Chapter 11 describes the rapprochement crisis, the psychological turmoil created by the necessity of integrating two fundamentally different ways of processing information. Chapter 12 describes the difficulties inherent in the term "object"; the argument is made that what are called "internal objects" within the framework of object relations theory describe the infant's first attempts at concept formation. (Thus "objects" are protoconcepts.) Chapter 13 describes the formation of complex affects, such as love and hate, and how they play a key role in phantasy[2] formation—the core of the dynamic unconscious. Chapter 14 describes some psychologically determined inhibitions in the process of thinking, which I conceptualize as thought dysfunctions. Chapter 15 discusses Freud's theory of psychosexual development as the unfolding of specific phantasies; it goes on to explore the surprisingly close connection among specific phantasies, the predominant motivational system, and the complex background mood. Chapter 16 describes the many ambiguities associated with various usages of the term "self"; the chapter concludes that what is usually thought of as the self is the result of achieving a relatively stable affective–symbolic integration.

---

[2] English psychoanalysts, particularly the Kleinians, have followed the recommendations of Susan Isaacs (1948) in using the *ph* spelling of phantasy to denote the more unconscious dimensions of the idea, while retaining the word fantasy to refer to the more conscious, daydream level of this activity. Except for the Kleinians, American psychoanalysts usually do not make this distinction. Although I am not a Kleinian and have many disagreements with her theories, I find the distinction a useful one and have used it throughout this book.

In summary, the essay "Is Primary Process Primary?" explores the hypothesis that the most important reason that psychoanalysis does not yet have a "satisfactory theory of affects" is that Freud's covert philosophic agenda, the subtext of his metapsychology, stripped affects of their process role. The second essay, "Affects as Process," develops the hypothesis that affects are the experiential representation of a nonsymbolic information-processing system that functions in animals and presymbolic infants. Using as examples six different motivational systems and the specific affects that serve as their monitors, chapters 1 through 9 of the second essay describe in detail how this system works. The balance of the essay describes the changes in human functioning that are secondary to the acquisition of the ability to use symbols (i.e., to think).

I

Is Primary Process Primary?

1

In the Beginning . . .

The roots of the difficulty in developing a theory of affects trace to the very beginnings of psychoanalysis. In 1893, Joseph Breuer and Sigmund Freud published the "Preliminary Communication" to *Studies on Hysteria*. In this historic paper, they summarized their theory that hysteria results from repressed sexual memories in the well-known phrase, *"Hysterics suffer mainly from reminiscences"* (p. 7). From this assumption, Freud and Breuer devised a cure through catharsis. Hypnosis, and later free association, were used to bring the repressed memory back into consciousness, thus releasing the "strangulated affect." The centrality of affect is well illustrated by this quotation:

> For we found, to our great surprise at first, that each individual hysterical symptom immediately and permanently disappeared when we had succeeded in bringing clearly to light the memory of the event by which it was provoked and *in arousing its accompanying affect,* and when the patient had described that event in the greatest possible detail and had put the affect into words. *Recollection without affect almost invariably produces no result* [p. 6, emphasis changed from original].

In this first formulation of psychoanalytic theory, patients became symptomatic because of the repressed, affect-laden experience and recovered when the affects were brought back into consciousness.

3

However, in a letter to Fliess dated September 21, 1897, Freud announced his discovery that his patients' traumatic memories of infantile seduction were not reports of reality experiences, but phantasies. With this discovery, Freud's interest shifted from affect to the agent that creates the phantasies: the instinctual drives *(Trieb)*. Affects were now considered "processes of discharge," occurring only when the drive was not carried through to completion (Freud, 1915c, p. 178). This shift of theoretical emphasis from affect to drive stripped affects of their process role, thereby creating the major stumbling block in arriving at a "satisfactory theory of affects." The interlocking assumptions about the nature of affect and drive create a serious methodologic problem; it is virtually impossible to examine affect theory without, at the same time, reexamining Freud's theory of drives. Assuming that one wishes to stay within the mainstream of psychoanalytic theory, there is virtually no choice but to attempt to unpack what Freud referred to as metapsychology, his grounding assumptions about the nature of the mind.

Trieb, translated as instinctual drive, is central to Freud's attempt to understand the nature of man. The origins of his use of this concept are not particularly obscure; in 1930 Freud wrote:

> Of all the slowly developed parts of analytic theory, the theory of the drives is the one that has felt its way the most painfully forward. And yet that theory was so indispensable to the whole structure that something had to be put in its place. In what *was at first my utter perplexity, I took as my starting-point a saying of the poet-philosopher, Schiller, that "hunger and love are what moves the world." Hunger could be taken to represent the drives which aim at preserving the individual; while love strives after objects, and its chief function, favoured in every way by nature, is the preservation of the species.* Thus, to begin with, ego-instincts and object-instincts confronted each other. It was to denote the energy of the latter and only the latter drives that I introduced the term "libido" [p. 117, emphasis added; the word "drives" has been substituted for "instincts"].

The work to which Freud refers is Schiller's famous—to an educated German—"Letters on the Aesthetic Education of Mankind."[1] In this work, Schiller described two main drives, the sensuous *(Stofftrieb)* and the formal *(Formtrieb)*. These two drives were then reconciled into an integral unity by the aesthetic or play drive *(Spieltrieb)*.

---

[1] This summary of Schiller's "Letters on the Aesthetic Education of Mankind" (1794–1795) was taken from *The Encyclopedia of Philosophy* (1967, "Schiller").

Schiller believed that Kant had erred by locating freedom in reason alone; his critique of reason as the only mode of freedom was incorporated into psychoanalytic theory through the concept of a dynamic unconscious. Accordingly, the concept of *Trieb,* an acknowledged derivative from Schiller, represents Freud's attempt to translate a poetic/philosophic conception of man into the language of science.

Thus, in the beginning, it was hunger (which Freud translated into the "instincts of self-preservation") and love (which became the libidinal drive) that move the world. From this early hypothesis, Freud (1905) went on to write *Three Essays on the Theory of Sexuality,* the cornerstone of his theory of development. Central to this theory is the hypothesis that the relationship between mother and infant can best be described as sexual: "No one who has seen a baby sinking back satiated from the breast and falling asleep with flushed cheeks and a blissful smile can escape the reflection that this picture persists as a prototype of the expression of sexual satisfaction in later life" (p. 182). Not surprisingly, this theory generated a good deal of controversy about whether or not infants were really experiencing sexual feelings; unfortunately, this controversy focused attention on the issue of sexuality, rather than on the more fundamental concept of drive. Freud's concept of the libidinal drive, inextricably interconnected with his theories about love and sexuality, lay at the heart of his reinterpretation of repressed traumas as phantasies.

As Freud worked with his patients and refined his theories, he came to attribute increasing importance to the phenomenon of "aggression." As early as 1908, Alfred Adler had hypothesized that aggression was an autonomous drive, but this viewpoint was initially rejected (see Laplanche and Pontalis, 1967, "Aggression"). With the 1920 publication of his famous essay *Beyond the Pleasure Principle,* however, Freud finally accepted Adler's hypothesis, at the same time expanding aggression into the concept of the death instinct. Together, libido (the life instinct) and aggression (the death instinct) constituted what has come to be known as the dual-drive theory. The instincts of self-preservation (i.e., hunger) were now regarded as part of the life instinct, or eros. To retranslate Freud back into the language of Schiller, it was no longer "hunger and love are what moves the world," but "love and hatred." As with the controversy about infantile sexuality, the controversies stirred up by Freud's concept of the death instinct were a formidable barrier that prevented any fundamental rethinking of the concept of *Trieb.*

Within the English-speaking world, another barrier was the unfortunate translation of the German word *Trieb* as "instinct." James Strachey (1966a) felt uneasy enough about this translation to comment:

> Hence my choice of "instinct." The only slight complication is that in some half-dozen instances Freud himself uses the German *"Instinkt,"* always, perhaps, in the sense of instinct in animals [p. xxv].

In *Freud and Man's Soul*, Bettelheim (1983) commented that this is hardly a "slight complication":

> Freud used the German word *Instinkt* when it seemed appropriate to him—to refer to the inborn instincts of animals—and he shunned it when he was speaking of human beings. Since Freud made a clear distinction between what he had in mind when he spoke of instincts, and what he had in mind when he spoke of *Triebe,* the importance of maintaining the distinction seems obvious [p. 104].

Freud himself certainly contributed to the confusion by approving the English translations of his work. But as Otto Kernberg (1982) has pointed out, it is too late to make a radical change in the definition of *Trieb;* I would further agree with Kernberg that the term is most usefully translated as "drive" or "instinctual drive." Therefore, throughout this essay, Strachey's translation of *Trieb* as "instinct" is revised to read "drive."

Basically, Freud's theory of drives comprises the generally accepted psychoanalytic theory of motivation. For example, Charles Brenner (1982), whose contributions come close to approximating the "classical position" within modern psychoanalytic theory, says, "drives . . . impel or drive the mental apparatus to activity in accordance with the pleasure principle. This is the role that Freud assigned to the drives in psychoanalytic theory. The drives provide impetus. They drive the mind to activity" (p. 11). A corollary of this position is that affects are secondary, or derivative. This, and other critical assumptions about the nature of mind, are deeply embedded within the conceptual language of drive theory and must be carefully teased out in order to critique Freud's theory of drives and affects in a meaningful way.

2

Freud, Darwin, and Descartes

From the beginning to the end of his career, Freud considered himself a scientist and psychoanalysis a science. At the beginning of the "Project," he wrote, "The intention is to furnish a psychology that shall be a natural science" (1895a, p. 295). At the end of his career, he concluded, "Psycho-analysis is a part of the mental science of psychology. . . . Psychology, too, is a natural science. What else can it be?" (1940b, p. 282). Despite overwhelming evidence to the contrary, a number of critics today maintain that Freud was really a humanist and that his image as a scientist is partially the result of Strachey's biased translation of his work. A number of critics, most notably Bruno Bettelheim (1983), have suggested that Strachey, in line with his logical positivist beliefs, tried to make Freud sound more "scientific" than he really was. As I do not read German, I cannot evaluate the problem myself, but after reading and rereading Freud and the secondary literature, I have come to the conclusion that Freud considered himself a scientist, but that his goal was to enlarge the scientific perspective to include much of what heretofore had been considered humanistic territory.

Unfortunately, part of Freud's conception of himself as a scientist entailed a contempt for metaphysics. In a letter to Werner Achelis, he wrote:

Other defects in my nature have certainly distressed me and made me feel humble; with metaphysics it is different—I not only have no

7

talent for it but no respect for it, either. In secret—one cannot say such things aloud—I believe that one day metaphysics will be condemned as a nuisance, as an abuse of thinking, as a survival from the period of the religious *Weltanschauung.* I know well to what extent this way of thinking estranges me from German cultural life [letter of January 30, 1927, E. Freud, 1960].

The effect of this attitude has been insidious. Inoculated with Freud's contempt for philosophy, subsequent psychoanalytic theorists felt free to ignore virtually all critiques from that direction. Although some philosophers, notably Ricoeur, attempted to maintain a friendly dialogue between the two disciplines, the general tendency has been to sever psychoanalytic theory from philosophy. This has been particularly unfortunate because, during the 1920s, Wittgenstein and his successors ("analytic philosophy") developed techniques for clarifying the meaning of concepts that, if applied to psychoanalytic theory, would have been particularly helpful.

Freud's metapsychology, an obvious play on the word "metaphysics," was intended to establish the theoretical ground for his psychological theories, analogous to the grounding role that metaphysics played for philosophy. Without a real understanding of the metaphysical assumptions that are present in his metapsychology, it is, I think, virtually impossible to understand either his theory of drives or his theory of affect. Freud's allusion to his metaphysical agenda is demonstrated by his frequent description of himself as a "dualist," a term he never defined. For example, Freud (1920) wrote:

Our views have from the very first been *dualistic,* and to-day they are even more definitely dualistic than before—now that we describe the opposition as being, not between ego-instincts and the sexual instincts but between life instincts and death instincts [p. 53].

In that passage, Freud is contrasting his "instinctual dualism" with Jung's "instinctual monism." The argument, however, has deeper roots. One cannot appropriate the language of metaphysical debate—terms such as "monism" and "dualism"—without evoking the philosophic debates from which these terms arise. As much as he later might deny it, Freud was clearly pursuing a hidden philosophic agenda. As early as 1896, Freud had written to Fliess, "I hope you will lend me your ear for a few *metapsychological* questions as well. . . . As a young man I knew no longing other than for philosophical knowledge, and now I am about to fulfill it as I move from medicine to psychology" (letter of April 2, 1896, Masson, 1985).

Metapsychology was Freud's attempt to construct a scientific metaphysics.

In considering Freud's use of the terms dualist and dualism, we have to step backward in time and remind ourselves of the origins of the term in the work of René Descartes. In his *Discourse on Method* (1641), Descartes hypothesized that animals differ from man in a fundamental way; all animals have feelings (affects), but only man has the power to reason, the *res cogitans*. The emotions, which he called "passions," belong to the body; as bodily phenomena, they belong to the material world, the *res extensa*. This philosophic point of view, known as rationalism, stresses the power of reason in understanding the world. It is also dualistic, in that it assumes that humans possess a faculty or process—the mind—that sharply differentiates them from the rest of the animal kingdom.

For Descartes, the mind is something that derives from God and is central to human existence; it operates independently of the human body and is a fully different sort of entity. The body, which contains the feelings or affects, is best thought of as a kind of automaton, which can be compared to the machines made by men. Within philosophy, the relationship between the rational mind and the mechanical body was referred to as the "mind–body" problem. As Howard Gardner (1985) says:

> In his discussion of ideas and the mind, sensory experience and the body, the power of language and the centrality of an organizing, doubting self, Descartes formulated an agenda that would dominate philosophical discussions and affect experimental science in the decades and centuries that followed. Furthermore, he proposed the vivid and controversial image of the mind as a rational instrument which, however, cannot be simulated by any imaginable machine— an image still debated in cognitive science today [p. 52].

The initial empirical responses by Locke, Hume, and Berkeley, the synthesis put forth by Kant, and the challenges to the Kantian synthesis were the principal milestones in the philosophic responses to Descartes. The successful assault on Cartesian dualism came, however, not from philosophy but from Darwin's theory of evolution. *On the Origin of Species* (1859) was widely interpreted as indicating that man was not all that different from the other animals. Hans Jonas (1966) commented, "Thus evolutionism undid Descartes' work more effectively than any metaphysical critique had managed to do" (p. 57).

The impact of Darwin's theories on Freud forms the point of departure for psychoanalytic theory. Freud (1917b) commented:

> In the course of the development of civilization man acquired a dominating position over his fellow-creatures in the animal kingdom. Not content with this supremacy, however, he began to place a gulf between his nature and theirs. *He denied the possession of reason to them,* and to himself he attributed an immortal soul, and made claims to a divine descent which permitted him to break the bond of community between him and the animal kingdom. . . .
>
> We all know that little more than half a century ago the researches of Charles Darwin and his collaborators and forerunners put an end to this presumption on the part of man. Man is not a being different from animals or superior to them; he himself is of animal descent, being more closely related to some species and more distantly to others. The acquisitions he has subsequently made have not succeeded in effacing the evidences, both in his physical structure and in his mental dispositions, of his parity with them [pp. 140–141, emphasis added].

Freud's comment that man "denied the possession of reason to them [animals]" constitutes a conscious rejection of Descartes's hypothesis that man differs from the other animals by the virtue of the power of reason. This attitude set Freud's metaphysical agenda: *his task was to maintain the dualistic perspective of Descartes, but at the same time to maintain the evolutionary continuity of Darwin.* In other words, Freud's metapsychology represents his attempt to establish a scientific, non-Cartesian dualism, one that could ultimately be derived from an "instinctual dualism," as the ground for his theory of mind.

In attempting to solve his central metaphysical problem, Freud faced a formidable task. While many mammals seem to possess emotions that appear to be similar to those in humans (e.g., rage, fear, disgust), they do not possess a reflective self-consciousness, the capacity to think, which Descartes called reason. Freud's solution to this problem was ingenious. While rejecting Descartes's specific dualism of reason and feelings, Freud maintained the dualistic perspective, the hypothesis that the mind is best understood as being governed by two processes. Freud's two-process model of the mind is set forth in "Formulations on the Two Principles of Mental Functioning" (1911), where he outlines the distinction between primary and secondary process. The essence of the paper is summarized in the title: there are two principles that govern human functioning, not one. While Freud did not define the term "process," his meaning is not particularly elusive: it means an internally coherent, integrated way of receiving, processing, and communicating information. Primary process is characteristic of the system unconscious, whereas secondary process typifies the conscious/preconscious system. In trying to appreciate the metaphysical agenda of Freud's work, it is important to recognize that the concept of primary process was the means by which he sought to maintain the "bond of community" with the animal kingdom. Thus, Freud responded to Descartes by retaining the hypothesis of the divided mind while maintaining that the critical dualism was not between affects and thought, but between two types of information processing: primary process and secondary process.

Freud's dualism of process gradually led him to think in terms of a dualism of structure, the "divided mind." Freud (1915c) laid the groundwork for this step when he formulated his three original metapsychological points of view: 1) the topographic, 2) the dynamic, and 3) the economic (pp. 172–176). Taken together, these original metapsychological points of view can be readily appreciated as three interlocking metaphysical assumptions: 1) the mind is divided (the topographic point of view); 2) the conflict within the divided mind gives rise to symptoms, character formation, or both (the dynamic point of view); and 3) the conflict can be quantified, measured in terms of energy (the economic point of view). These metapsychological postulates are really covert metaphysical assumptions setting forth Freud's premise of a divided mind, but one that can nonetheless be approached through a single biological and evolutionary perspective. From these postulates, Freud went on to assume that the dualism of structure could be derived from a dualism of antagonistic drive components. In 1920, Freud made this connection explicit: "It is merely that the distinction between the two kinds of drive, which was originally regarded as in some sort of way *qualitative*, must now be characterized differently—namely as being *topographical*" (p. 52).[1] Dualism of process was now linked to dualism of structure.

At this point, it is useful to compare Freud's view with that of Descartes. Descartes's influence was so great and so permeates Western thought that it has almost become the common-sense view of the mind. While there are many ways to parse the human spirit, the tripartite division of thought, feeling, and action (or behavior, as it now is called) is probably the most common. Proceeding primarily

---

[1] The word "drive" has been substituted for the word "instinct."

through introspection, Descartes assumed that thought and feeling were primary; action was held to be derivative, assumed to be the consequence of one of the other two. In the language of systems theory, both the *res cogitans* and the *res extensa* are systems, integrated processes by which an organism receives, stores, and communicates information. In effect, Descartes describes a feeling–thought model of the mind. These assumptions have passed into our everyday speech. For example, consider the following example: "I had an argument today with the boss. I felt so angry I felt like hitting him. I didn't. I could hardly stop myself but my better judgment told me not to. I knew I'd get fired." Here the dualistic assumptions are very clear. "I felt like hitting him" is the feeling, and "I knew I'd get fired" is the thought. The "I could hardly stop myself" is the conflict we experience. Thus, our introspective experience seems to strongly reinforce our belief that feeling and thought are two different modes of arriving at a decision; when they yield opposite conclusions, we are "in conflict." This sense of being torn by conflicting impulses is part of the experiential matrix that pushes us to think in terms of a divided mind. Translating Descartes into the language of systems theory, feeling and thinking are processes; action is not considered a process but a derivative of the other two. In the language of philosophy, action does not have metaphysical sanction.

Let us contrast this view with Freud's. As a philosopher-scientist, Freud faced the formidable task of integrating the scientific preference for observation (as opposed to introspection) into his theory. What the scientist observes is action (or "behavior"); in an inspired display of theory making, Freud's theory of drives *(Trieb)* represents his attempt to give the concept of action metaphysical sanction. This attempt is clearer in the French translation of Freud's work, where *Trieb* is translated as *pulsion,* impulse. At the most theoretical level, drives are not feelings, not affects; rather, they represent the impulse, the pressure, to *act.* Within the framework of metaphysics, it was the concept of *Trieb* that allowed Freud to establish an action–thought, as opposed to feeling–thought, model of the mind.

Freud's long apprenticeship as a neurologist and neurophysiologist may help us understand how he came to construct an action–thought model of the mind. At the time Freud was engaged in neurological research, one of the most fundamental observations about the nervous system was that the incoming nerves to the brain are sensory; the outgoing are motor. In summarizing this, Freud (1900) says, "Psychical processes advance in general from the perceptual end to the motor end" (p. 537). This observation was to be the point of departure for his metaphysical speculations. In the next paragraph, he goes on to say, "This, however, does no more than fulfil a requirement with which we have long been familiar, namely that the psychical apparatus must be constructed like a reflex apparatus. Reflex *processes remain the model of every psychical function*" (p. 538, emphasis added). Ten years later, he says, "This has given us the concept of a 'stimulus' and the pattern of the reflex arc, according to which a stimulus applied to living tissue (nervous substance) *from* the outside is discharged by action *to* the outside" (Freud, 1915a, p. 118). Thus, in a very schematic form, Freud's reflex-arc model of the mind leads from stimulus to "discharge by action."

Freud's theory of drives has often been called the "drive-discharge" model, as the concept of discharge is usually considered to be inherent in the concept of drive. A metaphysical perspective helps us to appreciate *why* this is so. Simply stated, drive stands for action while discharge stands for completion of that action. Thus, the metapsychological formulation of "drive-pushing-toward-discharge" gains added clarity when retranslated into the language of metaphysics as an "action-pushing-toward-completion." Thus understood, discharge becomes an implicit part of the definition of the term "drive."

The other half of Freud's action–thought model of the mind consisted of redefining thought *in terms of action.* In "Formulations on the Two Principles of Mental Functioning" (1911), he said, "It [thought] *is essentially an experimental kind of acting,* accompanied by displacement of relatively small quantities of cathexis together with less expenditure (discharge) of them" (p. 221, emphasis added). This formulation is usually expressed in the phrase that thought is "trial action." Implicitly, if secondary process is trial action, then what is restrained is the impulse to act; thought restrains action. Thus, at the metaphysical level both primary and secondary process have been conceptualized in terms of action processes. Freud then goes on to complete the model by addressing the role of affect:

> A new function was now allotted to motor discharge, which, under the dominance of the pleasure principle, had served as a means of unburdening the mental apparatus of accretions of stimuli, and which had carried out this task by sending innervations into the interior of the body (leading to expressive movements and the play of features and to manifestations of affect). Motor discharge was now employed in the appropriate alteration of reality; it was converted into *action* [p. 221].

Although this paragraph is rather murky, the net effect is to deprive affects of their process role by suggesting that they arise when action is blocked. This formulation led to the notoriously opaque section on "unconscious emotions" in the paper "The Unconscious," where Freud (1915c) says, "affects and emotions correspond to processes of discharge, the final manifestations of which are perceived as feelings" (p. 178).

It is in this short paragraph that Freud turns Descartes upside down. Drives push toward *action* (the metaphysical term); if this is done, there is the "appropriate alteration of reality." If the action is not completed, it goes to the interior of the body, "leading to expressive movements . . . and to manifestations of affect." In other words, blocked action leads to affect. In metaphysical terms, action is primary; it has metaphysical sanction. In contrast, affects are derivative, secondary; they have lost their process role and are now considered to be "processes of discharge." Here, I propose that stripping affects of their process role, their metaphysical sanction, has been the primary problem that has prevented the emergence of a psychoanalytic theory of affects.

It is interesting to speculate about why Freud chose to reject the Cartesian emphasis on the process role of affects rather than revising and updating it. Perhaps, as he implied, the reasons lay in his opposition to Descartes's sharp distinction of man from the rest of the animal kingdom. Another possibility is that Freud never really abandoned his neuroanatomic reflex-arc model of the mind. A third, intriguing possibility centers on German cultural consciousness and its emphasis on action. In Goethe's (1790) rendition of the Faust legend, Faust picks up the *New Testament* with the intention of translating it "with sincere feeling the sacred original into my beloved German":

> (*He opens a tome and begins.*)
> It says: "In the beginning was the *Word*."
> Already I am stopped. It seems absurd.
> The *Word* does not deserve the highest prize,
> I must translate it otherwise
> If I am well inspired and not blind.
> It says: In the beginning was the *Mind*.
> Ponder that first line, wait and see,
> Lest you should write too hastily.
> Is mind the all-creating source?
> It ought to say: In the beginning there was *Force*.
> Yet something warns me as I grasp the pen,
> That my translation must be changed again.
> The spirit helps me. Now it is exact.
> I write: In the beginning was the *Act* [lines 1220–1237].

In this soliloquy on metaphysics, Faust rejects the Word (Logos) as primary. In many ways, Freud's theory of drives can be understood as the attempt to provide the scientific underpinnings to the proud Faustian claim, "In the beginning was the *Act*."

In summary, René Descartes was the first modern philosopher to suggest that the human mind was most usefully conceptualized as using two fundamentally different processes. Within philosophy, powerful Cartesian assertions have set much of the agenda of Western philosophy. The Cartesian two-process model of the mind (Affect OR Thought → Action) has become so ingrained in our thinking that it has now become the accepted way of viewing the mind. Charles Taylor (1984) says:

> One has an ironic sense of how things have changed, when one reads Descartes advising his readers to ponder the Meditations seriously, and even to spend a month thinking about the first one, so difficult did it seem to him to break the previous mind-set and grasp the dualist truth. Today, philosophers of my persuasion spend years trying to get students (and decades trying to get colleagues) to see that there is an alternative. Cartesian dualism is immediately understandable to undergraduates on day one. The idea that the only two viable alternatives might be Hobbes or Descartes is espoused by many, and is a perfectly comprehensible thesis even to those who passionately reject it. They feel its power, and the need to refute it. Such was not the situation in the 1640s [p. 21].

Reacting to Descartes's proud claim that man was "different," and influenced by Darwin's theory of evolution, Freud sought to restore the bond of community between man and the animal kingdom, while at the same time creating a set of grounding assumptions for a "scientific dualism." These twin goals formed Freud's covert metaphysical agenda.

Freud's metapsychology (the new metaphysics) involved an inspired piece of philosophical theorizing: to turn Descartes upside down and create an action–thought model of the mind. Freud's mechanism for accomplishing this goal took the form of three interlocking hypotheses: 1) the theory of drives (action-pushing-toward-completion); 2) a corollary theory of thought formation as "trial action"; and 3) a revised theory of affects that reconceptualized them as "processes of discharge." This emphasis on action is prominent in his theory of thought formation. Secondary process, Descartes's reason, is "trial action." Primary process, the language of dreams and symptoms, is action discharged into the interior, unchecked by either perception or reason. These two formulations allowed Freud to construct an action–thought model of the mind that has acted as a controlling paradigm, exercising a powerful, unrecognized influence on subsequent psychoanalytic theorizing. The reason why we do not have a "satisfactory theory of affects" is that Freud's metapsychology deprived affects of metaphysical sanction.

3

Affects as Composites

Embedded within the Cartesian model of the mind is a very simple assumption: affects serve a primary information-processing role. Hunger is a signal to eat, thirst is a signal to drink, pain is a signal that something bad is happening to your body, fear is a danger signal. Other affects—rage, shame, lust, grief—carry other messages. Simply stated, affects form the core presymbolic information-processing system. Humans, possessed of the power to reason and thus the capacity for self-reflection, are not mere automatons responding to affective signals. The power of reason gives us the ability to override our animal nature and not simply act on our feelings; this capacity differentiates us from the rest of the animal kingdom. The conflict between what we think is best (our "better judgment") and what we feel like doing is the experiential substrate of the divided mind. The Cartesian model of the mind—as influential in Freud's time as it is today—forms the point of departure for all subsequent theorizing about affects.

Freud began to think about affects early in the course of his clinical work. As noted in chapter 1, Freud's initial therapeutic efforts centered on the recovery of the repressed affects connected with what he thought were traumatic memories. Freud's initial conception of affect was of a quantity of energy that accompanies the events of psychic life. In "The Neuro-Psychoses of Defence" (1894), he commented:

> I refer to the concept that in mental functions something is to be distinguished—a quota of affect or sum of excitation—which possesses all the characteristics of a quantity (though we have no means of measuring it), which is capable of increase, diminution, displacement and discharge, and which is spread over the memory-traces of ideas somewhat as an electric charge is spread over the surface of a body [p. 60].

The controversy that has arisen in regard to this oft-quoted sentence is whether Freud is using the terms "sum of excitation" and "quota of affect" as synonyms.[1] Sometimes overlooked and not fully appreciated in the sentence is the key phrase: "the memory-traces of ideas." Here is one of Freud's most important process assumptions: memories are stored in the form of *ideas* (i.e., thoughts). In other words, affects were regarded as something more ephemeral than ideas, as something that went through the process of synthesis, disintegration, and resynthesis, whereas ideas were somehow more permanent and could thus be stored.

In 1897, Freud discovered that his patients' traumatic memories were not reports of reality experience, but phantasies. In his attempt to account for the origin of the phantasies, Freud propounded his theory of drives *(Trieb)*. As set forth in the previous chapter, Freud's theory of drives gave action metaphysical sanction. As a result, affects were stripped of their process role (i.e., their metaphysical sanction). Consequently, Freud was required to reconceptualize affects so that they were subordinate to and derivatives of what he considered primary: drives (impulses to act) and thought. This hidden metaphysical agenda set forth the requirements for an acceptable psychoanalytic theory of affects. In three of the Papers on Metapsychology, Freud (1915a,b,c) discussed affects and attempted to resolve the theoretical problem; these papers, however, contained a number of internal contradictions and raised more questions than they answered.[2]

---

[1] For a discussion of this, see Strachey (1962a).

[2] Any discussion of the internal contradictions of those papers would take inordinate space, as it would require a sentence-by-sentence textual analysis of some very difficult material. As I regard Freud's foundational premises about affect to be fundamentally flawed, I do not think it would be worth the reader's time. For an excellent and sympathetic discussion of Freud's theories of affect,

As far as we know, Freud did not plan a paper on affects as one of the Papers on Metapsychology (Strachey, 1957a). Freud's failure to plan for a paper about affects cannot be regarded simply as an oversight on his part but must be examined as further evidence of his theoretical assumptions about affects. As already noted, Freud regarded affects as a secondary phenomenon that was subordinate to and derivative of other, more basic, processes; thus the discussion of affects would properly belong to a paper devoted to those processes. The working out of this assumption can be found in a lecture about affects given in 1917, approximately two years after he wrote the Papers on Metapsychology. In a lecture on "Anxiety," Freud (1916–1917) gave his most complete definition of an affect, in the process defining them as a composite of thought and impulse:

> And what is an affect in the dynamic sense? *It is in any case something highly composite.* An affect includes in the first place particular motor innervations or discharges and secondly certain feelings; the latter are of two kinds—perceptions of the motor actions that have occurred and the direct feelings of pleasure and unpleasure which, as we say, give the affect its keynote. But I do not think that with this enumeration we have arrived at the essence of an affect. We seem to see deeper in the case of some affects and to recognize that the core which holds the combination we have described together is the repetition of some particular significant experience. . . . To make myself more intelligible—an affective state would be constructed in the same way as a hysterical attack and, like it, would be the *precipitate of a reminiscence* [pp. 395–396, emphasis added].

When Freud says "the precipitate of a reminiscence," he is clearly suggesting a memory (i.e., "the memory-traces of ideas") and therefore a thought or idea. Thus, after struggling with the puzzle of affects in the Papers on Metapsychology, Freud reaffirms his most important assumptions about affects: affects are *composites* of some kind of "action impulse" combined with some mechanism that gives the action impulse its cognitive content.

In 1923, Freud wrote *The Ego and the Id,* which announced the structural, or tripartite, model of the mind. The need to understand the communications between the id, ego, and superego led Freud to reconsider the problem of affects. In 1926, he published *Inhibitions,*

---

see Green's article "Conceptions of Affect" (1977), prepared as a background article for the 19th meeting of the International Psycho-Analytic Association, which was devoted to affect.

Symptoms and Anxiety, in which he distinguished between traumatic anxiety and signal anxiety. Traumatic anxiety occurs when repressed libido forces itself through the stimulus barrier and overwhelms the focus of repression, resulting in a partial disintegration of ego functions; in contrast, signal anxiety is the reproduction, in attenuated form, of the anxiety reaction originally experienced in a traumatic situation. As André Green (1977) points out, "In a way, with the signal function of affect, the theory gave affective life the possibility of functioning in a way analogous to thought" (p. 138). In other words, signal anxiety serves a process function. In this conception, Freud anticipated by years the concerns of modern neurophysiologists and academic psychologists, who were to become increasingly concerned with the regulatory functions of the mind. In reexamining the concept of signal anxiety, one cannot help but be impressed by how close Freud came to a process theory of affects.

Why has a process theory of affects never been seriously considered? Some of the reasons have to do with the metaphysical assumptions about affects that are the subject of this essay. But there is another, extremely important reason—the rise of ego psychology within psychoanalytic theory. Although ostensibly concerned with conceptualizing more accurately the regulatory functions of the mind, the ego psychologists from Hartmann onward consistently did so while accepting the primacy of drives. This tendency was particularly noticeable in the work of David Rapaport. After Freud's death, Rapaport was arguably the most influential psychoanalytic theorist in the English-speaking world. Although Rapaport (1953) commented that "*affect charge* is conceptualized as a drive representation of the same order as the *idea*" (p. 489), he never really pursued the implications of this interesting hypothesis. The main thrust of his work was the attempt to work out all the apparent contradictions in drive theory. As Green (1977) said, "It is remarkable that in Rapaport, more faithful to Freud in letter than in spirit, the relationship of the affect to the signal never leads to a reflexion on the *sign* and in particular on language, in its relation to affects" (p. 140). Encyclopedic in his approach, almost obsessive in his attention to detail, Rapaport was much more invested in attempting to rationalize and reconcile any internal contradictions in Freudian theory than in pioneering a new conceptualization of affect. Straddling two fields—psychoanalysis and academic psychology—Rapaport helped insure that the predominant approach to emotions in both fields during the 1950s was drive oriented rather than cognitive. While he was alive, his pervasive influence made it unlikely that any significant new theories about affects would develop. After Rapaport's death, academic psychology experienced a reawakening of interest in new ways of conceptualizing affect, while psychoanalytic thinking about affect continued in its drive orientation until the challenge by self psychology (almost 20 years later) brought theorizing about affect to the foreground.

Freud's metaphysical assumption that "affects are composites" continued to have an important, albeit unrecognized, influence on theorizing about affects. As a practical matter, it is not possible to sketch, much less review, the development of affect theory post-Freud. In lieu of a comprehensive review, let me direct the reader's attention to *Theories of Emotion* (1980a) as an exemplar. The book, edited by Robert Plutchik and Henry Kellerman (1980a), includes 14 chapters by many of the leading theoreticians about affects, including Plutchik himself, Silvan Tomkins, Carroll Izard and Sandra Buechler, Richard Lazarus and his coworkers, George Mandler, Karl Pribram, and Charles Brenner. Many of these writers focus on what has come to be called the cognitive theory of emotion. As I will attempt to show here, the residuals of Freud's metaphysical theorizing, most particularly his view of affects as composites, show up more than 60 years later as the central tenets of the cognitive theory of emotion. My aim is not to criticize the theory or reject it outright, but simply to draw attention to how unrecognized metaphysical assumptions subtly and unconsciously influence the way we think.

The cognitive theory of emotion stresses the cognitive-evaluative function of the mind, "the continuous and automatic meaning analysis performed by the mental apparatus" (Mandler, 1980, p. 221). Cognitive theory emphasizes knowledge, how we come to know the world, how knowledge organizes our internal world, and therefore how we then react to the world-out-there. The cognitive theory of emotion considers affects to be complex, organized states. Central to the theory is that some sort of cognitive-evaluative process accompanies an emotion. Thus, Lazarus, Kanner, and Folkman (1980) define emotions as "complex, organized states (analogous to, not the same as, syndromes . . .) consisting of cognitive appraisals, action impulses, and patterned somatic reactions" (p. 198). The key concept in the theory is "cognitive appraisal"; the "cognitive evaluation" of Mandler (1980) and the "inferred cognition" of Plutchik (1980a) are but slightly different terms for the same process. Lazarus and his coauthors (1980) say that "in its fullest expression, a cognitively oriented theory states that each emotion quality and intensity—anxiety, guilt, jealousy, love, joy, or whatever—is generated and guided by its own particular pattern of appraisal" (p. 192). Thus, the appraisal itself becomes an integral part of the emotion. "Anger, for example, includes the attribution of blame for a particular kind of injury or threat, and guilt also involves such attribution of blame to oneself, with the further implication that one has not only done harm but has acted badly in accordance with personal standards of behavior" (p. 198). Thus, these attributions become more than the initial evaluation that precipitates the relevant emotions; they become embedded within the experience of anger and guilt. In other words: "Emotions not only involve an action impulse and somatic disturbances, but include as part of the emotional process and experience the cognitive appraisal on which they are based. Emotions and cognitions are thus inseparable, since appraisal comprises a part of the emotional reaction" (p. 198). Summarizing the work of Lazarus et al. as being representative of that of the cognitive theorists, Plutchik and Kellerman (1980b) say, "cognitive appraisals are fundamental precursors of all emotional states and . . . all emotions serve both an instrumental and expressive function" (p. xviii).

In many ways, these conceptualizations are similar to those of Brenner (1974), who considers affects a mixture of "ideas" (thought) and "sensations": "I believe that affects, whether pleasurable or unpleasurable . . . are complex mental phenomena which include (a) sensations of pleasure, unpleasure, or the mixture of the two, and (b) thoughts, memories, wishes, fears—in a word, ideas," adding, "Ideas and sensation together, both conscious and unconscious, constitute an affect" (pp. 534–535). The conception of affect as a synthesis either of "idea" and "sensation" (Brenner's formulation) or of "cognitive appraisals, action impulses, and patterned somatic reactions" (Lazarus's formulation) seems to be the working out of Freud's assumption that affects are composites. This formulation leads us automatically to the next question: what are affects composites of?

At the metaphysical level, the cognitive theory of emotion is a complicated working out of Freud's action–thought model of the mind that strips affects of their metaphysical sanction. Because of this switch, affects could no longer simply be thought of as nonsymbolic signals that, in and of themselves, conveyed information. This switch created a major theoretical problem: how do affects convey information? Brenner's answer is that affects are combinations that contain "ideas," a formulation that contains an obvious difficulty. The word idea—unless radically redefined—is usually used in connection with symbol usage (i.e., thinking). Affects are easily observable in animals (which are presumed to be unable to think) and infants long before the symbolic abilities come on-line. The way out of this dilemma was to look for some kind of "primitive thought" that was presumed to provide the cognitive content to affect. (This hypothesis is followed in detail in the next chapter.)

A far more difficult problem arises secondary to the subtle shifts in meaning attached to the word "cognitive." The word cognitive derives from the Latin word *cognoscere*, to know. If affects are process (the basic premise of the next essay), then the experience of any affect is itself cognitive because it adds to our knowledge about our body or the world. But, as used in the cognitive theory of emotion, the word "cognitive" slides toward being a hidden synonym for thought. For example, in a section entitled "Emotions and Cognitions," Plutchik (1980) says, "In the present context, *cognition will be considered as more or less synonymous with thinking* and will include such functions as perceiving, conceptualizing, and remembering" (p. 9, emphasis added). What is surprising is the power of the simple word "and." By entitling his section "Emotions *and* Cognitions," Plutchik subtly shifts the meaning of cognitive from a global term encompassing all types of mental activity into becoming an academic synonym for thought. This shift in meaning—already gaining acceptance—has several important consequences. Specifically, Plutchik's use of the word "and" implies that emotions are not "cognitions." By introducing a new vocabulary—"cognitions" for thought—all but the most careful reader will be led to believe that some progress has been made in resolving the longstanding thought–affect problem. This is not the case; it is simply translating the philosophic problem into the language of cognitive science. If one thinks in terms of a process theory of affects, then affects are not composites; they are simply *part* of the cognitive process.

4

The Search for Primitive Thought

In *The Interpretation of Dreams,* Freud (1900) demonstrated beyond any reasonable doubt that dreams have meaning and that if one understands the mechanisms involved, such as condensation and displacement, this meaning can be decoded. In the last chapter of *The Interpretation of Dreams*—the famous Chapter VII—Freud formulated the basic premises that served as the grounding operation for his theory of mind. There Freud defined two radically different modes of function in the "psychic apparatus," one of which he labeled as primary process and that held the key to understanding dream formation. In their excellent psychoanalytic dictionary, Laplanche and Pontalis (1967) comment:

> Freud's distinction between the primary and secondary processes is contemporaneous with his discovery of the unconscious processes, and it is in fact the first theoretical expression of this discovery. It [was first met with in] the "Project for a Scientific Psychology"; Freud developed it in Chapter VII of *The Interpretation of Dreams* and it always remained an unchanging co-ordinate of his thought [p. 339].

As we have seen, the distinction between primary and secondary process silently incorporated Freud's dualistic assumptions into psychoanalytic theory. That is to say, with this distinction, Freud reconceptualized the Cartesian distinction between body and mind as two different types of information processing.

Eleven years later, in "Formulations on the Two Principles of Mental Functioning," Freud (1911) attempted to clarify the distinction between primary and secondary process. Although Freud never defined the word "process" (he used it exclusively as part of the terms primary process and secondary process), his usage of the word makes it clear that he was describing a coherent, integrated system for processing information. Although Freud did not explicitly equate secondary process with thinking, it is virtually impossible to differentiate the two. In contrast, Freud makes it very clear that primary process is not the same as affect. This hypothesis, first laid down in the "Project" (Freud, 1895a), continued throughout his later work. One of the implicit assumptions of Freud's two-process model of the mind was that all information is processed by one of these two processes. The second assumption, clearly suggested by the word "primary," is that primary process antedates secondary process. The description and definition of primary process, however, continued to be obscure.

The use of dreams as the key for unlocking the secrets of the human mind had important and far-reaching consequences. Dreams are predominantly visual and, as Freud himself pointed out, words seldom appear in dreams. Thus, condensation and displacement are specific mechanisms for decoding the *visual symbolism* of the dream. As a consequence, the distinction between visual and verbal floats as a *leitmotif* through Freud's work. For example, Freud (1900) used the terms "perceptual identity" and "thought-activity" to denote the goals of primary and secondary process, respectively (p. 566). In the next sentence, Freud described perceptual identity as a type of "primitive thought-activity," thus linking the origins of "primitive thought" to perceptual experience. Although these terms did not appear again in Freud's writings, the idea that primary process is a type of primitive thought-activity persists throughout his work. For example, 15 years later in the paper "The Unconscious," Freud (1915c) contrasts the concreteness of "thing presentations" with the abstractness of "word presentations." These two sets of concepts (perceptual identity/thought-activity and thing presentation/word presentation) are basically variations on the same theme: the attempt to link the origins of thought to sensory (i.e., perceptual) experience. The empiricists such as Locke and Hume considered "ideas like superfaint copies of the real thing, with [internalized] images being faint copies" (Furth, 1969, p. 71). As some type of sensory experience is common to all animals, Freud's assumptions represent the acceptance of the basic empiricist assumptions about the origins of thought and a rejection of the Cartesian hypothesis that holds that reason is a faculty unique to humans. By linking the two terms (primary process; secondary process) verbally through the use of the word "process," Freud implies that the distinctions between the two are not all that great. Thus Freud can fulfill his hidden metaphysical agenda of maintaining the bond of "community" between man and the rest of the animal kingdom.

The problems inherent in the concept of primary process lay dormant in psychoanalysis for a number of years; they did not really begin to surface until an effort was made to synthesize the work of Freud and Piaget. Piaget, who some have called the second most important psychologist of the 20th century, intensively studied the cognitive development of the child. Piaget divided cognitive development into four major periods. The first is the sensorimotor period, which lasts from birth until about 16 to 18 months of age. During the sensorimotor period of development, the infant "lacks the symbolic function; that is, he does not have representations by which he can evoke persons or objects in their absence" (Piaget and Inhelder, 1969, p. 3). Piaget says that all the manifestations of the semiotic function—deferred imitation, symbolic play, the mental image, and language—make their appearance more or less simultaneously at around 18 months of age. (Piaget, following the lead of linguists, uses the term "semiotic function" to include any differentiated signifier.) If this conclusion is correct, and Piaget and his followers have produced an accumulating body of evidence that it is, then it exposes a huge deficit in Freud's theorizing. Primary process, however useful it might be in helping us understand jokes, dreams, and neurotic symptoms, is of no use at all in explaining simple types of behavior, such as how a child observes a piece of food, picks it up, and puts it in his mouth. Obviously, this information must be processed in some way. Only one conclusion is possible: *what Freud called "primary process" cannot be our first method of processing information*.

Piaget and Inhelder (1969) say, "The sensorimotor mechanisms are prerepresentational, and behavior based on the evocation of an absent object is not observed until during the second year" (p. 52). They add: "In the absence of language or symbolic function, however, these constructions are made with the sole support of perceptions and movements and thus by means of a sensori-motor coordination of actions, without the intervention of representation or thought" (p. 4). By saying that the sensorimotor period is "prerepresentational," what do they mean? Unfortunately, this question cannot be answered unless we are aware that the word "representative" carries a heavy epistemologic resonance in French philosophy (secondary to Descartes's expression "l'idée représentative").[1] These influences led Piaget (cited in Furth, 1969) to use the word "representation" as a synonym for thought.

> In fact, the word "representation" is used in two different senses. In the wide sense, representation is identical with thought, that is, with all intelligence which is not simply based on perceptions or movements (sensory-motor intelligence), but on a system of concepts or mental schemes. In the narrow sense, representation can be limited to the mental image or to the memory-image, that is, to the symbolic evocation of absent realities [p. 79].

In reading the work of Piaget, it is important to remember that, whichever usage is used, the term representation means some symbolic representation that is virtually identical to verbal thought. Consequently, when Piaget says that sensorimotor mechanisms are prerepresentational, he is simply saying that they take place prior to the ability to use language.

In its essentials, the concept of sensorimotor intelligence is the hypothesis of a prerepresentational (i.e., presymbolic) process that coordinates and regulates motor behavior. This leads to an obvious question: if symbols do not "coordinate the actions" during the sensorimotor period of development, what does? In other words, what serves the process function? Piaget never answers this question, other than to say that actions "are made with the sole support of perceptions and movements" (Piaget and Inhelder, 1969, p. 4). In effect, Piaget's theory of sensorimotor intelligence substitutes behavioral observations for process descriptions. Thus, although Piaget's observations of infant behavior are wonderfully detailed, they give us little or no feel for how the presymbolic infant actually "chooses" which action to initiate.

The difficulties in synthesizing the work of Freud and Piaget initially centered upon the issue of "representation." As just outlined, for Piaget the word representation means symbolic representation. This is not what the word means in English. The dictionary

---

[1] For an excellent review of the philosophic influences on Piaget's thinking, see the chapter "Piaget's Theory of Knowledge: The Nature of Representation and Interiorization" in Furth (1969).

definition of representation is "a likeness, image, picture, etc."[2] This ordinary-language definition is reasonably well captured by the definition in *Psychoanalytic Terms and Concepts* (1990), the dictionary published by the American Psychoanalytic Association: "A *psychic representation* is a more or less consistent reproduction within the mind of a perception of a meaningful thing or object" (p. 166). In other words, within the English philosophic tradition, a psychic representation is a concrete, but not necessarily symbolic, internalized reconstruction of experience. This definition fits the scientific evidence. From the moment of birth, infants, as well as all animals that are capable of paying attention, begin to construct a working map of their environment that includes the infant himself, significant others, as well as the important features of the inanimate environment. Learning the neurophysiologic mechanisms by which infants and animals construct this map is a problem that is well on the way to solution. What Piaget would call a schema would probably be called a representation in the English-speaking world.[3]

The deeper, more fundamental problem is to try to understand the control mechanisms of presymbolic infants (i.e., how do they process experience?). Piaget's description of sensorimotor intelligence as prerepresentational (by which he means presymbolic) does not begin to answer this question. Jerome Bruner (1964), one of America's leading psychologists, attempting to synthesize the work of Piaget and Freud, approached this issue through the problem of representation. He proposes three separate and distinct modes of representation. He calls the first mode of representation "enactive," implying that this stands for "encoded action"; this corresponds to Piaget's sensorimotor intelligence. The second mode of representation is "iconic," which Bruner equates with imagery; in this mode, Bruner clearly means to include Freud's primary process. The third mode, the symbolic (which is based on language), is equivalent to Freud's secondary process. In other words, Bruner attempts to reconcile the differences between Freud and Piaget by hypothesizing three separable systems through which information about the world is processed. Mardi Horowitz (1972) expanded Bruner's concept of three representational systems by hypothesizing that action is processed

---

[2] Unless otherwise noted, all dictionary definitions are from *Webster's Deluxe Unabridged Dictionary* (1979). For ease of exposition, formal citations for dictionary definitions are not used; nor are page references inasmuch as the alphabetical format of a dictionary makes this unnecessary.

[3] A further discussion of the concept of representation is contained in the section on "Memory, Schema, and the Concept of Representation" in chapter 9 of the next essay, "Affects as Process."

by a primitive type of thought, which he labeled "enactive thought" (p. 797).

Essentially, both Bruner and Horowitz were attempting to understand how behavior during the sensorimotor phase of development can be regulated, controlled, or processed. The difficulty with both Bruner's conception of the enactive mode of representation and Horowitz's concept of enactive thought is that they are essentially redundant. Simply put, action is represented in consciousness by encoded action. In effect, this translates the behavioristic assumptions of Piaget's work on the sensorimotor period into the language of representation by relabeling the description of a piece of behavior (action) as the *mode of representation*. In the Bruner/Horowitz model, thought is now subdivided into three subdivisions: ordinary thinking (secondary process), primary-process thinking (as illustrated by dreams), and an even more primitive type of "enactive thought" that controls actions. Related to enactive thought is the concept of "imageless thought." I do not want to review the famous "imageless thought" controversy, but merely to suggest that it carries the search for "primitive thought" to its logical conclusion. The problem with the concepts of enactive thought and imageless thought is that they are shadowy, elusive, and mysterious—concepts without a referent. As Bruner (1966) himself put it in another context, "Vague descriptions will never give birth to powerful theories" (p. 314).

The roots of this theoretical predicament are deeply embedded in Freud's reflex-arc model of the mind. In *The Interpretation of Dreams,* Freud (1900) wrote, "This, however, does no more than fulfil a requirement with which we have long been familiar, namely that the psychical apparatus must be constructed like a reflex apparatus. Reflex processes remain the model of every psychical function" (p. 538). The quasi-neurologic model of Chapter VII is, in many ways, a continuation of the speculations that he set down in 1895, but never published, the "Project for a Scientific Psychology" (Freud, 1895a). Although Freud later abandoned this model, "the *Project,* or rather its invisible ghost, haunts the whole series of Freud's theoretical writings to the very end" (Strachey, 1966b, p. 290). This is particularly so in the writings that are known as metapsychology. Consequently, one must have at least a rough working knowledge of the reflex arc in order to understand its influence on subsequent theory building.

The concept of the reflex arc grew out of the early 19th century experiments of Bell and Magendie, who found that the selective cutting of the dorsal roots of the nerves of a limb of a dog produced anesthesia of that limb without any marked change in the patterns of motor function that governed movement; selective cutting of the ventral roots produced paralysis without any alteration in sensitivity. These two investigators had taken advantage of the easily observable anatomic fact that every somatic peripheral nerve splits into two major divisions at its junction with the spinal cord: a ventral (toward the stomach) and dorsal (toward the back) root: "The results of these experiments were so dramatic that they became generalized in a 'law' (the Law of Bell and Magendie) which states that input and output from the central nervous system are carried by noninteracting pathways. Hence, input nerves are called afferents (*ad* + *fero* = to carry in) and output nerves are called efferents (*ex* + *fero* = to carry out)" (Pribram, 1971, p. 85). In reviewing this work, Pribram (1971) commented, "A long and often implicitly held generalization of the Law of Bell and Magendie holds that all afferents are sensory (i.e., connected to sensory receptors) and all efferents are motor (i.e., connected to contactile muscles) a generalization Sherrington made explicit in his famous fiction, the reflex arc" (p. 85). The model of the reflex arc, particularly when combined with the empiricist assumptions that linked thought formation to sensory input, created a formidable barrier to building a satisfactory theory of affects because of the assumption that efferents were not sensory; *therefore the regulation of motor activity could not be conceptualized in terms of affective processes.* Individually and in combination, these two assumptions were enough to prevent the exploration of the hypothesis that motor activity could be directly regulated by affective processes.

Recently, a way out of this dilemma was suggested by modern neurophysiology. The concept of the reflex arc has been revised, primarily because of new neurophysiological data that was not available to Sherrington. The central conclusion of the new neurophysiology is that movements are not only *initiated* but continuously *mediated* by sensory processes. The neurophysiologic experiments and reasoning that led to this conclusion are outlined by Pribram (1971, esp. chs. 5, 7, 8, 12, 13). This data can only be briefly sketched. Basically, further investigations have shown that one-third of the nerve fibers from the ventral root are not motor fibers. These fibers, which are called the gamma efferent system, are characterized by a small diameter and end in a group of specialized muscle receptors called muscle spindles. After the larger fibers of the ventral root have been dissected out and cut, stimulation of the gamma fibers shows that the function of the gamma efferents is not motor (p. 86). Because of the presence of the gamma efferent system, the neural control of motor behavior can no longer be conceptualized as output of a simple reflex arc. It must be considered to be a feedback type of circuit, which can be "tuned" by the gamma efferent system's acting as a feedback and feedforward mechanism. In short, it becomes a "biasable servomechanism."

Pribram also concludes that the motor cortex has a dual function and that a great deal of sensory information other than movement is encoded on it. From a series of elegant experiments, he concludes that the motor cortex is really a "sensory cortex for action" (p. 248). Rather than encoding either specific muscles or specific movements, the motor cortex produces an "Image-of-Achievement." The Image-of-Achievement, which is holographic in nature, is not much different from other sensory representations. The Image-of-Achievement is then converted to action, which is continuously updated through a neural holographic process much as is a perceptual image. He concludes that, "The model that emerges from these researches differs considerably from the conception of the motor cortex as a keyboard upon which the activities of the rest of the brain (and/or mind) converge to play a melody of movement. Rather, patterns of know-*how* here become encoded and make possible effective Acts, the external representations of brain processes" (p. 250). He later adds, "The Image-of-Achievement regulates behavior much as do the settings on a thermostat: the pattern of the turning on and off of the furnace is not encoded on the dial, *only the set-points to be achieved are*. Simplicity in design and economy of storage result" (p. 251, emphasis added). In other words, we choose *when, what, and where* we are going to move the set-points on the dial, but the mechanics of movement, the how, is mediated through the Image-of-Achievement.

To recapitulate, Pribram, who relabels the motor cortex a "sensory cortex for action," considers the how, the mechanics of movement, to be mediated by sensory processes. Although the neurophysiology is quite complex, Pribram has outlined a model of action that explains how an organism takes the set-points of movement (the where) and translates these set-points into smooth, coordinated movement. This model has freed psychology and psychoanalysis from the need to hypothesize a type of primitive thought to explain the mechanisms that control bodily movement; that question becomes the province of neurophysiology. Thus, we are left with a question that psychology should be able to answer: where, when, and why do we move? This is a question that can be framed in the language of motivation.

Within the hypothesis that affects represent an integrated system of nonsymbolic information processing, we can now refine the question: how are the set-points for an action represented in consciousness? How do we *experience* the if, when, and where of bodily movement? I suggest that the *impulse,* which we experience as our wanting to move from here to there, directs our bodily movements and is itself governed by affective processes. The impulse defines the "set-points on the dial." Neurophysiologically, the Image-of-Achievement translates a "want" into smooth, coordinated motor activity. As the infant develops, he gradually learns through a series of repetitive trials to make his body go where he wants to go, do what he wants it to. ("Where? There! I *want* to go *there*.") The stages of this repetitive learning of movement are well outlined by Piaget. As the infant becomes more proficient at bodily movement, the frustration at not being able to accomplish the movement lessens, thereby lessening the intensity of the governing affect. In time, we become so proficient at physical movement that the impulses of *wanting* to move are experienced at such low intensity that we usually do not pay much attention to them. They are there, though, just below the surface of our ordinary awareness, and, if we take the time to sort through the background noise, we can gain the experiential sense of how impulses guide our physical movement.

Let us briefly review the entire sequence of behavior. As will be developed in the next essay, the organism receives information from the body in the form of sensations. In addition, it receives a constant flow of information about the external world in the form of visual, aural, olfactory, and tactile data (perceptions). These are compared with previous experiences, which are monitored by feelings of familiarity or unfamiliarity. If we encounter the unfamiliar, we tend to pay more attention, which is focused by feelings of interest or curiosity, apprehension or fear. This information is organized into a number of motivational systems, which are monitored by a number of specific emotions, such as fear, rage, love, grief, disgust, pride, or shame. After all this information is synthesized and cross-correlated, we arrive at some type of response, which usually involves taking some kind of physical action. This action or group of actions is mediated through the Image-of-Achievement. What is represented in consciousness in Pribram's model of action are the "set-points on the dial." I suggest that we set the "points on the dial" through the impulse, which we experience as "wanting." In brief, the affective impulse guides our actions, with the brain translating the impulse into smooth, coordinated movement through a neural holographic process. Through this mechanism, it becomes possible to conceptualize the control of bodily movements as being directed by affective processes.

5

Is Primary Process Primary?

This essay started with a question, Is primary process primary? The answer to this question is simple and straightforward: No. It simply cannot be. Not if words mean what they imply. Not if the word "primary" means the first to arrive, and not if the word "process" is a shorthand way of describing an integrated way of processing information. Affects are our primary process. Specifically, affects are the experiential, nonsymbolic representations of our first information-processing system. This conclusion fits well with the work of Jean Piaget, who found that the capacity to use symbols does not emerge until approximately 15 to 18 months. Some of the mechanisms of how affects function as our first information-processing system are worked out in greater detail in the next essay, "Affects as Process."

The real question is not whether primary process is primary, but why the concept has not been subject to a more serious critique. It clearly demonstrates the powerful effect of a controlling paradigm on theory formation. Freud's theory of drive *(Trieb)* stripped affect of its process role. Consequently, affect was conceptualized as derivative, a process of discharge, arising when action was not carried forward to completion. Philosophically, Freud's theory of drive deprived affect of its metaphysical sanction. Secondarily, affects were conceptualized as composites, as mixtures of drive discharge plus some cognitive component. In turn, these conceptualizations led to the search for some type of primitive thought to explain the cognitive content of the affect. These foundational metaphysical assumptions, part of Freud's hidden philosophic agenda, were a significant hindrance in constructing a process theory of affects.

Another problem was the difficulty of trying to conceptualize how motor activity is controlled. A long-held neurophysiologic belief was that the design of the spinal cord was fairly simple: sensory in/motor out. This neurophysiologic model played a major role in forming Freud's reflex-arc model of the mind. Piaget dodged this problem by characterizing the sensorimotor period as prerepresentational and describing it in terms of behavior; doing so allowed him to avoid characterizing the infant's experience of the control systems. The effort by others to fill this gap once again led to the search for primitive thought. For example, concepts such as enactive thought (for encoded action) were proposed in an attempt to conceptualize the control system during the sensorimotor phase of development. A solution to this problem was found by Karl Pribram, who demonstrated that the motor cortex was really a *sensory cortex for action*. From this discovery, it is a short step to hypothesize that motoric activity can be controlled by affective impulses. This discovery broke a conceptual logjam, allowing us to construct an all-affect information-processing model of the mind.

II

Affects as Process

1

The Language of Affectivity

AFFECTS AND FEELINGS

The word "affect" is a term borrowed by psychoanalysis from German psychology. Laplanche and Pontalis (1967) define affect thus: "It connotes any affective state, whether painful or pleasant, whether vague or well defined, and whether it is manifested in the form of a massive discharge or in the form of a general mood" (p. 13). Within the framework of psychoanalytic theory, diverse emotions such as love, hate, and fear; bodily sensations such as hunger, thirst, and physical pain; and moods such as mania and depression are usually lumped together as affects. For example, David Rapaport (1953) allowed that "the term affect . . . will be used to stand for the terms 'emotion' and 'feeling' also, since there is no clear distinction in the literature in the use of these terms" (p. 476). Roy Schafer (1964) took a similar stance: "Nor will the terms *affect, emotion,* and *feeling* be differentiated; such efforts have been made, but there is no general agreement as to their merit" (pp. 275–276). The apparent preference for the more scientific-sounding term affect is sometimes justified on the ground that the terms of our everyday vocabulary—words such as feelings and emotions—are too difficult to define.

The difficulty with this approach is that, for most people, the word affect lacks any inner resonances; it becomes an awkward term, a mental footnote, constantly reminding the user, "Remember,

39

now, we are trying to speak scientifically." The use of such words as affect is part of the legacy of the effort, begun a century ago, to study the mind in a scientific way. The impetus for this change began in Germany, where, at the University of Leipzig, Wilhelm D. Wundt initiated the requirement for laboratory experience as an essential part of training for psychologists. At the time, this was regarded as a revolutionary innovation. *The New Psychology,* as it was called in the title of a book by Professor E. W. Scripture of Yale University, would follow the methodology of science (cited in D. Klein, 1970, p. 21). "Armchair psychology," Scripture's rather disparaging term for philo-sophic psychology, would be replaced by the new (i.e., scientific) psychology. One of the means of reaching this goal was to adopt a more objective terminology, free from the biases of everyday speech.

For most people, the word feelings usually includes any affective experience. The range of the word feeling is readily apparent if we examine the following three sentences: "I feel hungry"; "I feel angry at him"; "I feel like going to the movies tonight." In the first sentence, the word hungry describes a bodily sensation, similar to such experiences as thirsty, sleepy, hot, cold, or physical pain. In the second sentence, the word angry describes what most people would call an emotion, a class of feelings that would include love, hate, and fear, but not hunger, thirst, or physical pain. In the third sentence, "I feel like going to the movies," the emphasis is on how feeling can direct our behavior, what we commonly call an impulse. Basically, "affect" is the psychoanalytic synonym for the ordinary-language term "feelings." One of the primary goals of this essay is to attempt to clarify the language of mental experience as it is used in ordinary English conversation.

In reflecting about the origins of the term feelings, we immedi-ately notice that it is part of the language of the sense of touch. The reasons why we use the language of touch are worth speculating about. To begin with, touch is not a unitary sensing system; we now know that touch does not depend on a single "touch receptor." Rather, what we lump together as the sense of touch is really a combination of inputs from a number of specialized receptors such as pressure, light touch, cold, and pain. Therefore, to speak precisely, we must discriminate what it is that we are feeling; in other words, we must specify "It feels hot"; "It feels cold"; "It hurts." Furthermore, all these feelings share with one another the phenomenological quality of immediacy, of some impingement on our body. Just as feeling (as in the sense of touch) describes an impingement from the outside, our bodily sensations describe the sense of impingement on the sense of well-being from within. Thus, we can say, "I feel hungry," or "I feel thirsty," or "I feel tired." Consequently, it isn't surprising that we use the same word—feelings—to describe both. Perhaps our intuition partially guides us to the linguistic usage of the word "feelings" because, embryologically, the core brain receptors involved in sensation develop from the same neural crest tissue that forms some of the specialized sense receptors involved in touch, as well as some of the other sensory modalities (Pribram, 1971, p. 174). In any case, the word feelings, the language of the sense of touch, has broadened its scope so that it is commonly used to describe not only sensation, but all affective experience.

Today, the word feelings has acquired so many pop-psychology connotations that it is difficult to believe that the word could ever be taken seriously within the realm of psychoanalytic discourse. Therefore, despite the awkward, scientific connotations that the word "affect" carries, I think it is the best term available. As anyone who has studied language knows, the meaning of words shifts over the course of time, sometimes rapidly. Four to five hundred years ago, the word affect was used more or less as it is today, as a general, all-inclusive term meaning "feeling, desire, or appetite, as opposed to reason" *(Oxford English Dictionary I)*. For example, Sir Francis Bacon said, "The Affects and Passions of the Heart and Spirits are notably disclosed by the Pulse" (1626: *Sylvia,* 97: quoted from the *Oxford English Dictionary I*). Over the intervening period of time, however, this meaning gradually became obsolete. Perhaps, with the passage of time, the old meanings of the word affect will gradually be resurrected. If so, then the word will be reclaimed as part of our working vocabulary.

PERCEPTION AND "OBJECTIVITY"

In the Western world, people are usually thought of as having five senses: seeing, hearing, taste, touch, and smell. Two of these senses, seeing and hearing, collect information about the external world. The other three senses, taste, touch, and smell, do not ordinarily allow for an attribution of distance; the localization is to the receptor surface. Even with these receptor modalities, however, we sense that we are touching, tasting, or smelling something that is not ourself.

Thus, our skin becomes the boundary line between the "world-out-there" and the "world-within" (Pribram, 1971, p. 167).[1] Customarily we refer to the data about the world-out-there as perceptions. Perception gives us our picture of the external world, a world filled with sights, sounds, smells, and things that we can touch. In constructing a representation of experience, we tend to give priority to visual data, particularly when that data is reinforced by the sense of touch. The cross-modal correlation between sight and touch convinces us that something, a thing we call an object, is really there; it is not a figment of our imagination. In addition, we have developed an impressive array of adjectives to describe the various qualities of the things we can touch and see: size, shape, form, color, texture. Thus, our vocabulary allows us to focus our visual-tactile perceptions and to communicate them to others; when these observations match and can be measured and checked, then we can say that they have been consensually verified. In this process of verification, we have the beginning of what we call "objectivity."

Nouns are the first part of speech we learn. In the first 18 months of using words, we learn the names of things we can touch and see; we learn to distinguish cats from dogs, tables from chairs, men from women, babies from adults, trees from flowers. This priority of seeing-touching is contained in well-known sayings like "Seeing is believing" or "A picture is worth a thousand words." These seemingly simple sayings are a treasure trove that allows us a glimpse of the powerful unconscious assumptions that link the visual process to the origins of thought. For example, in Greek, the root word for idea and image is the verb "to see" (*The Encyclopedia of Philosophy,* 1967, "Ideas"). In part, Plato's theory of forms is the detailed working out of this assumption. Twenty centuries later, Freud's theory of hallucinatory wish fulfillment as the origin of thought is a likely continuation of this assumption. In our everyday speech, this connection is expressed in the phrase "I see" as an easy synonym for "I understand."

One of the primary reasons for our confidence in the cross-modal correlation of the visual and tactile information is that we have developed an extensive vocabulary that helps us sort and organize this information, thereby allowing us to communicate it to others. The rich and descriptive vocabulary we have for visual-tactile data

---

[1] The terms "world-out-there" and "world-within" were used by Pribram (1971) in his book *Languages of the Brain.* I suspect he adopted this terminology to avoid the philosophic thickets surrounding the term "reality." These terms are used in this book for the same reason.

is immediately apparent when we compare it with our other sensory modalities. For example, our olfactory sense is extremely powerful; we can detect trace quantities—one part in a billion—of the mercapto-purine placed in natural gas by the gas company to make it detectable (natural gas has no smell). Not only can we detect extremely small amounts of a substance, but we can also make exquisitely subtle distinctions. Perhaps the best demonstration of this is a pleasant evening with wine experts; in many cases, they can tell not only the winery but also the year the wine was bottled. Clearly, our olfactory sense is capable of minute and subtle distinctions. The problem begins when we attempt to communicate this information. For the most part, smells are usually described by their presumed origin—"It smells like an orange," "It smells like vanilla," "It smells like coffee." In a very few, select cases, we can say something a little more specific; for example, the word "fruity" begins to describe the aromatic esters associated with fruit. But in most situations we cannot even begin to describe an odor that is new to us; we simply have not developed a vocabulary that lets us communicate effectively about olfactory experience. In many ways, this is the same type of problem that crops up when we begin to talk about affects; we lack an agreed-upon vocabulary. In the ensuing sections of this chapter, I will attempt to sketch out the distinctions between different affective states, while trying, insofar as possible, to stay with ordinary-language usage.

SENSATION

In addition to our five special senses that we think of as constituting perception, we now know that we have a number of sense receptors deep within the core of the brain. These sense organs function by producing what Pribram (1971) calls "monitor images," which we experience as the easily recognized feelings of hunger, thirst, and so on. For example, hunger tells us we need more food, thirst tells us that we need more water, and smothering tells us that we desperately need more oxygen. Cannon (1932) christened these receptors "homeostats"; as he pointed out, the purpose of these monitors is to make sure that we maintain a stable internal environment. At birth, most of these core brain receptors are "wired in" and ready to provide specific information about our bodily needs. These sensing mechanisms form the core of a motivational system that regulates our physiologic requirements (Lichtenberg, 1989). The data from these inner sensing mechanisms, which Freud grouped together as the "instincts of self-preservation," is often referred to as sensations in the literature of experimental and physiological psychology. This usage, which parallels ordinary-language usage, is adhered to throughout this book.

All the sensations that measure our bodily processes—hunger, thirst, pain, tiredness—are experienced as moving up and down an intensity gradient. We have words to describe these variations in intensity. Let us consider a simple example: hunger, the feeling that measures our need for food. At one end of the spectrum we have the nice Scottish word "peckish," which means a little hungry, not quite ready for a real meal, but perhaps ready to snack (i.e., to peck at food). At the other extreme, "famished" means extremely hungry. (The word famine comes from the same root.) This variation in intensity allows us to grade our response qualitatively to fit the specific situation. Thus, if we felt famished, we would probably stop whatever else we were doing until we found some food. Some of our feelings—such as smothering and physical pain—are coded so that they escalate from silent to very intense in a great hurry; in this way, they act as an emergency alarm system. For example, if one should accidentally touch a hot stove, the pain overrides everything else until the problem is taken care of. These analogic gradients are a very economical method of prioritizing information and focusing our attention.

At this point, perhaps it is useful to clarify the distinction between symbols and analogs. A mercury thermometer is an excellent model of an analogic machine, constructed so that the height of the column of mercury measures the ambient temperature. The thermometer does not symbolize the temperature; it measures it. The concept of affects as analogs has been studied by Silvan Tomkins (1980): "the concept of affect as amplification has been revised so that the affect is now considered to be an analogic amplifier in much the same manner as pain is an analogic amplifier of the injury it amplifies" (p. 141). As an analog, the information is continuously available to us, although we may not focus on or pay attention to it when there is no problem. If we simply "tune in" to our bodies, we can usually feel how hungry, thirsty, or tired we are. These feelings, Freud's "instincts of self-preservation," provide a continuous readout of how our body is functioning. In short, sensations are conceptualized as the analogic measures of bodily processes, which then serve as the informational input of a motivational system that regulates our physiologic requirements (see Lichtenberg, 1989).

AFFECTS AND MOTIVATIONAL SYSTEMS

It is not sensations but the study of emotions that really interests us in the study of human beings. William James (1892) described anger, fear, love, hate, joy, grief, shame, and pride as the *"coarser emotions"* (p. 374). Tomkins (1962, 1963), building on Darwin's work, described nine primary affects: 1) interest, 2) enjoyment, 3) surprise, 4) distress, 5) fear, 6) anger, 7) disgust, 8) contempt, and 9) shame. A number of other theorists—Izard and Buechler (1980), Plutchik (1980), and De Rivera (1977) to name but a few—have similarly devised lists of "core emotions." While these lists vary somewhat from one another, they all have one thing in common: they all conspicuously omit the feelings that register bodily sensations, such as hunger, thirst, sleepiness, or physical pain. Thus, the differentiation of emotion from sensation seems rather well settled, a discrimination that we are already used to making.

The primary thesis of this essay is that emotions are the experiential monitor of complex motivational systems. By cross-comparing the affective intensity of feelings from competing systems, the organism has a simple, effective way of prioritizing information and thus reaching a decision, which, in turn, initiates a course of action. Consider the following example: a fairly hungry animal spots prey that may be difficult to kill. This situation exposes the hunting animal to the danger of being injured or killed. If fear overrides hunger, the animal will retreat and look for easier prey; however, if hunger overrides fear, the animal will attack despite the danger. In this example, a motivational system that regulates physiologic needs (hunger) is competing with a system that protects the body from harm (fear). Thus, the intensity of the competing affects allows for a quick means of prioritizing information and determining choice. This connection between emotions and motivational systems is illustrated by the etymologic history of the terms; both words are derivatives of the Latin word *movere* and its past participle *motivere*. In effect, we think of emotions as something that "moves" us to action.

Let us review how motivation has been handled within psychoanalytic theory. In many ways, the concept of motivational systems is implicit throughout the body of Freud's work, although it is deeply embedded in his understanding of the concept of drive *(Trieb)*. The acknowledged starting point of his theorizing about drives was the phrase from the poet Schiller, "Hunger and love are what moves the world." Hunger was the prototype of the "instincts of self-preservation." These bodily sensations form the core of a motivational system that regulates the body's physiologic requirements. Although not stated in the language of systems theory, Freud was saying that there are two fundamentally different types of motivation: 1) those that deal with the body's physiologic needs (e.g., hunger); and 2) love. In Freud's theorizing, "love" becomes the libidinal drive, which he conceptualized as being primarily sexual in nature. The other person, whom Freud (1915a) subsumed under the general term "object," was only the vehicle through which bodily needs were to be met.

Reacting to this viewpoint, the British object relations school reconceptualized the drive to form relationships as primary. In this revamped theory of drive, the pursuit of pleasure for itself (i.e., hedonism) was usually the result of the failure of what came to be called an object relationship (Guntrip, 1961). Dispensing with the language of drive theory altogether, John Bowlby (1969) went further and formulated a primary need for attachment. Working with a systems-theory approach, Lichtenberg (1989) has named this the affiliational system, one of his five primary motivational systems. Whether it is conceptualized as libido theory, object relations theory, attachment theory, or a motivational system, we are talking about the same phenomenon: the tendency of human beings to form long-term, relatively stable relationships. Within the conceptual framework being developed here, attachment (or affiliation) is the *observable* behavior of the motivational system, while affection or love is its experiential representation.

In 1920, Freud raised "aggression" to the status of a drive in his controversial essay *Beyond the Pleasure Principle*. On the basis of this theoretical revision, Freud might have concluded that man had three basic drives, rather than two: bodily needs, "love," and aggression. Freud's emphasis on "dualism" prevailed, however, and a new dualism was brought forward—between love (the life instinct) and aggression (the death instinct). At first Freud hesitated to place the self-preservative instincts in this scheme. Toying with the idea that the self-preservative instincts are part of the death instinct, he says that they are merely detours expressing the fact that "the organism wishes to die only in its own fashion" (Freud, 1920, p. 39). In the very next paragraph, however, he reverses himself and declares that the self-preservative instincts are a particular instance of the work of the life instincts.

What is clear in this discussion is that Freud did not even remotely consider a three-drive model. The only question was where to move the self-preservative instincts, thus preserving a dual-drive theoretical framework. In many important respects, Freud's dual-ism had more to do with form than with content, more with *how* we think than with *what* we think. On a number of separate issues, Freud thought in terms of conflicting, highly polarized forces. This emphasis on dualism added an aesthetic dimension to Freud's theorizing that has been relatively unappreciated. As in mathemat-ics, we expect our theories not only to be valid and useful in synthesizing the data (the criterion for most theories) but *elegant* as well. It is safe to say that if Freud had gone on to develop a three-drive model of the mind, the history of psychoanalysis would have been much different.

As a consequence of this emphasis on aesthetic form, the dual-drive theory—love (libido) and aggression—remained a central fixture in psychoanalytic theory for over half a century. This left psychoanalytic theory with a serious problem: how do we account for the vast repertory of behavior that has to do with competence and adapting to the environment? In some of his writings, Freud had touched on the subject and mentioned an "instinct for mastery" (1905, p. 193; 1920, p. 16). Expanding on this theme in the early 1940s, Ives Hendrick (1942, 1943a,b), in a series of papers on the "instinct to master," posited that there is "an inborn drive to do and to learn how to do" (1942, p. 40). These papers did not, however, lead to a revision of psychoanalytic theory, for to do so would have meant rethinking the dual-drive theory. In the early 1950s, Hartmann and his colleagues "solved" these problems by describing these behaviors as ego functions; the dual-drive theory was preserved by being said to be fueled by neutral (i.e., noninstinctual) energy. This led to the search for what Greenberg and Mitchell (1983) call "the elusive 'third drive' of the ego psychologists":

> The reason for this suggestive avoidance is inherent in the funda-mental premises of the drive/structure model. Freud's determinedly dualistic theory requires that *all* motivation be derived from origi-nally untamed, unmodulated sexual and aggressive energies. This interpretive stricture has seemed confining to many subsequent theorists; hence the idea of a third drive is attractive. Yet the explanatory domain of the "third drive" must always remain vague. To postulate phenomena which require the third drive is to suggest that the dual-instinct theory is not comprehensive enough. This has long been the argument of relational/structure model theorists, but it has no comfortable place within classical theory. The third drive appears to be each theorist's response to a perceived motivational

"missing link," but none has been quite willing to make that gap explicit or to tell us just how the third drive might fill it [p. 323].

While the circumlocutions of neutral, or noninstinctual, energy were sufficient to satisfy the dual-drive purists, they were insufficient to provide the theoretical grounding for the burgeoning field of infant research that was increasingly interested in the infant's interaction with and mastery of the environment. As a consequence, many infant researchers simply abandoned the language of drive theory altogether, leading to a body of literature that is usually referred to as developmentalist. The terminologic problems simply prevented a productive dialogue.

In 1989, Lichtenberg presented a new theory of motivation that synthesized the findings of contemporary infant research with psychoanalytic theory. In his book *Psychoanalysis and Motivation,* he outlines five primary motivational systems: 1) the need for psychic regulation of physiologic requirements (Freud's self-preservative instincts); 2) the need for attachment/affiliation (the core of the object relations critique of Freud's libido theory); 3) the need for exploration and assertion ("the elusive third drive" of the ego psychologists, which deals with mastery); 4) the need to react adversely through antagonism or withdrawal (Freud's "aggression," modified by later research on "fight or flight" responses); 5) the need for sensual enjoyment and sexual excitement (Freud's "libido"). Each of these motivational systems is grounded in the findings of infant research and illustrated with clinical data bearing on a variety of both normal and pathological conditions.

As Lichtenberg points out, the change from the term "structure" to "system" is quite important; the word "structure" connotes stability, while the word "system" connotes change and plasticity (p. 6). In bringing systems theory to the study of human motivation, Lichtenberg has provided the conceptual tool for organizing the vast array of data into a coherent, easy-to-understand framework. Although the term systems theory may be somewhat intimidating in the abstract, we are quite used to thinking this way. When we talk about the human body, we usually refer to specific systems: the cardiovascular system, the gastrointestinal system, the endocrine system, and the reproductive system. In an automobile, we have the power train, the electrical system, the air conditioning system, the braking system, and so forth. At its bare essentials, systems theory is a conceptual tool that allows us to sort through vast arrays of information and classify it (and thus think about it) by function.

Inevitably, Lichtenberg needed to integrate affects into his work on motivational systems. Quoting Sandler, he states that affects are the prime motivators of human behavior (p. 259). Then he goes on to say, *"Cross-sectionally, affects provide the principal means of identifying moment-to-moment shifts in motivational dominance"* (p. 260, emphasis added). In other words, affects tell you which motivational system you are in. This statement appears in the chapter on "Model Scenes, Affects, and the Unconscious," which focuses primarily on the clinical usefulness of a motivational-systems approach in working with patients. At the time that he wrote this, I believe that Lichtenberg was unaware that he had given us the Rosetta stone for developing a "satisfactory theory of affects." Not only are affects a nonsymbolic language, they are *the* language of motivational systems. They provide the affective signal, not only to the organism itself but to others as well, indicating what motivational system is operative. For example, let us examine the process of feeding. In most species, the sensation of hunger signals that it is "time to eat"; this feeling usually leads to the search for food. When something potentially edible is found, another set of feelings signals whether the food is good or bad. The meaning and the adaptive function of the emotion "disgust" can hardly be mistaken: "The food is bad." The opposite of disgust might be described as the "yummy" feeling, a response that sometimes leads people to describe food as "mouth watering." After eating, we usually experience the feeling of satiety, a feeling often accompanied by a sense of relaxation as well as a number of physiologic changes. Thus, our feelings and emotions work together, as a nonsymbolic "vocabulary," simplifying a vast complex of neurophysiologic data into relatively simple, easy-to-understand signals. Motivational systems, with affects serving as their experiential monitors, provide us with a useful, straightforward method of conceptualizing human motivation. In summary, I believe that Joseph Lichtenberg has provided one of the conceptual tools for unraveling the puzzle of affect.

I do disagree with Lichtenberg on one specific point. In reviewing the work of Silvan Tomkins, with a particular focus on the study of disgust, shame, and contempt and their relation to what I will call the competence/mastery system, I came to the conclusion that fear and rage represent two very different motivational systems. The affect of fear acts as the signal of a system designed to protect the physical safety of the organism; the danger may be a physical one, such as fire or heights, or it may be the danger of a predator. The message that fear conveys could not be more clear: Danger! Protect yourself! In some cases, such as a baby chick's fleeing at the sight of a cardboard cutout resembling a hawk, the response is wired in; in other cases, social learning plays a much larger part. In short, fear is exclusively defensive in nature and activates a series of behaviors designed to provide physical self-protection.

In contrast, rage serves as the monitor of what I call the competitive/territorial system. While it is certainly true that we become angry when attacked, the primary purpose of aggression, and its affective signal of anger and rage, is not defensive. Aggression serves the very specific adaptive function of allocating scarce resources, such as food, mates, and territory, among members of the same species. This is sometimes done by fighting but, more often, by the threat of fighting, as both parties can usually determine in advance who will be the winner. This knowledge, shared by members of the group, leads to the avoidance of fighting through the establishment of dominance hierarchies. I suggest further that the emotions of pride and shame play a major role in communicating these dominance hierarchies. In humans, swaggering pride conveys a clear message, "I can beat you"; while the eye-avoiding emotion of shame conveys a gesture of submission, "You are right, I won't fight with you." Taken together, aggression (the behavior) and rage (the affective monitor indicating that the animal is "fighting mad") constitute a motivational system that I would describe as the competitive/territorial system. As elaborated in chapter 7, I think that the confusion between the competence/mastery and competitive/territorial motivational systems is secondary to our discomfort with and disapproval of "aggression."

THE DYNAMIC CONTOURS OF AFFECTS

As noted in the discussion of hunger, affects, as analogs, are experienced through a range of intensity. This intensity gradient, which applies equally to sensations, moods, and emotions, is so much a part of affective experience that Tomkins described his nine primary affects by pairs of words, so as to capture the idea of an affective range. Thus Tomkins describes distress → anguish; fear → terror; anger → rage; shame → humiliation, and so on. These experienced changes in intensity, the analogic representation of complex sensing systems, allow us to make quantitative distinctions. Thus, the intensity of our hunger signals how much we need food; the intensity of our fear measures the dangerousness of the situation. The intensity variations give us a simple, economical mechanism for prioritizing information: the loudest, most intense affect is the one that gains our attention and thus activates the behavioral sequences of the motivational system.

Affective experience, however, entails more than simple intensity gradients. We often describe affective experience as "surging," "fading," "fleeting," "bursting," or "exploding." For example, we talk about a "surge of anger" or a "burst of determination." In describing these qualities, one cannot help but be impressed by the remarkable similarity to the notational system for musical emphasis. Thus affects could be easily described as "crescendo" or "decrescendo." Daniel Stern (1985) has introduced the term "vitality affects" to describe this kinetic, dynamic quality of affective experience, which he differentiates from the "categorical affects" such as joy, sadness, fear, or anger (pp. 53–61). Even though the term vitality affects is clear enough within the context of Stern's work, in one respect it is an unfortunate choice for such an important concept, for it may suggest to the unwary that one is talking about different affects, rather than about the *different qualities* of the same affect. The phrase "dynamic contour," borrowed from music, seems to be equally descriptive of this change in intensity and much easier to master terminologically. Hereafter it will be used throughout this book.

Stern hypothesizes that the dynamic contours of the affective experience may be a key to understanding how infants begin to attach significance to certain elements of the huge amount of information that comes to them from a number of sensory systems. This is one of the most important aspects of his work.

> For instance, in trying to soothe the infant, the parent could say, "There, there, there . . . ," giving more stress and amplitude on the first part of the word and trailing off towards the end of the word. Alternatively, the parent could silently stroke the baby's back or head with a stroke analogous to the "There, there" sequence, applying more pressure at the onset of the stroke and lightening or trailing it off toward the end. If the duration of the contoured stroke and the pauses between strokes were of the same absolute and relative durations as the vocalization-pause pattern, the infant would experience similar activation contours no matter which soothing technique was performed. The two soothings would feel the same (beyond their sensory specificity) and would result in the same vitality affect experience [p. 58].

In this example, the two experiences of a stroking mother and a separate "there, there" mother become yoked into a single, soothing mother through the linkage of affective form. Stern goes on to say, "No matter whether an object was encountered with the eye or the touch, and perhaps even the ear, it would produce the same overall pattern or activation contour" (p. 59). This, he suggests, may give us an answer to the question of how affects, through the process of attaching significance to a specific patterning, begin to organize our responses to the complexity of experience.

These dynamic contours, so obvious when we simply tune into our body, so difficult to express in language, help us to begin to understand why it is so difficult to arrive at a "satisfactory theory of affects." Affective experience has many of the qualities of music, and music simply does not translate well into language. Imagine the difficulties of trying to tell someone about a Mozart symphony or a Beethoven string quartet. Language does particularly well in describing visual-spatial data—things that we see and touch—particularly when they aren't changing very much over a period of time. It allows for a consensual validation of what is seen, and we can talk with confidence about "objects." But with music—and in this respect affects are very much like music—things are always in constant flux. This creates all sorts of difficulties in communication, particularly inasmuch as no one else has access to our inner experiences. These difficulties are further compounded by the fact that, as adult human beings, our affective experience is subtly, but significantly, influenced by the capacity for symbolic thought. Thus, inexorably, the study of more complex affects in all of their experiential manifestations becomes virtually synonymous with the study of the human mind.

SUMMARY

Affects are our first language. Specifically, affects are conceptualized as the experiential representation of a nonsymbolic information-processing system that can serve as the central control mechanism for all aspects of behavior. One of the most important functions of affects is to let us know which motivational system is dominant at any particular time. A cross-comparison of the intensity of the affects between competing motivational systems provides a simple, "user friendly" mechanism for prioritizing information and thus choosing which motivational system to activate.

2

Moods

Inside the womb, the unborn infant experiences the gentle rhythms of the rest–activity cycle and responds to distress (unpleasure) with arousal and increased activity. The continuously nurturing environment of the womb serves to protect the unborn infant from experiencing much in the way of thirst, hunger, heat, cold, or physical pain. As we now know from such experiments as shining a bright light into the fetus's eyes, it can react to uncomfortable stimuli with a clearly recognizable distress reaction. Somewhat surprisingly, we now have evidence that even a fetus can learn. In one experiment, mothers read *The Cat in the Hat* to their unborn children six and a half weeks before birth; after birth, the neonates would suck to hear their mothers reading that book but not another (DeCasper and Fifer, 1980). By the time the infant is ready to face the world, the inner sense organs, monitored by such feelings as thirst and hunger, are "on-line" and ready to operate. At the time of birth, a major reorganization takes place as the infant separates physically from the mother.

The infant has often, and wrongly, been conceptualized as existing during the first eight weeks of life in some sort of a precognitive, presocial, preorganized phase of life (Mahler, Pine, and Bergman's, 1975, autistic phase). These assumptions, however, have been entirely disproved; and the newborn infant's ability to pay attention to the outside world, learn about it, and respond to it with adaptive responses has been documented by numerous observers and is no longer open to question. (For an excellent review of this literature, see Lichtenberg, 1983.) As the neonate spends increasingly more time in the awake state, he must learn to synchronize his own internal rhythms to the day–night rhythm of the earth; in addition, he must learn to "entrain" his hunger patterns to the feeding patterns of the caretaker. Lichtenberg (1989) eloquently describes the world of the well-cared-for infant:

> The infant moves progressively through states of sleep, alert aware-ness, quiescent awareness, drowsiness, fussiness, and crying. The caregiver intuitively responds to the changing states, observing the presence of hunger; elimination and the need for diaper changing; the response to eye contact, tactile stimulation, being spoken to and cooed to, and the response to being rocked or left alone. The combina-tion of the infant's preprogrammed, state-organizing functioning and the caregiver's organizing responses creates a mutual regulating system of sensitivity previously unrecognized. On one hand, a well-organized newborn can pull an inexperienced mother toward the caregiving the infant needs. On the other hand, extremely subtle alterations in timing can move the infant toward longer daytime wakefulness and longer nighttime periods—within the first weeks. . . .
>
> The picture that emerges from this subtle interregulating system of baby and mother in the first weeks and months is one of a relative unity of experience. In this relatively smooth unity, the passages from state to state have a consistency, a rhythm, that begins life with a smoothness not evident when therapists reconstruct infancy from the standpoint of the origins of symptoms or of personality distur-bances. When the fit between infant and caregiver is good, changes of state and the internal and external regulations that bring them about proceed in a seamless manner. *Affects are associated with each state, some positive*, such as interest and enjoyment; *some negative*, such as anger, crying, and distress. When mutual regulation is successful, and state moves smoothly to state . . . both partners experience a positive overall affective coloration [p. 32, emphasis added].

I think that Lichtenberg accurately describes the smoothly shifting states of the life of a neonate together with their affective coloration, and I would emphasize one particular point that he makes: "Affects are associated with each state, some positive . . . some negative." The problem arises in trying to fit these behavioral observations— about which almost all observers would now agree—into a useful theoretical framework.

As Stern (1985) has said, the neonate's experience appears to be both "unified" and "global" (p. 67). This is what René Spitz (1959) was trying to describe when he spoke of the "coenesthetic" organization of the neonate. These observations have led many observers to prefer the concept of "state" in describing the affective life of the neonate (see esp. Wolff, 1960, 1966). As Emde, Gaensbauer, and Harmon (1976) have pointed out, state is a "low-level" concept, but one that is "subject to ready operational definition" and has been useful chiefly because it allows for prediction (p. 29). They define states as "constellations of certain patterns of physiological variables and/or patterns of behaviors which seem to repeat themselves and which appear to be relatively stable" (p. 29). They classify 12 neonatal behavioral states, four of which occur while the infants are awake, five during REM sleep, and three during non-REM sleep; the four awake states are "crying-awake," "fussy-awake," "alert-inactive," and "alert-active" (p. 167).[1] It is important to recognize that "state" is not really a contrasting concept to that of affect; rather, state entails a set of behavioral descriptions and observations while "affect" focuses on the inferred internal experience. The preference of many authors for the concept of "state" in describing the neonatal period may stem from the fact that the infant's affective response patterns are too global and diffuse to be considered "discrete" emotions. Consequently, they are difficult to classify and to fit into currently available theories of affect.

In the following pages, I present the hypothesis that the global affective response patterns that accompany the infant's state are best understood as moods. Like the concept of state, mood is a "low-level" concept. The word itself certainly suggests a general feeling tone, rather than the specificity connected with a discrete emotion such as sadness, anger, or fear. For example, if an employee says, "The boss is in a bad mood today," most people will understand what is meant. In talking about the boss's bad mood, the employees have ruled out that the boss is simply upset about something in particular. On the contrary, they are predicting that the boss probably will react with irritability, perhaps even with anger, to a minor annoyance. To be in a bad mood implies something quite different from being angry at someone or something. Webster defines mood as "a particular state of mind or feeling; humor, or temper." This diffuseness is captured in Edith Jacobson's (1957) definition of mood: "In fact, moods seem to represent, as it were, a cross-section through the entire state of the ego, lending a particular, uniform coloring to all its manifestations for a longer or shorter period of time. Since they do

---

[1] The five REM sleep states are sleep, drowsy, sucking, fussing, and crying; the three non-REM sleep states are sleep, drowsy, and sucking.

not relate to a specific content or object, but find expression in specific qualities attached to all feelings, thoughts, and actions, they may indeed be called a barometer of the ego state" (p. 75). In this definition, Jacobson captures the global, diffuse characteristics of a mood, qualities that differentiate moods from emotions.

Moods can, and often do, serve as a communication both to the mother and to the infant. The infant distress syndrome, a mood that can be observed in all infants, is an excellent example. The cause of the distress can be physical (hungry, hot, tired, cold) or environmental (bright lights, loud noise); but sometimes the fussiness emerges for no discernable reason. Whatever the cause, distress vocalizations communicate a clear message to the mother: "Something is wrong. Fix it!" In most cases, a good mother will be able to decipher the meaning of the infant's cry and attend to it. If the infant's needs are met, the infant will often move from a distressed to a contented mood. In contrast, the contented mood that accompanies the alert-inactive state signals the caretaker, "I'm OK. Nothing needs fixing right now." From the subtle variations in the quality of the infant's cry, empathic mothers not only can gradually learn that something is wrong but also, in many cases, intuitively know what that something is. They have begun to learn the infant's affective language, encoded within the specific dynamic contours of the distress cry.

FOUR NEONATAL MOODS

The major hypothesis of this chapter is that moods are our first central affective processing unit. They are on-line at birth, prior to the development of the capacity for emotion at eight weeks. Four specific moods—interest, contentment, distress, and surprise—provide the neonate with the core of his first information-processing system, organizing information about the world. The interrelationships of these moods can be more easily understood when one sees that they form a rough matrix with two coordinates: inner–outer and good–bad. One axis of the matrix focuses our attention: interest and surprise focus us toward the outer world, while contentment points inward. Distress may direct our attention either way, although, at the very beginning of life, it tends to point inward because it usually arises secondary to some unmet physiologic need. The other axis of the matrix adds a qualitative assessment to the experience (good–bad). Contentment and interest are clearly positive, whereas distress is clearly negative. Surprise, however, is more difficult to assess. Tomkins (1962) and Izard (1991) classify it as a neutrally valenced affect, serving a "reset" function. On the other hand, Sroufe (1982) conceptualizes the surprise–startle response as the beginning of the "wariness–fear system," which develops through a period of obligatory attention (three to six months) into the fear response, as manifested by the stranger anxiety syndrome, at eight months (p. 582). It may very well be that the hard-wired startle response, present at birth, is initially experienced as a negative affect (as Sroufe suggests). As the newborn matures, the physiologic startle response may gradually lessen, thus allowing surprise (a mood) to emerge, thus acquiring a more neutral valence. In summary, these four moods, in connection with perceptual, proprioceptive, and physiologic sensations, are sufficient for the neonate to begin to map his world.

In commenting about the endogenous component of some of the fussiness, Emde and his colleagues (1976) note, "All babies cry when hungry or in response to pain, but unexplainable crying also occurs. This form of crying, usually referred to as 'fussiness,' causes bewilderment even in experienced mothers" (p. 80). In extreme cases, this fussiness may come to the attention of the pediatrician as infantile colic. Emde et al. found that fussiness occurred in *all* the infants studied and was "largely independent of variations in mothering" (p. 80). Speculating about this nonspecific fussiness, Emde agreed with Bowlby that the evolutionary purpose seemed to be to ensure mother–infant attachment; they also agree that this putative evolutionary strategy appears to be counterproductive, as it causes "bewilderment even in experienced mothers" (p. 80).

The difficulty with this line of reasoning is that it does not consider that "endogenous fussiness" (the distress reaction) begins as *a message without content*. Then, through the process of learning, the specific content becomes connected to the message. The message itself is clear: "Something is wrong!" In the beginning of life, the infant certainly does not "know" what the problem is. More often than not, the problem has to do with physiologic distress; the infant is cold, tired, wet, or hungry. Even when the cause may be in the external environment, such as a very loud noise activating the startle response, the infant is probably reacting to an uncomfortable level of auditory stimulation rather than worrying about something "out there." In any case, he must rely on the caretaker to try to find the specific cause of the distress. The important thing is that the distress signal is a message not only to the mother, *but to the infant as well*. Through the caretaker's appropriately responding to the cause of distress, the infant not only learns something about relationships, but also begins to link the message (fussiness leading to distress) with the specific content of the message (e.g., "I'm hungry!" "I'm thirsty!"). One of the first things the infant must learn is where the problem is located. For example, the hunger signal, accompanied by the distress reaction, followed by the ministrations of the mother, followed by the relief of hunger and distress, helps the infant to begin to differentiate the inner world of physical sensations from the "world-out-there." This is one of our first steps in assembling our affective vocabulary.

During the alert-active state, the infant displays an interest and curiosity in the world around him, manifested by the characteristic facial expression of "eyebrows down, track, look, listen" (Tomkins, 1962, p. 337). In Tomkins's classification, interest–excitement is one of nine primary affects; three of these primary affects—interest–excitement, distress–anguish, and surprise–startle—appear to be moods. Interest serves the developmental function of focusing the infant's attention on the outside world; this interest initiates exploratory activity, first with the eyes, and later, when possible, with the body. The mood of interest–excitement accompanying the alert-active state helps the infant accomplish one of the major developmental tasks of the neonatal period: he must construct a map of the world-out-there, all the while learning to separate this whole domain from the inner world of physiologic self-regulation. In addition, the increased alertness in the face of the infant is likely to engage the mother's interest, thereby initiating a reciprocal interaction that serves as the beginning of a nonverbal communication system between the mother and infant.

Tomkins considers surprise–startle as one of nine basic affect states, with the easily recognizable facial expression of "eyebrows up, eyes blink" (p. 498). Interestingly, the affect of surprise fits the definition of a mood; it begins at birth, probably building on the hard-wired startle response. Further research may show that the startle response is the hard-wired anlage of surprise in the same way that endogenous fussiness is the anlage for distress. In Tomkins's classification of primary affects, surprise–startle is neither positive nor negative; it is the single affect that is classified as neutral (pp. 498–508). The function of surprise is to clear the mind of preceding information; it signals that something new is happening. Neurologically, this tends to "clear the channels." Tomkins calls this a "reset" function, similar in design to the radio or television announcement that says, "We are interrupting this program to bring you this special news bulletin. . . ." In the infant, when all the world is new, the surprise–startle response is relatively frequent, but as we grow older, less and less surprises us. In contrast to the distress syndrome, which, at least initially, directs the infant's attention inward, the surprise–startle response usually focuses the infant's attention on the outer world, as that is where most of the surprises come from. The interrelationship of interest and surprise is intricate, and, in certain circumstances, they may activate one another. For example, if the rise in interest–excitement exceeds a critical threshold value, it may activate the startle response. In the adult, the "double take" is perhaps the best example of this phenomenon; specifically, a sudden increase in comprehension may activate the surprise response, which, in turn, evokes a further increase in interest.

The affect of surprise pushes us to reexamine some of our assumptions about moods. Surprise, almost by definition, lasts only a very short time, and we are used to thinking of moods (such as depression in an adult) as relatively long lasting. For example, in *Psychoanalytic Terms and Concepts* (1990), published by the American Psychoanalytic Association, mood is defined as follows: "A relatively stable and long-lasting affective state, evoked and perpetuated by the continuing influence of unconscious fantasy" (p. 9). This definition reflects the conventional thinking about moods. The further connotations of this definition are that what we call moods are secondary to some type of psychodynamic constellation; and that they do not emerge early in life, inasmuch as they are a derivative of the capacity to form unconscious phantasies. Both of these conventional assumptions direct our attention away from another, more interesting, possibility: normal (not pathological) moods may be our first affects that serve a central information-processing function.

While interest, surprise, and distress are commonly used words for easily recognized affective states, finding a term to describe the mood that accompanies the alert-inactive state presents a number of problems. The two terms that are most frequently used—satisfaction and pleasure—have specific theoretical connotations that make them unsatisfactory. "Satisfied" or "satisfaction" seems to describe some sort of pleasure in the general sense but carries with it theoretical baggage that is our legacy from Freud. As mentioned in the first essay, Freud's theory of drive began with his reworking of Schiller's aphorism "hunger and love are what moves the world"; the term "satisfaction" appears to have been taken from the satiety that we experience when our hunger needs are met. Freud (1915a) commented, "The aim [*Ziel*] of an instinct is in every instance *satisfaction*, which can only be obtained by removing the state of stimulation at the source of the instinct" (p. 122, emphasis added). Thus, if the term satisfaction were limited to the motivational system that regulates our physiologic requirements, it would be reasonably applicable inasmuch as this motivational system operates primarily by removing specific deficits manifested by feelings such as hunger, thirst, and tiredness. Human beings, however, are much more than our physiologic needs; and, as countless critics of Freud and the drive-discharge model have pointed out, a deficit theory does not even remotely begin to account for the higher aspirations of man. Therefore, we cannot use the term satisfaction without conjuring up the ghosts of drive theory, for the term subtly implies a deficit theory of motivation, suggesting that some specific need or group of needs have recently been met.

"Pleasure" is another word that is sometimes used to describe the mood that accompanies the alert-inactive state. The problem with the word pleasure is that it has two similar, but quite distinct, meanings. One of these meanings is suggested by the first dictionary definition of the word: "the gratification of the senses or of the mind; agreeable sensations or emotions: . . . satisfaction: opposed to *pain*." Here, pleasure is used as a synonym for any positively valenced affect, as Freud used the term in talking about the pleasure principle. Pleasure, however, is also commonly used as a synonym for a specific kind of emotional experience, as when we experience the emotion of joy or delight. This sense of the word pleasure is captured by the fourth dictionary definition: "a thing that gives delight and satisfaction; that which pleases." This type of pleasure seems to be the emotion of enjoyment, or, more simply, joy. This discrete emotion— one of Tomkins's nine primary affects—emerges at eight weeks of age and is manifested by the social smile. Therefore, if we were to retain the word "pleasure" to describe the mood that accompanies the alert-inactive state, then it would create a certain awkwardness in our thinking, as we would always have to footnote mentally how we are using the term. Are we thinking of pleasure as a synonym for any positively valenced affect, or do we mean a specific "pleasurable" affect, such as joy or delight? Perhaps we might learn to live with the awkwardness that this ambiguity creates, but I suspect that it is this type of ambiguity that has created so much difficulty for psychoanalytic theory. Many critics—especially those outside the field of psychoanalysis who have attacked Freud's description of man as "pleasure seeking"—fail to understand that Freud was using the term in a restricted sense as a mental regulatory principle rather than describing a specific affect.

My own choice for the name of the mood accompanying the alert-inactive state would be the word "contentment." This term avoids many of the theoretical problems of "pleasure" and "satisfaction," while at the same time providing a reasonably accurate phenomenologic description of the mood that accompanies the alert-inactive state. Furthermore, the word contentment implies a relaxed state, suggesting the inwardly focused transition from wakefulness to sleep (and/or REM) states. For most species, sleep is a very specific physiologic need. When our other physiologic needs are met (satisfied, to use Freud's language), then sensations of tiredness plus feelings of safety and contentment signal that it is time for sleep. One of the advantages of the word contentment is that it does not suggest that something is coming to an end (i.e., that a need has been satisfied); rather, it suggests that life is an ongoing process and that the focus of attention is shifting from outer to inner.

In summary, in much of the early literature on neonatal development, primitive moods are referred to as states. Focusing attention on the observed *behavior* (states) rather than on the internal *process* (the affect) that accompanies the behavior created a major difficulty in building a process theory of affects. Translating these behavioral observations into the language of affect—fussy-awake (mild distress); crying-awake (much distress; Tomkins's anguish); alert-active (interest); alert-inactive (contentment)—helps us understand what is going on in the infant's mind. The lack of an adequate theory of normal moods has played a major role in preventing the emergence of a process theory of affects.

MOODS AND THE TRIUNE BRAIN

Very little discussion is to be found in the psychoanalytic literature about the concept of mood as an organizing concept; whatever discussion there is is generally limited to a specific kind of mood disturbance such as depression or mania. Edith Jacobson's (1957) paper on "Normal and Pathological Moods" stands as a lonely exception to this neglect. The problem is that moods are easy enough to describe but difficult to account for theoretically. Many of the difficulties stem from the language and embedded assumptions of the classic drive/structure model, which deprived affects of their processing function. Consequently, it became almost impossible to conceptualize normal moods as serving a primary affective processing (i.e., signaling) function. As a consequence, moods, both normal and pathological, could be described clinically but could not be accounted for theoretically.

The concept of moods and states as organizers traces its neurophysiologic roots to Paul MacLean's (1949) concept of "the triune brain." MacLean reviewed James Papez's neuroanatomic work on emotions and rescued it from relative obscurity. Papez had identified three separate levels of development: the stream of movement, the stream of feeling, and the stream of thought. MacLean renamed the neurological network subtending the stream of feeling the limbic system. (Limbic means "hemming in" or "bordering around"; anatomically, the limbic system, the old mammalian brain, enfolds the more primitive *corpus striatum*.) Since then, this concept has won almost universal acceptance as describing the central neural network of the emotions. (For a review of MacLean's work, see Konner, 1982, pp. 146–151.) In 1952, MacLean went further and identified the frontal lobes of the neocortex as "the report and control center" for the limbic system. As a result of this work, MacLean was named head of the Laboratory for Brain Evolution at NIMH. Over the course of three decades, his theory of brain structure and evolution demonstrated that the human brain contains three important evolutionary levels: the reptilian brain, the old mammalian brain, and the neocortex. Hence, the triune brain. These three "biological computers" are noticeably distinct in their structure and chemistry; they can be differentiated by the Golgi method of staining brain tissue (Hampden-Turner, 1981, p. 80).

Each of these three systems has its own characteristic method of processing information. Konner (1982) describes these differences:

> The first is the "reptilian brain," which in lizards and other reptiles is the dominant and controlling circuitry, and which corresponds to the *corpus striatum* and related structures in the human brain—the circuit that figured prominently in Papez's "stream of movement." But MacLean's contribution has been to show that this structure, whether in reptiles, birds, or mammals, is not concerned with mere control of movement, but with the storage and control of "instinctive" behavior; the fixed action patterns and innate releasing mechanisms of the ethologists. This helps explain why reptiles and birds, in which the *corpus striatum* is the most highly developed part of the brain, seem (much more than mammals) to have behavioral repertoires consisting of stereotyped behaviors and responses: a lizard turning sideways and displaying its dewlap as a threat, for instance,

or a bird repeating over and over again the same territorial song. It isn't that mammals have no such behaviors, but rather that birds and reptiles have so little else.

The second collection of circuits is called "the old mammalian brain," a designation that comes from evidence that it arose with the evolution of the earliest mammals. This, in effect, is the limbic system, and corresponds to Papez's "stream of feeling." In primitive mammals such as rodents and rabbits, it occupies a much higher percentage of the cerebral mass than it does in higher mammals such as monkeys. According to MacLean, it is this circuit that, without replacing the "instinctive" functions of the striatal or "reptilian" circuitry, gives those functions an emotional coloring they would otherwise not have [pp. 147–148].

Here let us focus on one part of the model. The ancient, basically reptilian brain has been hardly touched by evolution; it flourished in the age of dinosaurs and is found in the alligators, lizards, and turtles of today. In humans, the reptilian brain consists of the matrix of the brain stem, midbrain, basal ganglia, and much of the hypothalamus and the reticular activating system. MacLean's contribution was to demonstrate that the reptilian brain is concerned not merely with the control of movement, but with the storage and control of "instinctive behavior" (Freud's *Instinkte*), the fixed action patterns and innate releasing mechanisms as described by ethologists. I would suggest that *moods can be conceptualized as the primary affective representation of the reptilian brain*.

In MacLean's model of the triune brain, the biobehavioral reorganization that takes place at eight weeks marks the ascendance of the old mammalian brain and its predominance over the reptilian brain. The observations that first pointed to this reorganization were done by Spitz and have been carried forward by Emde and his colleagues in Denver. In his work *A Genetic Field Theory of Ego Formation*, Spitz (1959) directed our attention to the issue of infant discontinuities. The issue can be stated fairly succinctly: is development best conceptualized as a continuous process with the gradual accretion of learned responses, or should it be conceptualized as sometimes discontinuous with abrupt changes resulting in major reorganizations? Emde and his coauthors (1976) agree with the central proposition of Spitz's theory, which held that rates of development are uneven.

There are certain periods when both behavioral and physiological development proceeds at an increased pace. These times of rapid change are reflected in the emergence of new levels of organization and are followed by periods of slower change when developmental gains are consolidated and further differentiation begins to take place. Development is not only a process of steady accumulation; from the observer's point of view, it can be seen to occur in jumps [p. 6].

Viewing development as episodic or discontinuous, Spitz favors psychoanalytic theories of development that emphasize successive stages (Emde et al., 1976, p. 7). The biobehavioral shift at eight weeks is, I suggest, a discontinuity (within Spitz's use of the term) produced by the old mammalian brain's achieving dominance and taking control of the more primitive reptilian brain. This hypothesis links MacLean's neurophysiologic model of the triune brain with the infant observational data of Spitz, Emde, and others.

The emergence of the social smile at approximately eight weeks, accompanied by the recognizable emotion of enjoyment, signals that a major reorganization of the psyche is taking place. From this time on, our core emotions, each monitoring the information from a complex motivational system, will become the predominant forces in determining behavior. Stern (1985) eloquently describes these changes:

> The age of two months is almost as clear a boundary as birth itself. At about eight weeks, infants undergo a qualitative change: they begin to make direct eye-to-eye contact. Shortly thereafter they begin to smile more frequently, but also responsively and infectiously. They begin to coo. In fact, much more goes on during this developmental shift than what is reflected by increased overt social behaviors. Most learning is faster and more inclusive. . . . Almost everything changes. And all observers of infants, including parents, agree on this [p. 37].

Spitz (1965) called the eight-week smiling response one of the three "organizers" of the personality. Emde and his coauthors (1976), following the work of Spitz, coined the term "biobehavioral shift." Describing this shift as biobehavioral reorganization is especially apt, because it represents a reorganization of *how* we process information. The infant will now develop a number of motivational systems to deal with the world-out-there. The core emotions, now coming on-line, are the monitors of these specific motivational systems and have very different messages; the varying *intensities* of the specific affects, however, allow us to correlate and compare the incoming information from the various systems. A cross-comparison of the affective intensity from competing motivational systems gives us a simple, effective method of prioritizing information; a response to the "loudest signal" then initiates a course of action.

SUMMARY

Moods can be distinguished from emotions both observationally and through introspective experience as well. Observationally, emotions are less diffuse, more discrete, than the more global moods. At birth, four specific moods—interest, surprise, distress, and contentment—are the core feelings that organize the neonate's information about the world and guide his responses to it. These early affective responses are seldom, if ever, labeled as moods. More often than not, the original organization of normal moods is described in terms of states (i.e., behavior) or are dismissed as "affect precursors." Neurophysiologically, moods are the representations of the more primitive "reptilian brain"; the more discrete responses, which we think of as emotions, depend on the coming on-line of the limbic circuitry of the "old mammalian brain."

A theory of normal moods is very much needed. In one sense, moods are the bastard stepchild of affect theory, existing somewhere in the limbo between biologic psychiatry and psychoanalytic theory. (Within the psychoanalytic literature, whatever attention is paid to moods usually focuses on complex adult mood disturbances such as depression or mania.) It is highly unlikely that we will be able to develop any in-depth knowledge of mood disturbances until we adequately understand the baseline normal moods from which they emerge. The problem of developing an adequate theory does not appear to be due to the complexity of the subject matter, but to our unexamined preconceptions about moods.

3

Lust, Libido, and Love

Without any doubt, love is one of the most fascinating and complex of human emotions. Since the beginnings of recorded history, poets and troubadours have sung of it, painters have painted it, and playwrights and novelists have written about it. When we think of romantic love, images of Tristan and Isolde, Lancelot and Guinevere, and Romeo and Juliet are likely to come to mind. Almost everyone is aware of how the vagaries of romantic love have shaped the course of history. Helen of Troy, Antony and Cleopatra, and the six wives of King Henry VIII are among the better known examples. Given the power of love (and sex) to shape not only our imagination but our lives, it was inevitable that philosophers, psychologists, and psychoanalysts would attempt to understand it.

In his initial formulations about drive theory, Freud (1915a) seemed to be saying that the other person was only the vehicle through which bodily needs were to be met. Reacting to this viewpoint, the British object relations school reconceptualized the drive to form relationships; the pursuit of pleasure for itself was the result of the failure of the object relations (Guntrip, 1961). Dispensing with the language of drive altogether, John Bowlby (1969) formulated a primary need for attachment. More recently, Lichtenberg (1989) described the affiliational system as one of five primary motivational systems. Whether it is conceptualized in terms of libido theory, object relations theory, or attachment theory, or as a motivational system, we are talking about the same phenomenon: the

67

propensity of human beings to form stable relationships. What makes human love different from animal pair-bonds is our capacity for idealization. Therefore, any reasonably complete theory of human behavior must account not only for the attachment or the affiliation (where reasonably good animal models exist), but also for the idealization that is so often a part of romance. Idealization, a uniquely human capacity, is the defining characteristic of romantic love.

LIBIDO AND ATTACHMENT

Freud's concept of libido (or, if you will, of libidinal attachment) is vague. As Laplanche and Pontalis (1967) wrote, "A satisfactory definition of libido is difficult to give. This is not only because the theory of libido evolved hand in hand with the different stages of the drive theory, but also because the concept of libido itself has never been clearly defined" (p. 239). In 1921 Freud tried to define the relationship between libido and love:

> Libido is an expression taken from the theory of the emotions. We call by that name the energy, regarded as a quantitative magnitude (though not at present actually measurable), of those instincts which have to do with all that may be comprised under the word "love." *The nucleus of what we mean by love naturally consists (and this is what is commonly called love, and what the poets sing of) in sexual love with sexual union as its aim* [p. 90, emphasis added].

In other words, Freud starts by saying that the word "love" is often used to describe a sexual relationship. He then goes on to say that psychoanalytic research has demonstrated that all relationships—self-love, the love between parents and children, friendship, love of humanity—are also sexual. He argues "that language has carried out an entirely justifiable piece of unification in creating the word 'love' with its numerous uses, and that we cannot do better than take it as the basis of our scientific discussions and expositions as well" (p. 91). About half a page later, Freud says that the term love, which he has just finished defining as sexual, is virtually synonymous with "emotional ties" (p. 91). The essence of Freud's libido theory is expressed in those two statements: love in the "wider sense," what ethologists call attachment, is assumed to be basically sexual in nature.

The result of this theorizing is not clarity but confusion. For most people, including most psychoanalysts, the concept of libido is little more than a vague theoretical abstraction, sort of a mushy amalgam of love and lust. Let us, then, briefly review the observations and reasoning that led Freud to his conclusion. Freud had discovered that, before reaching the age of puberty, children have sexual feelings about their parents. These feelings, accompanied by unconscious phantasies, often occur in a constellation that Freud called the Oedipus complex. In its positive form, the Oedipus complex consists of feelings of sexual attraction for the parent of the opposite sex, and rivalrous feelings—even a desire for the death of the rival—toward the parent of the same sex. In the negative Oedipus complex, the situation is reversed: there is love of the parent of the same sex and rivalrous or jealous feelings toward the parent of the opposite sex. The peak of the oedipal feelings comes between the ages of three to five or six years; their decline signals the child's entry into the latency period. The Oedipus complex has been described in a great variety of cultures, including those where the conjugal family is not predominant. In classical psychoanalytic theory, the internalized prohibitions against these sexual and murderous feelings give rise to the superego. Today, almost every clinician recognizes the validity of Freud's observations about what might be called "the family romance." The disagreements—and there are serious ones—surround the issue of the extent to which the Oedipus complex and the superego play a fundamental role in creating what we call psychic structure.

A sharp distinction must be drawn between Freud's *observations* about the existence of childhood sexual feelings and his *theory* of infantile sexuality. No serious researcher questions the validity of Freud's observations concerning the existence of prepubertal sexual feelings. The child's sexual feelings are an important developmental milestone to which the parent must respond. How the parent responds to the child's prepubertal sexuality will substantially influence how the child, when he grows to adulthood, will approach sexual relationships. From his observations about childhood sexuality, Freud drew an extremely important theoretical conclusion: *the relationship between a parent and child can best be described as sexual in nature.* It is this theoretical conclusion, rather than his clinical observations, that is known as his "theory of infantile sexuality."

Freud's theory of infantile sexuality, characterizing the child as moving through well-demarcated stages of psychosexual development, became the organizing premise for his theory of development. The infant begins with the oral phase (0–18 months) and then moves to the anal phase (18–36 months), the phallic or oedipal phase (3–6 years), and the latency phase (6–12 years) before undergoing the "transformations of puberty," which change him to an active sexual being in the usually accepted sense of the word. In this theory, the term sexual is used in its broadest sense, more or less as a synonym for pleasurable. During the oral period activities such as nursing or thumb sucking are defined as sexual activities. During the anal period, defecating (or willfully not defecating) is similarly defined as sexual. It is important to note that Freud considered *all* feelings of closeness, love, and affection, not just the specifically sexual feelings of the oedipal period, to be sexual in nature; this is the core assumption of his theory of infantile sexuality.

The central question raised by libido theory can be easily stated: although sexual feelings certainly do arise in children, is the child's need for a relationship most accurately characterized as sexual in nature, or is the childhood sexuality of the oedipal phase simply an important developmental milestone that must be handled within the parent–child relationship? In trying to arrive at an answer to this question, it may be helpful to attempt to formulate the question in the language of ethology.[1] Most ethologists try to state their conclusions in terms of observable behavior, rather than in the language of drives or emotions (i.e., they tend to avoid terms that lead to inferences about inner states). Thus, attachment is the term usually used to describe any type of observable, long-term relationship. Similarly, pair-bonding is the term usually used to describe relatively stable male–female *sexual* relationships that are formed to reproduce and to raise the young (Konner, 1982, p. 267). Thus, the question implicit in libido theory would be whether or not the attachment of the infant to the mother is part of a developmental continuum that ends up in pair-bonding. In other words, libido theory would suggest that mother–infant attachments represent an early form of pair-bonding.

In 1935, Konrad Lorenz published his famous monograph *Der Kumpan in der Umwelt des Vogels*, which is usually translated *The Companion in the Bird's World* (cited in Konner, 1982, p. 294). In this work, he described the various types of "companion relationships" that develop in birds. The book classifies five types of companion

---

[1] One of the goals of this book is to synthesize our knowledge of child development with what we know about animals. Since one cannot be expert in all fields, I have relied upon the excellent integration of the ethology literature in *The Tangled Wing* (1982) by Melvin Konner. Although this book is more than 10 years old, I still consider it the best presentation of this material available.

relationships: the parental companion, the infant companion, the sexual companion, the social companion, and the sibling companion. In each category, a number of species are covered. These relationships are real, ubiquitous, strong, often quite long lasting, and in most cases essential to survival or reproduction (Konner, 1982, p. 294). The process of imprinting is perhaps the best example of how hard-wired instinctive behavior can be. Lorenz found that in some species of birds, an infant would "imprint" and then follow any object that is available. Ordinarily, the object followed was the mother, but if the mother was not available, some of the ducklings imprinted on Lorenz, and one, in an unusual case, on a big orange ball. The more frequently the infant follows, the more it wants to follow, and, after a certain point, punishment tends to increase rather than decrease its impulse to follow the mother—exactly contrary to the predictions of learning theory (p. 295). In this respect, imprinting is an archetypal example of a behavior that we would call instinctive (Freud's *Instinkte*). Once Lorenz's experiments were repeated and verified, it was natural to wonder whether attachment behavior develops in primates, particularly in humans.

Harry Harlow's work with rhesus monkeys provides a model of attachment closer to the human one. In the early 1950s, Harlow began his work on affectional systems in an effort to determine "the nature of love." In a series of now classic experiments, Harlow reared monkeys in total social isolation, with food being dispensed through a plastic bottle. These experiments are now so well known that the phrase "Harlow's monkeys" has become part of our psychological vocabulary. The monkeys reared in total isolation were definitely abnormal, as manifested by behaviors of rocking, self-clasping, self-biting. At adolescence, the time of sexual activity in normal monkeys, both males and females were inept; if the females were artificially inseminated, they were negligent mothers or even brutal toward their offspring. An infant monkey placed in a cage with a wire cylinder with a milk-dispensing nipple and with a sloping cylinder that was covered with a warm terry cloth would spend almost all its time with the terry-cloth surrogate and would go to the wire cylinder only to feed. When a frightening object was introduced into the cage, the monkey invariably went to the cloth cylinder, not to the wire cylinder with the nipple. The tendency to form attachments is so strong that a socially isolated infant monkey will form an attachment to a long-haired dog, clinging to it, riding on its back, and generally interacting with it (Mason and Kinney, 1974). In general, the monkeys reared by cloth-covered surrogates did better (i.e., had fewer abnormal behaviors) than did the monkeys reared in total social isolation; they were, however, more abnormal than monkeys raised by normal mothers. These findings have been confirmed by primatologists the world over.

Lorenz's work with birds and Harlow's with monkeys demonstrate that attachment behavior is instinctive (wired in) rather than simply the result of social learning. The adaptive purpose of attachment is straightforward and obvious: the infant needs to stay close to the mother for sustenance and protection; the mother needs to guard her progeny lest they would die. After reviewing the work of the animal behaviorists, one would inevitably conclude that the human infant's attachment to the mother is likewise instinctive, as much a part of human nature as walking or talking. Although an infant's experience will inevitably affect the character of his attachment to the mother, the *need for the attachment* to the mother is independent of any specific experiences. Framed in the language of systems theory, the need for attachment operates as one of our most powerful motivational systems. If one is in search of ultimate answers, there is no really specific "reason" that we form attachments; we form them for the same reason that fish swim and birds fly.

SEXUALITY

With this as a background, let us examine the spectrum of sexual and reproductive behavior among the vertebrates. Within the animal kingdom, sexuality is one of the easiest types of behavior to understand because it is the type of behavior that we consider instinctive (in Freud's sense of *Instinkte*, not *Trieb*). Bowlby (1969) has listed the four main characteristics of behaviors that are conventionally termed instinctive:

> a. it follows a recognisably similar and predictable pattern in almost all members of a species (or all members of one sex);
> b. it is not a simple response to a single stimulus but a sequence of behaviour that usually runs a predictable course;
> c. certain of its usual consequences are of obvious value in contributing to the preservation of an individual or the continuity of a species;
> d. many examples of it develop even when all the ordinary opportunities for learning it are exiguous or absent [p. 38].

Under these criteria, sexual and reproductive behavior among animals clearly are excellent examples of what we think of as instinctive.

Instinctive behavior—whether sexual or nonsexual—does not operate all the time; rather, it requires some kind of a releasing stimulus to activate the program. During the last 25 years, we have come to understand a great deal about how specific stimuli— pheromones, hormones, visual displays, mating calls—play a major part in activating sexual behavior. In any case, once the program is activated, the mating dance begins. The details of these programs— the courtship rituals, the display behaviors, the rutting tournaments— are infinitely varied and endlessly fascinating. The ring dove, a strongly pair-bonded, tree-living African bird, demonstrates many of these mechanisms.

> It has been shown that pair formation requires an elaborate, pro-longed courtship period in which the male bows and coos to the female. Watching this behavior—or for that matter a film of it— directly stimulates the pituitary gland of the female (through an unknown brain pathway) to secrete luteinizing hormone, which in turn stimulates the ovary to produce increases in the blood level of progesterone and estradiol, the hormones that will prepare her, physically and behaviorally, for breeding. After that they build a nest together and copulate, and the female gestates and lays the eggs.
>
> The male's initial behavioral gestures are a function of his own testosterone level, which when it rises presumably alters the respon-siveness of neural circuits controlling bowing and cooing. But the female's physiological changes depend on the male's movements. . . . the weight of the female's oviduct can be plotted as a function of the male's testosterone level, a powerful physiological effect in which the intervening variables are behavioral. Both male and female sit on the eggs, and this experience stimulates each of them to develop "crop milk," a specialized baby food produced in the crop, a side chamber of the esophagus. This they regurgitate in response to the newly hatched young [Konner, 1982, pp. 270–271].

These details demonstrate how, in a single species, nature has provided for the propagation and care of the young.

In most species, there is a time—annually or semiannually in most birds and mammals, monthly in monkeys and apes—when the hormonal level elicits the cooperation, if not the enthusiasm, of the female. This is the time of estrus or, more colloquially, when the female is "in heat." These cycles are regulated by complex neuroendocrine mechanisms. In the majority of monkeys and apes, there is a monthly surge of female sexual posturing and invitational behavior directed toward sexually active males (p. 276). In some cases, such as the savannah baboon, there are distinctive physical manifestations as well, such as color changes and/or swelling of the genital regions. These mechanisms, fascinating in their diversity, are easy enough to understand: a releasing stimulus, usually hormonal, activates the prewired program that leads to reproduction. That is, a specific, easily recognizable affect serves as the signal that the sexual/ reproductive program is now engaged. This affect has a very clear message: it's time for sex. Thus, as hunger may serve as the stimulus to a complex set of behaviors that eventually results in feeding, feelings of sexual arousal lead to behaviors that begin with courting and eventually culminate in reproduction.

In all sexually reproducing species and especially among vertebrates, many facts about the males can be predicted by the degree to which they participate in, or abstain from, the care of their progeny. In the pair-bonding species—including about 8,000 species of birds, small South American monkeys called marmosets, the gibbons or lesser apes, and a few members of the dog family such as coyotes and bat-eared foxes—the male contributes substantially to the care of the young. In these species, males and females tend to be approximately the same size and color, without fancy appendages, and grow at approximately the same rate. They mate in pairs on a long-term basis, sometimes for life (Konner, 1982, p. 269).

At the other end of the spectrum is a quite different story; males differ markedly from females and take little interest in infants and juveniles. They are usually larger than females, are more floridly conspicuous, possess more dangerous weapons, and are slower to mature. For example, the male may be triple the weight of the female as in the elephant seal, or have fantastic display coloration as in the peacock, or have antlers for prancing and battering as in white-tailed deer. These species are often called "tournament species" because competition for females varies from intense to fierce and is often concentrated in an annual breeding "tournament." In these species males do little or nothing to care for the young. An extreme example is the elephant seal; fights between the enormous males in the colony frequently result in injury and death to newborn pups.

In comparison with tournament species, pair-bonding species tend to have a fairly close physical resemblance between males and females, low variability in male reproductive success, high male investment in offspring, a low degree of promiscuity, and relatively unspectacular competition among males. In contrast, tournament species have large, florid males, high variability in male reproductive success (a few males copulate with large numbers of females, while many males lose out entirely), little or no direct care of offspring, high promiscuity or polygamous mating, and intense male–male competition (Konner, 1982, p. 269). Although any number of jokes might be made about the point, human beings belong to the pair-bonding end of the spectrum. In the tournament species, the infant outgrows the attachment to the mother and more or less goes his or her own separate way; reproduction and infant care take place without the benefit of pair-bonding.

As one surveys the wide variety of sexual behavior and infant-rearing patterns in mammals (particularly the large number of tournament species where mother–infant attachment does not lead to any kind of stable male–female relationship in adulthood), it becomes increasingly difficult to hypothesize that mother–infant attachment is simply the prelude to a pair-bonding sexual relationship in adulthood. To the extent to which human beings are similar to other pair-bonded animals, there is no ethological reason to consider the attachment between a human infant and his mother either as sexual in itself or designed to be a prelude to later sexual relationships. From the ethologic data, one can conclude that, within the rest of the animal kingdom, attachment and sexuality are very different behavioral programs. Human sexuality, however, is markedly different from that of any other species; consequently, animal models cannot serve as a basis for understanding human relationships, sexual or otherwise.

AFFECTION ("LIKING") AND LOVE

Each motivational system has an accompanying affect or affects that signal the organism: "You are in this system." We do not need to know the exact content of an animal's (or an infant's) experience of a certain affect; all we need to know is that the signal is strong enough and distinct enough to be distinguished from the other signals. From the work on animals and infants, which includes both detailed observations and the measurement of physiologic variables, there is every indication that affects serve this signaling function. Therefore, we can reasonably assume that some specific affect signals the attachment (or affiliational) process. In this section, we will explore the assumption that love—not the idealizing, capital "L" Love of which the poets sing but the small "l" love of affection or liking—is that affect. This hypothesis parallels one of the dictionary definitions of the word love as "a strong affection for or attachment or devotion to a person or persons." In other words, attachment is the behavioral process we can observe; affection or liking (small "l" love) is the affective signal of the attachment.

As soon as a baby opens his eyes, he starts to bond with the mother. (For the mother and father, the attachment may begin even before conception.) After eight weeks, the mother becomes even more important, as the infant clearly demonstrates a preference for her company over anyone else's. This mother–infant bond, the experiential base of all later affiliations, represents the beginning of one of our most powerful motivational systems, which undoubtedly is the model for all future relationships. As will be explored in the next chapter, the mother's capacity to communicate a sense of joyousness about life not only influences how the infant will approach future relationships but also helps shape some very basic attitudes toward life itself. In addition, the relationship with the mother is very much needed to help the infant master the emotion of fear, which emerges at approximately eight months. The emergence of the capacity for fear makes the infant much more vulnerable to a grief reaction secondary to the loss of the mother. If the mother fails to protect the infant, he may very well carry the legacy of this failure into adult life in the form of an underlying fearfulness or mistrust of life. These inferences, which are certainly compatible with Harlow's experiments with monkeys, are reinforced by data from both infant observation and psychoanalysis (Lichtenberg, 1983). During the first 18 months of life (Freud's oral period), the affiliational system is the motivational system of primary importance (with the qualification that during the neonatal period—the first eight weeks—the mother's attention to the infant's physiologic needs, rather than the relationship itself, seems to be more important).

As with many motivational systems, the affective monitor of the affiliation system is bimodal: affection measures the intensity of the attachment while grief signals its loss. For example, we know that the loss of an avian pair-bond partner leads to a response that looks, in many respects, very much like human grief (Konner, 1982, p. 328). Lorenz observed that in ducks and geese, the loss of a partner often resulted in persistent and repetitive searching that lasted for days and was followed by a period of maladaptive behavior. From the work of Spitz (1965) on hospitalized infants, we also know that infants deprived of essential human contact can experience severe depression. From these observations, we can conclude that 1) relationships are a vital necessity for the infant; 2) the presence of the relationship is reflected by some signal such as affection; and 3) the loss of the relationship leads to something that looks like grief or depression.

If during this period of time the mother is suddenly absent, the infant experiences a profound grief reaction. If the absence is prolonged, or if—as Spitz and Wolf (1946) demonstrated—the infant is placed in an environment with little, if any, stimulation, the infant may develop a failure-to-thrive syndrome and ultimately die. These facts demonstrate the critical importance of the relationship for the developing infant. In animals that form adult–adult pair-bonds, the loss of the pair-bond partner often leads to a reaction that we easily recognize as grief. In the animal kingdom (excluding human beings), the loss of the adult pair-bond partner causes a more profound grief reaction than the loss of an infant. We can hypothesize that animals, lacking the symbolic function, do not build up the same kind of attachment to infants as humans do.

Affection has its beginning as the affect that signals the importance of any enduring relationship. We can infer its existence in most, if not all, of the pair-bonded species, for the loss of the partner leads to something that looks very much like grief or depression. In humans, the addition of the emotions of joy and fear, particularly the need for the mother to help the infant master fear, adds a dimension to the affective component of the relationship far beyond that found in birds. If the relationship with the mother is good enough, then the feelings about her can generalize into a feeling of basic trust, a complex mood that signals that life itself is good. If, on the other hand, the relationship is not good enough, then the person may take steps to protect himself against further relationships, which can be seen in the schizoid and paranoid personality disorders. I view these personality styles as mood disorders. The cognitive content of these mood disorders is clear: relationships are bad and/or dangerous and are to be avoided.

The ability to form a good-enough affectionate relationship provides the foundation for love, but affection and love are not the same. In our everyday speech, we often use the word love to refer to almost anything we value. People speak not only of loving their spouses, children, best friends, and country, but also of loving a piece of music, a movie, or cherry pie. This plasticity of our definitions is one of the glories (or, depending on your point of view, the misfortunes) of human language. While this may be easy enough to live with on a day-to-day basis (where the context provides clues to the meaning), it causes a real difficulty if we are attempting to acquire a deeper understanding of the nature of human relationships. Actually, the distinction between affection and romantic Love is one that we are used to making and is often expressed as the difference between liking and loving someone. In evaluating someone as a potential spouse, we may hear a person say, "Well, I really like him a lot. He's a great friend, but I don't really think that I love him." On the other hand, we occasionally hear someone say, "You know, I am madly in love with this guy, but I don't even really like him." (Clearly, this is an ominous prognostic sign for the relationship.) It appears, then, that the difference between liking (or affection) and love is not simply one of intensity; there are subtle, but very real, differences in quality. What are these differences? This is the question that must be answered if the distinction is to have any real meaning.

Affectionate relationships are something we share with many other species, but human love is more than liking someone, even intensely, for it includes the capacity for idealization of the loved one. This capacity for idealization is what can transform a warm, affectionate relationship (love) into the idealizing, romantic Love of the poets. It is the process of symbolic thought that allows us to idealize, that catalyzes the transformation of affection into Love. Basically, Love is affection combined with the *idea* that the loved person is good. The capacity to idealize is an integral component of the ability to use symbols, the most obvious manifestation of which is the arrival of speech at approximately 18 months of life. The old saying "absence makes the heart grow fonder" is a glowing tribute to the power of idealization freed from the constraints of the reality of daily contact. The role that idealization plays in Love is an important one clinically, for, as is well known, a person may very well "fall in love" with an idealized image of a person, rather than with the person himself or herself. "Falling out of love" six months or a year after marriage is the result of the diminution of the idealization, the result of living together, day by day. Thus, it is the capacity to idealize our beloved that gives us the power to transform affectionate bonds—a capacity we share with many species—into romantic Love.

SUMMARY

Human beings are different from the rest of the animal kingdom in their capacity to use symbols, a capacity that creates complex affects, core affects combined with ideas. (A discussion of complex affects is

contained in ch. 13, "Love, Hate, and the Dynamic Unconscious.")
Not only love, but hate, envy, greed, wonder, compassion, and many,
many more are examples of complex affects. In addition, the ability
to think gives humans the power to imagine something different
from what is. We are not imprisoned by reality. We can imagine
many things: unicorns, demons, gods, the beginning and the end of
the universe. As children, we can also imagine being married to or
murdering a parent. It is the power of the imagination to create
stories that catalyzes the emergence of infantile sexuality during the
oedipal period. The existence of childhood sexual feelings and fantasies should not be taken as evidence that the relationship between
parents and children is sexual. Rather, the existence of these fantasies demonstrates that human beings, once they have acquired the
ability to use symbols, often, perhaps even always, use the body—
feeding, defecating, sexuality—to symbolize their experience of that
relationship.

There is no reason to describe the relationship between mother
and infant as sexual. During the first 18 months of life—Freud's oral
period—the child experiences many feelings toward the mother
including all or almost all the core affects such as interest–excitement,
joy, fear, and anger. As will be developed in chapter 9, complex
moods, such as trust and mistrust, are the representation of the
presymbolic character structure. During the first 18 months of life,
the most important experience for the infant is the quality of the
relationship with the mother. The basis for calling the relationship
sexual derives from Freud's bold assertion that the nursing experience is sexual. As will be discussed in the next chapter, I suspect that
it is the similarity of dynamic contours of the affects connected with
nursing and sexual intercourse that led Freud to this conclusion.

4

Contentment, Excitement, and Joy

In much of Freud's theorizing, three positively valenced affects—
contentment, excitement, and joy—are lumped together as "pleasure." A substantial part of the problem of differentiating among
them is that what Freud called pleasure is inextricably interwoven
with both his theory of infantile sexuality and his theory of instinctual drives. Because of the heavy theoretical burden that sexuality
carries in both of these theories, it has been very difficult for
psychoanalysts to adequately understand human sexuality, which
radically differs from the biologically driven, animal sexuality.

CONTENTMENT

Contentment is one of four neonatal moods that are present at birth
and help the newly born infant begin to organize his experience of
the world. (The other three are interest, surprise, and distress.)
While interest and surprise tend to focus the infant's attention on
something in the world-out-there, the distress syndrome and
contentment have an inward focus. During the neonatal period
(birth to eight weeks), distress is almost always secondary to physiologic distress. The infant is hungry, thirsty, cold, hot, or in pain;
"outer world" events such as a loud noise probably cause their
distress because of an uncomfortable level of auditory stimulation,

not because the infant has some worry or fear about something "out-there." Freud called these physiologic needs the instincts of self-preservation; in Lichtenberg's classification of motivational systems, they are considered within the motivational system that regulates physiologic requirements.

In the paper "Instincts and Their Vicissitudes," Freud (1915a) said, "The aim [*Ziel*] of an instinct is in every instance satisfaction, which can only be obtained by removing the state of stimulation at the source of the instinct" (p. 122). When used to describe the motivational system that regulates our physiologic needs, a drive-discharge model works reasonably well because this system is deficit driven (lack of food → hunger → distress). When all these physiologic deficits are "satisfied," this satisfaction (a behavioral description) will be signaled by the feeling of contentment whose message is "everything is OK with my body." In summary, what Freud called "satisfaction" seems to be derived from a model that primarily concerns the body's physiologic needs. The satisfaction of these needs is often signaled by feelings of contentment.

Presymbolically, contentment carries the reasonably simple message that "my bodily needs have been taken care of." After one has acquired the ability to think, contentment acquires a secondary, more important, meaning as a global signal about how life is going. As such, it plays a complex and exceedingly important part in affect development. The parents play a key role, particularly in helping the child develop a tolerance for negative affects, such as sadness or grief. If something bad happens—the dog dies, a friend gets angry and ends the friendship, a family member is hurt or dies—the parents have to help the child understand that experiencing sadness or grief does not mean that "something is wrong *with him or her*" but, rather, that feeling bad is the appropriate response to a distressing event. Learning that one can be content and still be unhappy is the beginning of wisdom; helping the patient understand this plays a part in almost every therapeutic experience.

INTEREST–EXCITEMENT

Interest–excitement is easy enough to recognize, both in ourselves and in others. In ourselves, we experience a heightened alertness, our attention focused intently on something by the "mind's eye." In others, we can observe the slightly furrowed brow with the eyes fixed and tracking the object. As one of the four moods present at birth, interest focuses our attention on the outside world, catalyzing our ability to learn about and interact effectively with our environment. Interest–excitement is generated primarily by something we need, such as food, sex, or the urge to explore new territory. As Tomkins (1962) points out, interest and excitement guide us and support the necessary and the possible: "One's sexual drive and one's hunger drive can be no stronger than one's excitement about sexuality or about eating" (p. 342). In every species, prewired programs guide the organism in selecting what, when, where, and (in the case of predators) whom to eat. Frogs are interested in catching flies, herbivores in grazing, predators in catching their prey, and so on. Except in human beings, sexual and reproductive behavior is similarly preprogrammed. When these physiologic needs are satisfied, there is generally a shift of focus from the outside world to the inner, and the organism moves to the relaxed, contented mood of the alert-inactive state. Behaviorally, this shift may be manifested by an activity such as dozing, perhaps as a prelude to sleep.

The capacity to begin to regulate our moods emerges much earlier than might be expected. By the age of four or five months, most infants are beginning to be able both to stimulate and to soothe themselves. Escalona (1963) described this development as follows:

> One of the interesting things about bodily self-stimulation is that the very same behavior sometimes has a soothing effect, whereas at other times it is excitatory. As early as age four months babies are seen not only to comfort themselves by sucking (as even newborns do) but also to suck or chomp so vigorously as to create increasingly high states of excitation. From about age five months onward, some babies "cradle rock" in rhythmic fashion when distressed or tired, and this may lead to a reduction in bodily tension and to a more contented state of mind. Yet they may also start to rock while alert and unoccupied (one is tempted to say bored) and work themselves up to high peaks of excitation. In young infants tactile self-stimulation is very common, but it is difficult to say whether it tends to be excitatory or soothing. Most often it appears along with other signs of increasing tension as, for instance, in the universal and more lasting pattern of rubbing the eyes when tired. Yet some infants can be seen to "entertain themselves" by stroking, scratching, or pinching portions of their skin with every appearance of mild pleasure, but no distinct signs of heightened tension [pp. 226–227].

These observations illustrate how the infant engages in behaviors that purposefully evoke specific affects, the prototype of what will later come to be known as "self-regulation." The early emergence of these discrete patterns convincingly demonstrates how affects serve as the central control signals that guide and regulate the infant's behavior.

Escalona noted that, at times, infants engage in behavior that seems designed to counteract what could be interpreted as boredom. For animals living in the wild, the naturally occurring interactions with the environment cause enough stimulation that we seldom observe what we think of as boredom. Only in the atypical circumstances of captivity (a large animal relentlessly pacing a too-small cage in a zoo) do we observe behavior that suggests the contrary. Domesticated animals also experience mild boredom, primarily because life has become too easy. For example, domesticated cats, freed from the need to provide food for themselves, spend a great deal of time either napping or asleep; at times, our cat will irritably scratch the wallpaper or carpet if no one is paying attention to her. The reasons why boredom occurs in human beings and seldom, if ever, in free-living wild animals are extremely important. Because of the advances of civilization, human infants are raised in circumstances that approximate the life of domesticated animals. Consequently, the parents must attempt to design an environment that supplies an optimal amount of stimulation.

After we reach the stage of development where we can be guided by our ideas rather than solely by our affects, a more complex problem emerges. Through the use of will power, we can force ourselves to pay attention to something that we are not really interested in or excited by. For example, our better judgment may tell us to study for an exam even though we hate the subject or our tact prevents us from interrupting a boring conversation. Thus, we are constrained from doing what animals would do: cease paying attention to what they find uninteresting.

One way to combat the feeling of boredom is by actively seeking what are known as thrills. As vocations involving considerable physical danger progressively vanish from modern life, avocations that physically challenge the individual—sports such as skiing or mountain climbing—can become something of a substitute. Or, rather than the active mastery of activities that involve complex physical skills, passive thrills can be sought. At a harmless level, the thrill rides of an amusement park generate these feelings. At a less harmless level, such spectacles as the Roman "games," bear baiting, and public executions generate similar feelings. (Some would put boxing and auto racing into this category.) These thrills, of course, do not generate the pride that comes from the mastery of physical danger; in that sense, they are bought on the cheap. Reckless driving, gambling, needless financial risk taking, promiscuity, and, perhaps for some, mindless violence become activities that can generate, however fleetingly, a sense of excitement that is only a pale substitute for the ability to enjoy life.

ENJOYMENT– JOY

At approximately eight weeks of age, infants undergo a dramatic change as they begin to make direct eye contact. Shortly thereafter, they begin to smile not only more frequently but also more responsively and infectiously. As Stern (1985) has said, "The age of two months is almost as clear a boundary as birth itself" (p. 37). This dramatic shift correlates with the level of neurologic maturation. Prior to the shift, the infant is governed primarily by the reptilian brain, whose major affective representation is the global, diffuse mood. Subsequent to the shift, the infant begins to experience the more discrete emotions as the old mammalian brain superimposes its organization on the older, reptilian brain. Joyfulness, manifested by the social smile, announces that the infant can now experience emotions.

At one time, many people assumed that social smiling suddenly appeared out of the blue and was without precursors. Careful observation, however, indicated otherwise.

> During the early weeks we saw facial expressions which often puzzled us—a bilateral upturning of the corners of the mouth occurring sporadically in a variety of behavioral states. Mothers tended to make light of these early smiles and to ignore them; they referred to some of them as "gas expressions" and to others as "smiling at the angels" [Emde et al., 1976, p. 71].

Emde and his colleagues found that this form of smiling was not the result of external stimulation, but seemed to occur spontaneously as one of many endogenously determined physiologic patterns (p. 72). Other behaviors, such as nutritional sucking, fussing, and crying, were also observed and exhibited similar EEG patterns. Thus, careful observation has shown that the social smile has its anlage in the early endogenous smile.

The exogenous smile, not present at birth, begins in an irregular fashion during the first or second month and increases in specificity and importance throughout the first year. During the period in which the smile is irregular, from one and a half to two and a half months, a variety of stimuli—visual, kinesthetic, auditory, tactile—will elicit it (p. 76). Emde and his coworkers outline the course of development of the social smile:

> We might think of this age as one during which there is nonspecific smiling, or smiling in response to multiple stimuli. There is a flowering of the response, the infant smiling in response to "everything," but it is not predictable. . . . After this, from two and a half to three months, the regular social smile occurs. Now smiling is best elicited by visual stimuli, especially the human face, although it increases in response to stimuli in other modalities as well. During the next phase, at three months and after, there is early differentiated smiling. Smiling becomes more specific within the visual modality, requiring a three-dimensional stimulus configuration, and soon there is more smiling in response to the mother's face than to others. Concomitantly, smiling becomes rare in response to nonvisual stimuli [p. 76].

As the young infant begins to smile regularly in response to people, social interaction begins. His mother, father, brothers, and sisters are delighted by his beaming response. He is proudly exhibited to friends, "who no longer feel they always have to tiptoe in the house of a sleeping baby. Instead, he smiles engagingly at everyone, his eyes brightly fixated on those of the person who looks at him" (p. 86). About two weeks after the regular social smile begins, a cooing vocalization is added to the baby's communicative repertoire. With the onset of the social smile, affective communication is now possible. The mother usually experiences "delight and a feeling that her infant is delighted" (p. 86). Obviously, the interactive experience of joyfulness plays a major role in opening up affective communication between mother and infant. One might say that joy is part of the glue of the bonding process.

As Emde and his colleagues have commented, "The dramatic shift from virtually no exogenous smiling to a surge of nonspecific smiling before smiling becomes specifically social, the fact of the flowering itself, seems to argue for a strong maturational thrust in smiling onset" (p. 88). In other words, the smiling is the *result*, not the cause, of the maturational shift. The biobehavioral shift that occurs at eight weeks in human infants is easily observable in other mammals. The house cat is a reasonably good animal model for this biobehavioral shift. In reviewing a number of experiments, Emde et al. conclude that the cat's "postnatal development is more rapid than the human's but similar events occur" (pp. 19–20). The neurophysiologic basis seems to be correlated with the progressive encephalization of the neural controls of wakefulness and sleep, allowing control to shift from the brain stem to higher level forebrain mechanisms (p. 20). Thus, the observable shift in organization of the psyche from moods to emotions is correlated with a neurophysiologic change. In kittens, this shift is manifested by the onset of purring; as with humans, this capacity does not begin at birth. Emde et al. comment, "The newborn kitten, like the newborn human, has a distress vocalization-quiescence organization; purring has its onset only later" (p. 92). Similarly, tail wagging in dogs has its onset at approximately three weeks, not at birth (pp. 92–93). Thus, the smiling response in human infants, purring in kittens, and tail wagging in puppies are all manifestations of the same biobehavioral shift that signals the coming "on-line" of the circuitry of the old mammalian brain. Inferentially, these observations of a biobehavioral shift offer strong support for MacLean's (1949, 1952) hypothesis of the triune brain.

An analysis of the social smile in terms of communication is most illuminating. The distress cry, the predominant affective communication during the first two months, gives a universal and peremptory message: "Come quick! Change what's happening." Ordinarily, the intuitive mother is able to respond either specifically, by feeding the baby or changing a diaper, or nonspecifically, by comforting, stroking, or rocking. More often than not, the effect of the mother's successful intervention is to bring an end to the interaction and return the infant to an inwardly focused state. The only time the interaction continues is when the mother fails, and then we move to the escalating cycle of a "colicky baby" and frustrated mother. On the other hand, smiling does not result in this type of vicious circle; it gives a universal message, but it is not a request for change. It says, "Keep on with what you are doing. I like it." Thus the smile, once it has moved from the endogenous to the exogenous phase, becomes a reciprocally reinforcing positive interaction. In terms of the specific goals of parenting, one of the parent's tasks is to facilitate the infant's experience of joy.

Interest–excitement is an easy affect to understand because it makes us interested in and excited by the very things (food, sex) that are necessary for life to go on; joyfulness is difficult to understand because we are not sure of its specific adaptive function. One of the difficulties is that joy is rarely experienced as a "pure culture" but is usually blended with a number of other feelings. The developmental research of Emde and others strongly suggests that in the very beginning joyfulness is the result of physiologic maturation, but it is an affect that is easily triggered through the process of playful interactions with the mother with the net result that it becomes part of their relationship. Joy, however, is more than an affect generated between individuals and situated within the context of a relationship. For example, many types of play incorporate elements of joyousness. Perhaps the best example of this is rough-and-tumble play, an activity observed both in children and in some of the more intelligent animals ("playful as a kitten"). One can see in this activity a blend of both excitement and enjoyment, as well as the beginnings of the development of the skills that may be used in fighting as an adult. Thus, we often find joy as part of an affective blend, where it may very well serve as a reinforcer for activities that we recognize as having a specific adaptive usefulness. Recognizing that joy is often connected with play—whether the social playfulness between mother and infant or the rough-and-tumble play of young children—does not, however, really help us, because the adaptive function of play, like joy, also remains something of a mystery.

For a fortunate few individuals, pure joyfulness can be experienced at the high-intensity end of the spectrum. Many creative adults have left accounts of childhood feelings of a certain kind of joyousness that felt like a mystical union with Nature. Bernard Berenson (1949) described this experience as "some instant of perfect harmony" (p. 18).

> In childhood and boyhood this ecstasy overtook me when I was happy out of doors. Was I five or six? Certainly not seven. It was a morning in early summer. A silver haze shimmered and trembled over the lime trees. The air was laden with their fragrance. The temperature was like a caress. I remember—I need not recall—that I climbed up a tree stump and felt suddenly immersed in Itness. I did not call it by that name. I had no need for words. It and I were one [p. 18].

These special states of joyousness—"Intimations of Immortality" as Wordsworth called them—are relatively rare and tend to be limited to persons who, in later life, become artists or poets, or develop a special affinity for the spiritual life. In a letter to Freud, Romaine Rolland suggested that this "oceanic feeling," rather than a belief in God, was the true source of religion; Freud (1930) responded that he could not discover the feeling in himself and "could not convince myself of the primary nature of such a feeling" (pp. 64–65). Although he seemed to give lip service to the idea that these feelings might simply represent a type of experience unavailable to him, the underlying tone of Freud's discussion of religious experience is to dismiss it as some kind of regressive aberration. This tendency to subtly pathologize ecstatic states has left theorists with a very real ignorance of the full range of joyful experience. This lack, in turn, has been a major handicap in developing a comprehensive theory of affects. These ecstatic states are not regressive but are the experience of intense joyfulness. Perhaps because of our ambivalence about the subject, the psychoanalytic literature contains remarkably few studies devoted to the emergence of the capacity for joyfulness.

"PLEASURE"

The impairment of the ability to experience joy is a common problem, not only for patients, but for all people. Quite simply, most people do not take the time to pause to "smell the flowers," to enjoy the countless small pleasures that life has to offer. A substantial part of the problem is that the capacity for real enjoyment is, in many respects, a cultural achievement that must be nourished by the educational process. This is true whether we are talking about the ability to enjoy relationships, play, sexuality, the arts, leisure, nature, or—ultimately—life itself. I suspect that a substantial part of the problem is that both interest–excitement and enjoyment–joy are positively valenced but distinct affects. They are often lumped together in our minds, as well as in psychoanalytic theory, under the all-inclusive category of "pleasure." The failure to discriminate between these two affects causes a number of problems, both theoretical and practical.

In psychoanalytic discourse, Freud used the term pleasure to describe any positively valenced affect. Part of the difficulty is that the term has two distinct definitions: 1) as a word to describe positively valenced affects (what Henry Krystal, 1988, calls hedonic tone); and 2) as a synonym for enjoyment, as in "It's a pleasure to see you." Both excitement and joyfulness, for example, would be considered "pleasure" under the first definition of the word, but would be easily distinguished from each other by the second definition. These usages are similar enough to cause a great deal of intellectual confusion, and we often oscillate between the two meanings of the term unless we mentally footnote how we are using them. These semantic difficulties are compounded by the fact that Freud's theory of pleasure was built around sexuality, with the orgasm implicitly serving as the primary model. This theoretical model complicates the problem, since sexuality in adult humans contains elements of at least three positively valenced affects: excitement, enjoyment, and contentment (usually in that order). Let us, then, examine Freud's theoretical treatment of the positive affects.

One of the key assumptions of Freud's (1905) theory of infantile sexuality is that most, if not all, of the infant's pleasurable/sensual experiences are sexual in nature. The erotogenic zones, usually defined as the skin or the mucous membranes of the oral, anal, genital, or mammillary areas, give a sexual character to the experiences connected to these zones (p. 182). Later, Freud (1940a) seemed to be saying that virtually the whole body could function as an "erotogenic zone" (p. 151). Although the details of these formulations were vague then and are still vague today, the net result is that Freud seemed to consider all pleasure, once one understood the underlying displacements from the erotogenic zones, as sexual in nature. In respect to the equation of pleasure and sexuality, Freud's theory was heavily influenced by his observations of the characteristic dynamic contour of intercourse. As we noted earlier, the dynamic contours of affective experience—Stern's (1985) "vitality affects"— are remarkably similar to the crescendo/decrescendo patterns of music. If one were to diagram the affective sequence of intercourse, the foreplay would be the slow building of sexual excitement, and the orgasm would be a sudden rush of enjoyment, followed by a relaxed feeling of calm and contentment. The dynamic contour of excitement → enjoyment → contentment is so much a part of sexual experience that, in effect, it becomes its signature. The hunger → feeding → satiety sequence demonstrates a similar dynamic contour. From his observations of the similarity of the dynamic contours of the two experiences, Freud (1905) drew a conclusion that had immense importance for psychoanalytic theory:

> No one who has seen a baby sinking back satisfied from the breast and falling asleep with flushed cheeks and a blissful smile can escape the reflection that this picture persists as a prototype of the expression of sexual satisfaction in later life [p. 182].

In this sentence, Freud is clearly referring to patterning of affective response. In essence, he is arguing that the similarity of dynamic contour of the two affective sequences (nursing and intercourse) can be interpreted to mean that the "oral satisfactions" connected with nursing *are* sexual in nature.

In developing his theories about sexuality, Freud (1905) placed his primary emphasis on the orgasm, saying "A certain amount of touching is indispensable (at all events among human beings) before the *normal sexual aim* can be attained" (p. 156, emphasis added). In Freud's terminology, the "normal aim" is ejaculation/orgasm leading to reproduction. The implication of Freud's theory is that sexuality should be considered a biologic need, similar to hunger; while foreplay is sometimes necessary ("A certain amount of touching is indispensable"), the emphasis is clearly on ejaculation. Adopting one of the everyday meanings of tension as a synonym for excitement, Freud used the phrase "tension buildup" to describe the gradual increase of sexual excitement during foreplay. In the adult male, the increase in excitement during sexual intercourse almost always ends with ejaculation, which is virtually synonymous with orgasm; in contrast, the female may or may not reach orgasm. Freud conceptualized the postorgasm feelings of relaxation as the "discharge of tension," a term that evokes sexuality through its unconscious links to ejaculatory discharge. By using the same word—*tension* buildup/*tension* discharge—to describe the feelings both prior to and after the orgasm, Freud leads the reader to believe that we are dealing with the same affect—pleasure—in a crescendo/decrescendo form.

Almost 20 years later, Freud (1924a) began to have doubts about this formulation:

> Pleasure and unpleasure, therefore, cannot be referred to "an increase or decrease of a quantity (which we describe as "tension due to stimulus"), although they obviously have a great deal to do with that factor. It appears that they depend, not on this quantitative factor, *but on some characteristic of it which we can only describe as a qualitative one*. If we were able to say what this qualitative characteristic is, we should be much further advanced in psychology. Perhaps it is the rhythm, the temporal sequence of changes, rises and falls in the quantity of stimulus. We do not know [p. 160, emphasis added].

In beginning to differentiate the qualitative from the quantitative factors and thus moving away from describing all positively valenced affects as pleasure, Freud was moving toward a process theory of affects. At the time he wrote this paper, however, he was 80, and perhaps he sensed that he did not have the time to radically revise his theories.

An impairment of the capacity for enjoyment, whatever the cause, leaves one with the feeling that something is missing from life. One of the ways to deal with this sense of loss is to attempt to substitute the experience of excitement for enjoyment. Some of the more obvious ways, the generation of "thrills" through the use of drugs, gambling, affairs, even violence, were mentioned in the section on "Interest–Excitement." But there are other, more subtle, culturally sanctioned ways of doing the same thing; one of the easiest is to simply immerse oneself in work, the dynamics of a workaholic. This has many forms—the 30-year-old lawyer working a hundred hours a week to become a senior partner in a law firm, the "Super Mom" spending all her time schlepping kids to and from their activities, or the young executive—male or female—caught up in the corporate "rat race." The long-term hope is that, after one is successful enough, then one will finally begin to be able to enjoy life, an illusion that is strongly reinforced by our culture. But work is not the only place where one can find the workaholic; some people adopt lifestyles that are its functional equivalent. Whatever the specifics, the key phrase seems to be "too much; too fast," and what once was exciting gradually begins to feel hectic, if not frantic. Part of the problem is that a number of activities may generate both excitement and enjoyment, making it difficult to distinguish between the two. But they are not the same. Excitement tends to become more intense as we speed up; in contrast, joy often, but not always, becomes more intense as we allow ourselves to slow down. At the core of their being, what humans long for is to enjoy life. In the long run, if joy is absent, it leaves people with a vague, undefinable feeling that they are missing out on what life has to offer.

HUMAN SEXUALITY AS PLAY

"Man is only truly human when he plays." When we hear this aphorism, it intuitively feels correct to us. The problems begin when we attempt to understand why, because this seemingly simple statement contains within it an exceedingly complex view of human development. John Huizinga (1938), a Dutch historian, begins his book *Homo Ludens* ("playful man") with this delightful description:

> Play is older than culture, for culture, however inadequately defined, always presupposes human society, and animals have not waited for

man to teach them their playing. We can safely assert, even, that human civilization has added no essential feature to the general idea of play. Animals play just like men. We have only to watch young dogs to see that all the essentials of human play are present in their merry gambols. They invite one another to play by a certain ceremoniousness of attitude and gesture. They keep to the rule that you shall not bite, or not bite hard, your brother's ear. They pretend to get terribly angry. And—what is most important—in all these doings they plainly experience tremendous fun and enjoyment. Such rompings of young dogs are only one of the simpler forms of animal play [p. 1].

In contrast to sexuality, playfulness ordinarily is limited to the more intelligent animals; for example, the primates; the seagoing mammals such as whales, porpoises, and dolphins; and the terrestrial carnivores are noted for their ability to play. These two characteristics—playfulness and intelligence—may very well have evolved in concert, each strengthening the other in ways that are not yet fully understood. In our attempt to link specific affects with identifiable motivational systems, joy seems to be the emotion that is most closely associated with play. Returning to the aphorism "Man is only truly human when he plays," I suspect that we endorse it because it places the feeling of joyfulness at the center of human aspirations.

Play has always been difficult to understand from an ethologic perspective, primarily because the goals of play are not "of obvious value in contributing to the preservation of an individual or the continuity of a species" (one of Bowlby's, 1969, four criteria of instinctive behavior). Thus, as Huizinga (1938) says, the attempts to define the adaptive value of play have shown a striking variation and include the following: the discharge of superabundant vital energy; the "imitative instinct"; the "need" for relaxation; preparation for the serious work of life; practice in exercising restraint; the urge to dominate; the sublimation of destructive impulses; "wish fulfilment" (p. 2). In reviewing the extensive literature about the function of play, Konner (1982) says, "To summarize a great deal of print about how to define play, I think that to say that it is an expenditure of energy that looks both impractical and pleasurable would not, despite its brevity and vagueness, do violence to the literature on the subject" (p. 246).

One of the difficulties in understanding play is that the positive feelings accompanying it, including both excitement and enjoyment, become recruited into the other motivational systems, where they function as a reinforcement or a reward. For example, interactive smiling between mother and baby is obviously pleasurable, and it is not much of a stretch to call this a type of game or play. Freud's (1920) delightful vignette about his grandson is another example; he hypothesized that the game of "disappearance and return" (p. 15) helped the infant master the fear and anxiety that occurs with separation (pp. 14–16). Without much doubt, play and playlike activity can be of great use in cementing the relationship between mother and child. Play, however, is not simply restricted to relationships. The predatory behavior of the big cats is an excellent example. As will be developed in chapter 7, hunting is usually carried out in a playlike mode. Mothers often bring back half-dead prey, which their young then kill and eat. "They lead cubs and kittens on expeditions whose main purpose seems to be to acquaint the young with stalking. And they partially kill prey on the hunt, leaving the young to finish the job and intervening only if the prey is about to escape" (Konner, 1982, p. 247). Play fights, or rough-and-tumble play, is displayed in virtually all mammalian juveniles. This kind of play, both vigorous and highly arousing, usually does not result in injury although it sometimes can; however, it contains components, both behavioral and physiological, that are later used in the serious fights of adulthood. Thus, practice hunts and rough-and-tumble fights are clearly play but also serve an educative function in developing skills that will be used in adulthood.

The ease with which excitement and enjoyment can become intermixed with other behaviors illustrates some of the difficulty in sorting out exactly what are our primary motivational systems. This brings us back to the question of sexuality. Sexuality in animals is, as noted in the previous chapter, relatively easy to understand because it functions as a discrete motivational system. Pheromones, hormones, and behavioral signs such as visual displays and mating calls activate complex instinctive programs that lead to courtship rituals, mating, and reproduction. In turn, the birth of the offspring leads to programs that govern how the mother (and sometimes the father) raises and cares for the young. Human sexuality, however, is markedly different from that of other species. A major difference— and it is an impressive one by evolutionary standards—is that human females do not experience "heat," or estrus. Their sexual responsiveness is not governed by the neuroendocrine clock and is distributed more or less randomly over the days of the year, with the exception, in some cultures, of a somewhat lowered receptivity during the days of menstrual flow. (There is no way to tell whether this diminished receptivity is the result of subtle neuroendocrine differences or of cultural bias against having sexual relations with a woman who is considered "unclean.")

But there is another, less obvious but more important, distinction between animal sexuality and human sexuality that has to do with the emotion of joy. In the animal world, the capacity for enjoyment is restricted to but a few mammals, primarily the most intelligent. But even in those species that can experience joy, sexual activity takes place without feelings of enjoyment. The animals are not playing when engaged in sexual activity; it is a program to be run, a need to be satisfied. One does not have to be a highly trained ethologist to arrive at these conclusions; one simply has to listen to the neighborhood cats at night to hear the noise of their "lovemaking." It is evident that the emotion of joyfulness begins as something that is quite distinct from and independent of the rudiments of the sexual/reproductive system. It is in human beings and in human beings alone that sexuality and joyfulness are connected.

At times, the impulse for sexual intercourse in human beings is biologically driven; however, most of the time other factors far outweigh the biological. As a result, human sexual activity cannot be conceptualized as taking place primarily to satisfy a physiologic need (although feelings of lust or "horniness" may serve as the trigger or stimulus to initiate sexual activity). For example, performing well sexually may be a major source of self-esteem (the competence/mastery system). When a long-married couple decides to spend a romantic weekend away from work and the kids, their decision has more to do with the quality of their relationship (the affiliational system) than it does with sex. At the other end of the spectrum, therapists who work with sexual dysfunctions know that, more often than not, apparent sexual dysfunction turns out to be a relationship dysfunction. Virtually every therapist has treated a female patient for whom sexuality became a means for being cuddled, held, protected, "loved," or escaping from an intolerable home situation. For that woman, sexuality is a means for mastering (sometimes by escaping from) an exceedingly frightening situation. At the other end of the scale, we have begun to hear the phrase "trophy wife" to describe the woman of exceptional beauty, talent, and intellect who is sought by outstandingly successful corporate executives; in this situation, competitive strivings, the desire to be successful (or at least appear to be), may be a primary motivational factor. At a darker level, we now know that rape is not motivated primarily by sexual feelings but is primarily a symbolic act of revenge. It is clear that human sexuality can become intricately interwoven with any and all of the motivational systems and, along the way, can acquire a multiplicity of meanings.

It is difficult to assess the part the orgasm plays in human sexuality and its relationship to the emotion of joy. As mentioned before, when animals are engaged in sexual activity, feelings of joyfulness appear to be absent, even in the few mammalian species that are capable of experiencing this emotion (excitement, yes; enjoyment, no). In contrast, the human orgasm is often experienced as high-intensity feelings of joy. For many people, the orgasm itself, the joyous bridge from excitement to contentment, may be their only experience of high-intensity feelings of joy. It may be that the joyful component of human sexuality, coupled with the ability to connect sexuality with feelings of affection and love, most clearly distinguishes human from animal sexuality. Because of the inclusion of this joyful component, human sexuality is most usefully conceptualized as a specific type of play, not as a biologic need.

Therefore, sexual intercourse in human beings is a specific sequence of three positively valenced affects: the foreplay crescendo of sexual excitement; the orgasm proper with its intense feelings of joyfulness; and the feelings of relaxation and contentment that rapidly follow. This sequence suggests that the orgasm itself serves as a catalyst, perhaps operating at a primarily organic level, that shifts us from one specific affect (sexual excitement) into another (relaxed contentment). Following this line of reasoning, Margo Anand (1989) has written about how sexuality can become not only more pleasurable but an art form and a spiritual discipline. Building on her knowledge of Tantric yoga—the sexual yoga from India and Tibet—she suggests a number of exercises that can lead to disconnecting the link between the orgasm and ejaculatory discharge. This disconnection enables an indefinite prolongation of the orgasm, which she calls "the streaming reflex," experienced as ecstasy and bliss. This ability, reached by behavioral exercises rather than by meditation, may have important implications for understanding some of the ecstatic states of saints and mystics.

In summary, the differentiation of three positively valenced affects—contentment, excitement, joy—helps us to better understand human sexuality. In the rest of the animal kingdom, sexuality is driven primarily by sexual excitement and is carried on without noticeable feelings of joy or behaviors suggesting playfulness. Human sexuality is markedly different from animal sexuality (where the obvious adaptive purpose is "the preservation of the species"). Through the use of symbols, human beings can detach sexuality from its biologically driven program and connect it with other motivational systems, where it can acquire a variety of meanings. The orgasm plays a very important part in our thinking about positively valenced affects. For many persons—probably most—the orgasm is their only experience of high-intensity feelings of joy. Consequently, it serves as an implicit model of what the affective range of human experience can be. Within the context of a loving relationship, sexuality is most usefully thought of as a very specific type of play.

SUMMARY

By lumping three positively valenced affects (contentment, excitement, joy) together as "pleasure," Freud's theorizing complicated our ability to build a satisfactory theory of affects. A specific deficit in Freud's theorizing is his failure to appreciate adequately the importance of joy. Enjoyment–joy, one of Tomkins's (1962) nine basic affects, is very different from interest–excitement and is one of the key feelings associated with play. Part of the problem in differentiating excitement from joy is that they are complexly interconnected in play and that the adaptive purpose of play has always been difficult to understand. In contrast, the purpose of those activities that generate feelings of pure excitement is usually obvious; they allow us to survive as individuals (food, relationships) or as a species (sexual excitement). At the clinical level, the differentiation of excitement from joy is important because too many people who pursue activities that are exciting have lost the capacity to experience joy. While excitement is easy enough to induce in oneself (drugs, thrills, manic activity, violence, etc.), joy is much more difficult to counterfeit. The capacity for joy—whether in the context of a relationship, play, sexuality, art, or simply while living life—is an ability that is cultivated rather than something you can go out and get. I think that one could safely say that very few people who are able to really enjoy life ever come to therapy. If this observation is correct, then it has important implications for formulating the goals of the therapeutic process.

5

Fear

Fear, one of Sylvan Tomkins's (1962) nine basic affects, is one of the easiest emotions to understand because its message is so clear: Danger! Protect yourself! Within the animal kingdom, danger comes from two primary sources: 1) physical dangers, such as fires or heights; and 2) predators. Among the range of protective responses in various species, one fact is immediately obvious: the lower the animal is on the phylogenetic scale, the greater its use of preprogrammed, instinctive (in the sense of *Instinkte*) responses. For example, Tinbergen and Lorenz observed the reflexive, fearful crouch of a chick before a hawk, or even before a cardboard silhouette of a hawk. They concluded that the crouching constituted a classic innate releasing mechanism, both in muscle contraction and emotion (see Konner, 1982, pp. 208–235). This hard-wired response has obvious adaptive usefulness, for it allows for self-protective measures to be taken long *before* the infant is able to learn from experience. Even as we move up the phylogenetic scale, these fears are still highly specific. Konner (1982) comments:

> A looming object (or a simulation of one) can cause startled crying in even the youngest of human infants; and the edge of a cliff (or an optical illusion that looks like one) will cause fear not only in human infants but in a wide variety of vertebrate infants, *including those with no experience of heights* [p. 221, emphasis added].

99

These experiments, and countless others, demonstrate that not only humans, but virtually all vertebrates, are preprogrammed to respond in a protective manner to threats of bodily injury. Fear is the affect of a motivational system that attempts to protect an organism from physical harm or destruction.[1]

In human infants, the anlagen of these protective responses begin at birth with the startle response and the infant distress syndrome. Although distress responses can be triggered by a variety of environmental stimuli such as loud noises and sudden movements, in all probability the reaction is simply the response to physiologic overload (i.e., the noise is too loud). In any case, distress signals, both to the infant and to the caretaker, that something is wrong. Distress responses are common in a wide variety of species, and all carry the same message: "Mother, come quick!" (e.g., the yelping of young puppies). It is important to recognize, however, that the infant distress response is not the same affect as fear. Tomkins (1962), for example, distinguishes between distress–anguish and fear–terror. The difference between distress and fear plays a key role in understanding what we call anxiety (see chapter 6).

At approximately seven to nine months of age, the more-specific fear response emerges. Before this age, fear, for all intents and purposes, is nonexistent. The onset of the fear response is easily recognized and is manifested by what is called "stranger anxiety" or "eight-month anxiety." The child reacts with a cry at the approach of an unfamiliar person, even one approaching in a friendly fashion. This response occurs in virtually every culture and class that has been studied throughout the world.

> In infants from the professional class and the working class in the United States, in infants in an Israeli kibbutz where mother-infant contact is by our standards quite limited, in rural and urban Guatemala, and among the !Kung San of Botswana, who have the closest, most intimate, and most indulgent mother-infant relationships ever systematically described, the rise of separation fear and stranger fear occurs during the same age period. There are large cross-cultural variations in the percentage of infants who cry at any give age, in the age at which the percentage reaches its peak, and in the steepness and duration of the subsequent decline with further

---

[1] Joseph Lichtenberg (1989) includes both fear and rage within a more inclusive "aversive motivational system." The fundamental rationale for this classification is that he considers aggression (often accompanied by the affect of rage) as primarily defensive in nature. I strongly disagree with this conclusion; my reasoning is set forth in chapter 7.

growth. But the variations in the shape and timing of the rising portion of the curve between the ages of six and fifteen months are minor or nonexistent; cultural training does not much accelerate or decelerate the change [Konner, 1982, pp. 222–223].

This fearful response to strangers is quite specific and is easily differentiated from the more global distress vocalization of infancy, the fussiness and crying of the "infant distress syndrome." The consistency of the development of the fear response cross-culturally suggests some maturational change that is independent of the quality of maternal care.

Experiments have been designed that convincingly demonstrate the onset of this "fear system" in children. Perhaps the most dramatic of these experiments is the "visual cliff" (Campos et al., 1978). Any psychoanalytic theory concerning the origin of fear will have to account for the data generated by this set of experiments. The visual cliff is an experimental apparatus originally designed to study depth perception in infants, but it has proved to be very useful in demonstrating the onset of fear. The experimental apparatus is a large, glass-covered table divided into two. One half of the table, the "shallow side," has a textured surface immediately under the glass. The other half, the "deep side," has a similar surface under it, but it is nearly four feet below the glass. With this apparatus, depth perception and fear is inferred from the presence of wariness or distress when the infant is perched directly over the glass covering the deep side, and from the absence of fear when the infant is over the shallow side. When five-month-olds were placed on the deep side of the cliff, their looking was associated with cardiac deceleration and there was no behavioral distress. When nine-month-olds were placed on the deep side, their looking was accompanied by cardiac acceleration, often with overt distress (p. 152). The inference from these experiments is that the nine-month-old infants were feeling afraid and that this response was absent in the five-month-old infant. This experimental result confirms the data of infant observation: fear, in the usually accepted sense of the term, does not begin until approximately seven to nine months of age.

Animal experiments and observations have also demonstrated the onset of this fear system. In both puppies and kittens, distress vocalization begins at birth, but fear of strangers in novel situations begins at about five weeks (see Emde et al., 1976, p. 125). Perhaps Sackett's (1966) studies with monkeys provides the most convincing evidence that fearfulness depends on maturational rather than social factors. He raised eight rhesus monkeys *in total social isolation* from birth; once a week each monkey was shown the same set of slide-projected photographs of other monkeys in various poses. Beginning at two months and peaking at about three months, pictures of monkeys in threat poses resulted in distress vocalizations and disturbance behaviors such as "fear, withdrawal, rocking, and huddling." These disturbances were seldom, if ever, observed before two months and began to wane at four to five months. Pictures of monkeys in other poses did not result in this type of response. In mammals, the emergence of the fear response is an important developmental milestone; moreover, the evidence strongly suggests that the fear response is caused not simply by separation from the mother but by an underlying maturational process that is independent of the physical presence or absence of the mother.

The emergence of this fear response constitutes an advance in cognitive maturation, because it signals not only that "something is wrong" but that "something is wrong *out there*." In other words, the fear response helps locate the problem and is therefore more useful than the distress response. Fear, though, is also a more painful response than distress and is therefore potentially more toxic. With the onset of the ability to feel fear, the distress response does not disappear; rather, we continue to experience it in the feelings we label as distress, frustration, being upset, or anxiety.

"STRANGER ANXIETY": PSYCHOANALYTIC ASSUMPTIONS

The fear response, an easily observed developmental milestone, must be accounted for theoretically. Freud's allegiance to the dual-drive hypothesis led him to think in terms of two primary motivational systems. If one begins with this assumption, fear cannot be considered as primary; therefore, it must be considered a derivative of one of the two major drives. If one begins with these theoretical preconceptions, one eventually comes to the conclusion that fear begins with the fear of the prospective loss of the relationship with the mother (i.e., fear is a derivative of the libidinal drive). Labeling the emergence of the fear response as "stranger anxiety" or "eight-month anxiety" hides an important theoretical assumption in the terminology as it implies a developmental connection between anxiety and fear. This issue is of particular importance in psychoanalytic theory because Freud used anxiety as the paradigm for all affects.

His assumption, which was never really spelled out, was that if we understood anxiety, then we had the key to understanding other affects.

What is the relationship between fear ("stranger distress") and separation from the mother (object loss)? A long-held hypothesis is that stranger distress is, in the final analysis, a reaction to maternal loss. The origin of this hypothesis traces back to Freud (1916–1917):

> A child is frightened of a strange face because he is adjusted to the sight of a familiar and beloved figure—ultimately of his mother. It is his disappointment and longing that are transformed into anxiety— his libido, in fact, which has become unemployable, which cannot at that time be held in suspense and is discharged as anxiety [p. 407].

In 1926, he repeats this formulation:

> Only a few of the manifestations of anxiety in children are comprehensible to us, and we must confine our attention to them. They occur, for instance, when a child is alone, or in the dark, or when it finds itself with an unknown person instead of one to whom it is used—such as its mother. These three instances can be reduced to a single condition—namely, that of missing someone who is loved and longed for [p. 136].

Freud goes on to say, "Here anxiety appears as a reaction to the felt loss of the object" (p. 137), emphasizing the helplessness and dependence of the child "when his ego is immature" (p. 142). Spitz (cited in Emde et al., 1976), elaborating on these comments of Freud, postulated that "when the infant compared the unfamiliar face of the stranger to memory traces of the mother, anxiety resulted from the realization that this person was not the mother and that 'mother is gone'"(p. 109). In short, the Freud/Spitz hypothesis is that "stranger anxiety" is caused by fear of the loss of the mother.

Let us review the situation from the beginning. By the age of four months, the infant clearly demonstrates that he knows his mother as compared with a stranger. He is more responsive to her, and her presence is signaled by an increase in smiling, cooing, and general bodily activity (Emde et al., p. 96). In addition, the mother is more easily able to feed and soothe the infant. Although the four-month-old infant can discriminate between mother and others, he does not avoid the stranger or protest his approach with a cry. This leads to the very interesting question: why does the crying at the sight of a stranger emerge only at seven or eight months when the discrimination between mother and others is established at four months? This was the data that had to be accounted for by subsequent theorizing.

Selma Fraiberg (1969) sought to overcome this theoretical difficulty by hypothesizing that the achievement of object permanence (in the Piagetian sense of the term) is the maturational step that is necessary before stranger distress can occur. She used Piaget's stages of sensorimotor development as the reference point. (During stage three, out of sight is literally out of mind; during stage four, out of sight is no longer out of mind. Thus, in stage four, the infant has developed "object permanence.") Fraiberg's hypothesis links stranger anxiety to a specific step in cognitive maturation. Allan Compton (1980), working within a more specific psychoanalytic framework, continued with this line of theorizing. He suggested that not only object permanence (for which he used the psychoanalytic equivalent term "lasting object cathexis") but also a sense of time ("future tense") were necessary for stranger anxiety to occur.

In many ways, the work of Fraiberg and of Compton represents a continuation of the theory that stranger distress is basically a reaction to object loss but with the modification that object loss cannot be said to occur until the infant has reached the stage of object permanence. Both Compton and Fraiberg share the assumption that stranger anxiety can be accounted for exclusively by certain events of psychological maturation and that somatic factors are not necessary as part of the explanation. The Fraiberg/Compton model represents what might be called an "all-psychological theory of stranger anxiety."

Emde, who worked with Spitz in Denver before Spitz left for Geneva, was very much influenced by Spitz's (1959) book *A Genetic Field Theory of Ego Formation* and set out to test the hypothesis that separation anxiety is primarily caused by object loss (p. ix). The study showed that stranger distress was an expectable developmental event, occurring at a mean age of 8.4 months and reaching a peak intensity soon after onset. In contrast, distress on separation from the mother "tended to occur much more erratically, to be isolated in time, and depended much more on the context of the separation (relative strangeness of the environment and the presence of exacerbating circumstances such as fatigue, illness, and previous experiences of separation)" (Emde et al., 1976, p. 115). Emde and his colleagues concluded that the "earlier notion that stranger distress is primarily an expression of fear of maternal loss seems no longer tenable" (p. 117). They based their conclusion on two important facts:

1) the infants often demonstrated stranger distress even when the mother was present; and 2) stranger distress occurred in a high percentage (62%) of cases *prior* to the occurrence of separation distress. The authors concluded, "It is hard to reason that the infant shows distress in response to a situation in which he [the infant] must infer a loss (i.e., stranger = prospective mother-loss) when he fails to show any distress in response to the actual loss itself (mother leaving)" (p. 117). They concluded that stranger distress and separation distress "are clearly separable phenomena with different developmental courses" (p. 117).

Emde and his colleagues set out to test the hypothesis that the achievement of stage-four object permanence is necessary before the full stranger distress response occurs. The tests were conducted as follows:

> Beginning at four months, each home visit included a filmed testing for object permanence in the manner of Piaget. We used a favorite toy of the infant and cloth screens for covering it, and tested until the upper limits of the infant's abilities were clearly reached. After our study was completed, a rater, uninformed about our correlational interests, scored all films for test passes and failures. Onset of stranger distress was determined from two other independent raters' assessments of the filmed social-interaction series. Global judgments were used for this analysis, based upon observations of pronounced frowning, fussing, or crying in response to the stranger's approach.
>
> The results were clear-cut. Of the 13 cases in which there were no data gaps in the monthly ratings, eight infants showed stranger distress before passing [into] stage four; overt stranger distress occurred in the same session in which the infant failed to search for the hidden toy under the cloth [p. 105].

From this experiment, Emde and his colleagues concluded that object permanence was not a necessary prerequisite for the development of stranger distress (p. 106). This conclusion confirmed the earlier work of Scarr and Salapatek (1970). Thus Emde's work seems to cast serious doubt on the hypothesis that object permanence is a necessary prerequisite for the development of stranger anxiety.[2]

It is a virtual certainty that the onset of the fear response coincides with neurophysiologic changes in the nervous system,

---

[2] Other investigators, for example, Bell (1970), have distinguished object permanence from person permanence. These experiments do not, however, significantly alter Emde's conclusion that stranger distress cannot be explained by maternal loss.

which affect both the quality and the intensity of the fear response. Konner (1982) calls attention to the studies of Flechsig and later of Yakolev, which indicate that myelinization is still occurring in the axons that may be presumed to be used in the "fear response."

> During the period represented by the rising portion of the fear curve, the brains of human infants go through a rapid process of myelin deposition in all the major fiber tracts of the limbic system: the fornix, connecting the hippocampus with the hypothalamus; the mammilothalamic tract, connecting the hypothalamus with the anterior nucleus of the thalamus, and thence with the cerebral cortex; and the cingulum bundle connecting the cortex with the hippocampus. These large fiber bundles—the fornix is as massive as the optic nerve, which brings one-third of all external sense impressions into the brain—constitute the key paths of the Papez circuit, the core of the limbic system or "old mammalian brain," and there is thus a real sense in which the "stream of feeling" cannot be said to be properly functional until they are at least substantially myelinated. Another myelination event at this age, which is outside the limbic system and might have relevance to the growth of the social fears, occurs in the striatum, a principal portion of the "reptilian brain" believed by MacLean and others to account for much of the neural causation of fixed action patterns generally. To the extent that crying at separation and at the appearance of strangers constitutes a fixed action pattern triggered by an innate releasing mechanism, striatal myelination may play a role in its outset [p. 223].

Konner then goes on to conclude that the myelinization of the major fiber tracts of the limbic system plays a major role in the onset of the fear response:

> If Papez and his numerous intellectual descendants are at all right, then the myelination of the major fiber tracts of the limbic system during the second half-year of life could result in a quantum advance in the capacity to *feel*, above and beyond the parallel advances that may be occurring in cognitive capacity and in the regulation of innate behavior patterns. The very cingulum bundle that has little or no myelin at four months of age and a great deal at twelve is the bundle that is lesioned by psychiatric neurosurgeons to treat some intractable cases of phobia. It is difficult to imagine that the "lesion" caused by the absence of myelin at four months can have nothing to do with that age-group's relative fearlessness. . . . These developmental changes are primarily maturational and under fairly close control by the genes [p. 225].

The emergence of the stranger response syndrome at approximately eight months in virtually *all* infants in *all* cultures leads one to the conclusion that it is dependent on neurophysiological maturation; separation from the mother may trigger the fear response but does not cause it.

The importance of the onset of a true fear response at approximately eight months correlates quite well with Spitz's work on anaclitic depression. In 1946, Spitz and Wolf first described the syndrome of anaclitic depression, characterized by diminished activity, loss of appetite, a failure to thrive, and withdrawal, as one of the consequences of mother–infant separation during this critical period. Schaffer and Callender (1959) confirmed their findings, noting that there was a marked shift in hospitalized infants' reactions after seven months of age. Before the age of seven months, separation from the mother produced little distress; strangers' attentions were easily accepted in the hospital, and the return home was accomplished relatively easily. After seven months, separation from the mother was protested vigorously, the infants would show substantial distress and negativism while in the hospital, and the readjustment to home was accomplished only with great difficulty. Both studies emphasize the loss of the mother and note that the timing of the separation appears to be critical. As Emde and his colleagues (1976) point out, the timing seems to be determined by the emergence of the fear response syndrome. Separation from the mother prior to the emergence of this syndrome (i.e., before the infant is able to experience real fear) has few, if any, serious consequences. On the other hand, separation from the mother at the height of the fear response syndrome may lead to a severe disturbance in the infant and, if the separation is prolonged, to anaclitic depression.

In reviewing all of the evidence—the correlation of myelinization with the emergence of the fear response, Spitz's work on anaclitic depression, the visual cliff experiments, Emde's work, and the cross-cultural studies—what emerges is that stranger distress can no longer be explained simply as a reaction to maternal loss, either external or internal. What does seem to be the case is that the three events—stranger distress, person permanence, and object (inanimate) permanence—are part of an underlying maturational process. These events are usually synchronous, but in some cases, they may not be. This is basically the conclusion reached by Emde and his coauthors (1976): "We believe that the infant's developing attachment to his mother and his developing cognitive capacities are of obvious importance in the emergence of stranger distress. But more is needed to explain its occurrence. We hypothesize that *the added factor is a maturational one* and that it controls a further differentiation of emotionality, namely the onset of a capacity for 'fearfulness' " (p. 122, emphasis added). Thus, neurophysiologic maturation catalyzes the change from the simple bit of cognitive knowledge "mother is gone" to the easily recognized experience of fearfulness at the approach of strangers when, "Mother is gone!"

SUMMARY

Fear is an affect that sends a clear and unambiguous signal: "Danger!" As such, it serves as the key affect in a motivational system designed to protect the organism from physical destruction. In human infants, the onset of the ability to experience fear begins at approximately eight months; the overwhelming evidence is that the timing of the onset of this response is secondary to neurophysiologic maturation. This experience of fearfulness brings about an important shift in the mother–child relationship. The infant's message to the mother in the face of stranger distress is something like, "I feel secure only with you, mother. Please don't leave me alone with strange people" (Emde et al., 1976, p. 131). Separation from the mother during this time may have a disorganizing effect upon the infant. These findings suggest that the critical factor in the mother's absence is the infant's loss of her function to soothe and comfort him in the face of an upsurge of stimuli that, for the first time, he is experiencing as frightening. In turn, this fear leads to feelings of helplessness in the infant. Thus, the function of the mother can be conceptualized as helping the infant, partially through her presence and partially by example, to master this fearfulness. The function of the mother in soothing and comforting the infant during the flowering of the fear response syndrome may be one of the crucial ingredients of the attachment process; correspondingly, her failure to fulfill this function may have serious repercussions for the infant.

If the mother is successful in her task, then the infant gradually becomes able to soothe himself. Over an extended period of time, the mastery of fear leads to the virtue that we call courage. As Walter Kaufmann (1961) points out, courage may take two forms: 1) the courage to face physical danger (which may even mean risking death); and 2) the courage to think for oneself and to challenge established authority.[3] If the mother fails at her task, the infant, now grown to an adult, will need to find some other way to avoid feeling too much fear. One way is simple: learn to avoid situations that involve too much risk. Risk may take many forms: sports that are physically challenging, relationships that demand real intimacy, taking chances in one's professional life, or thinking creatively. To avoid taking these perceived risks, the person learns to "play it safe," often with a concomitant emotional, physical, and psychological constriction or deadness of the personality. In addition to avoiding risk, a person may seek self-soothing through drugs, drug substitutes (such as food), inauthentically dependent relationships, or the submersion of individuality into a group such as a cult. These mechanisms may lead to additional feelings of deadness, which, in turn, may lead to attempts to counteract the feelings of deadness by generating excitement, sometimes by taking foolish risks. Sorting out the results of hidden feelings of fear is, for the therapist, a very complex task.

---

[3] As Kaufmann points out, a culture may value one but not the other; among his examples, he describes prewar Germany, which highly valued courage and personal self-sacrifice but ostracized and excluded those who sought to challenge established authority.

6

Anxiety and Traumatic States

Freud's hypotheses about anxiety played a critical, as well as confusing, role in the development of his theory of affect. Part of the difficulty in trying to follow his theory is that the English word "anxiety" does not carry with it the ominous connotations of the German word *Angst*. Strachey (1962b) was well aware of the translation problem.

> The word universally, and perhaps unfortunately, adopted for the purpose has been "anxiety"—unfortunately, since "anxiety" too has a current everyday meaning, and one which has only a rather remote connection with any of the uses of the German *"Angst"* [p. 116].

Strachey, pointing out that a translator is driven to compromise, noted that, in some of the earlier translations of Freud into English, *Angst* was translated as "morbid anxiety" (p. 117). As Strachey says, the problem Freud was struggling with was trying to find out "whether, and if so why, *'Angst'* is sometimes pathological and sometimes normal" (p. 117). In this chapter, I will try to demonstrate that what Strachey refers to as "normal anxiety" and as "pathological anxiety" are two very different affects. Labeling them and thus thinking about them as variants of the same affect—anxiety—has led to a great deal of confusion, which in turn has been a major hindrance to the development of a psychoanalytic theory of affect.

ANXIETY–PANIC

Pathological anxiety—what we sometimes call an anxiety attack—
is easy to describe and define. When we think of an anxiety attack,
we think of a fear, often without apparent content, that overwhelms
a person and prevents him from functioning effectively. In ordinary
English, the word panic—"a sudden, unreasoning . . . fear, often
spreading quickly" (dictionary definition)—closely approximates
what we think of as "morbid" (i.e., pathological) anxiety. Freud
(1895b) listed many of the somatic symptoms that often accompany
an anxiety attack: heart palpitations, shortness of breath, sweating,
tremors and shivering, diarrhea, vertigo, paresthesias (numbness
and tingling sensations of the extremities), fears, and agoraphobia.
These symptoms are almost exactly the same as those described as a
panic disorder in the DSM-III-R (American Psychiatric Association,
1987). In summary, what people often refer to as anxiety attacks or
panic, Freud described as an anxiety neurosis. In the modern
psychiatric literature, this is what is often diagnosed as a panic
attack. To sharpen the distinction between "normal" and "pathological" anxiety, I will use the term anxiety–panic to refer to what
Strachey calls the feelings associated with an anxiety attack and
"pathological anxiety."

I propose that anxiety–panic is the affect that signals the
approach of disrupted or traumatic states of mind. This definition is
compatible with what we know about how the body works. Physical
pain on our skin indicates that something bad is happening or about
to happen on the surface of our body (a burn, a cut, etc.); aches and
pains tell us about troubles in the musculoskeletal system; arthritic
pains tell us about joint problems; gastritis or ulcer pains tell us
about our GI system; angina tells us about our heart, and so on.
Anxiety–panic is a specific affective signal that warns us when the
mind—the report and control center of the human nervous system—
is approaching a traumatized state and thus is in danger of not
working effectively.

Like all feelings, anxiety–panic ranges through an intensity
gradient. Thus, mild feelings of anxiety are a signal that we are
approaching the limits of the amount of stress that we can effectively
cope with. If we are able to take steps to reduce the stress that we are
under, the feelings of anxiety will subside and the disorganized state
will clear; if, however, we are not able to escape from the situation
and it worsens, then we will experience a traumatized state of mind

accompanied by feelings of panic. Krystal (1988) gives this excellent definition of the traumatized state of mind as "a paralyzed, over-whelmed state, with immobilization, withdrawal, possible deperson-alization, and evidence of disorganization. There may be a regression in any or all spheres of mental function and affect expression" (p. 142). The regression includes not only affective blocking, but a restriction of the ability to function in everyday life due to the inhibition of the processes of memory, imagination, association, problem solving, and planning (p. 153). Thus, the mind-jamming feeling of panic is part of the phenomenology of a traumatized state of mind in the same way that intense physical pain accompanies physical trauma. The word panic is an excellent one to describe this state, for it clearly suggests that the ability to cope effectively has been compromised and the organism is no longer able to respond effectively to the situation.

What is it that leads to a traumatized state of mind? As Freud (1926) pointed out, one of the key ingredients seems to be the feeling of helplessness in the face of a dangerous situation (p. 166). Real external danger, signaled by feelings of fear, usually triggers a specific sequence of behaviors that are designed to cope with the threat. In response to fear, the most appropriate behavior is either to flee or prepare to fight (the "fight or flight" response). The fear, however, may escalate to the point where it becomes toxic; this affective overload leads to the jamming of the mind thus blocking effective coping responses. Consequently, as Freud points out, "There are two reactions to real danger. One is an affective reaction, an outbreak of anxiety. The other is a protective action" (p. 165). In other words, we have an anxiety attack when we feel so helpless that we cannot respond effectively (i.e., take "protective action"). As Freud says, "We shall then have good grounds for distinguishing a traumatic situation from a danger-situation" (p. 166).

Where the situation appears hopeless and death inevitable, a surrender response—triggered by feelings of panic—may mute the horror of the situation. As Krystal (1988) points out, this surrender pattern is not necessarily maladaptive, but can be a way of securing a "merciful, painless death."

When the wild dogs of the Serengeti Plain of Tanzania hunt for zebra (a prey nine times larger than they), the lead dog grabs the zebra by the fleshy upper lip whereupon "the victim would cease its thrashings and stand quietly as the rest of the pack dispatched it" [p. 116, quoting Malcolm, 1980].

At times, this surrender response may also be triggered in situations where effective action could be taken; a deer frozen in the headlights of a car is an excellent example of this process.

In human beings, feelings of extreme helplessness may lead us to surrender to what appears to be an unavoidable peril. In response to extreme conditions—war, concentration camps, severe physical or sexual abuse—normal persons attempt to close off the horror of the experience by shutting down their affective responses through the process of psychic numbing. Krystal details numerous examples—the Katyn Forest massacre, the Nazi death camps—where captives simply cooperated "in an automatonlike fashion" with their killers (pp. 143–145). They had simply reached a point where their emotional and physical resources had become exhausted. During the Korean War, some American prisoners simply gave up, went over to a corner of the room, lay down, and in a few hours or days, were dead. These examples document a well-known fact: if a person loses the will to live, physical death may soon follow.

One of the most important contributions that Krystal makes is his fundamental rethinking of how to classify the affects connected with traumatic states (pp. 43–49). He points out that we usually think of *two* developmental lines of affects, positive and negative. The positive, "pleasurable" line includes the affects of excitement, security (safety), contentment, joy, pride, tenderness, and love; the negative or "distress" affects include pain, anger, guilt, shame, disgust, fear, and jealousy. Krystal suggests that it is most useful to consider the affects connected with traumatic states as a third line of affective development, rather than simply as a derivative of the negatively valenced affects. As outlined by Krystal, this line of affective development begins with infantile depletion states such as marasmus and failure to thrive and ends with various constellations of experiences that accompany severe traumatic states. If the traumatic state is not interrupted, it can lead to any, or all, of the following: 1) the surrender pattern; 2) catenoid reactions with symptoms of despair and physical symptoms of tiredness, weakness, and lack of resistance to physical illnesses; 3) affective blocking; 4) continuation of "emergency regimes"; 5) alexithymia; 6) cognitive constriction; 7) irrational fears; and 8) a dead-to-the-world reaction (pp. 156–166). If one accepts the usefulness of Krystal's formulation, then anxiety–panic belongs with the affects connected with traumatic states.

In proposing this definition of anxiety–panic as part of the phenomenology of traumatic states, we are faced with the problem of defining "trauma." As the word is used in psychoanalysis today, there are two definitions. One definition, modeled on the war neuroses, concentration camp phenomena, and, as we increasingly recognize, severe physical, sexual, and/or psychological abuse during childhood, refers to an "unbearable situation" that leads to a disorganization of a person's ability to cope. In contrast, we also use the word "trauma" to include any experience that is not conducive to a child's optimal development; as Krystal points out in critiquing the work of Kris and Khan, this definition of trauma encompasses almost everything (pp. 139–140). Anna Freud (1967) acknowledged the problems created by this dual usage:

> Like everyone else, I have tended to use the term "trauma" rather loosely up to now, but I shall find it easier to avoid this in the future. Whenever I am tempted to call an event in a child's or adult's life "traumatic," I shall ask myself some further questions. Do I mean that the event was upsetting; that it was significant for altering the course of further development; that it was pathogenic? Or do I really mean traumatic in the strictest sense of the word, i.e., shattering, devastating, causing internal disruption by putting ego functioning and ego mediation out of action [p. 241].

This shifting definition of trauma is a good example of what is called linguistic drift. As psychoanalysis discovered that the events of childhood played a much more important role in shaping adult character than anyone might have known, educated people began to hear the phrase "psychic trauma" (even if they were unaware of the details of the theory). As a consequence, some of us began to use the word "traumatic" rather than "upsetting" or "distressing" because it is a novel, more pithy, way of expressing ourselves. ("I had a traumatic experience today; I got stuck on the freeway for over an hour.") As the word traumatic (and trauma) began to shift meanings so that it became a synonym for distress, it became less and less useful as a way of accounting for the etiology of psychopathology.

As Krystal (1988) points out, we need "a better definition" of the concept of trauma (p. 139). If trauma is limited to what is "shattering" and "devastating"—war neuroses, concentration camp phenomena, massive physical and/or sexual abuse—then we are likely to miss the more subtle manifestations of traumatic states. What is needed is an *operational definition* of traumatic states. I suggest that our behavioral response points toward a definition. In line with the basic premise of this essay, affects are presymbolic signals that convey information; the organism uses these affective signals to

appraise the situation and take effective action. Defined operation-
ally, a traumatized state occurs when a person is unable to respond
appropriately and effectively to a situation; in turn, this inability to
respond is signaled by anxiety–panic. As Stolorow and Atwood
(1992) say, anxiety functions as a signal for these "rock-bottom
dangers" (p. 26). If we reserve the term trauma for those situations
that evoke anxiety–panic, then we have defined both in operational
terms. This is the definition of traumatic anxiety Freud (1926)
proposed, but which has been lost due to the shifting meanings of
"trauma."

PANIC DISORDERS:
A DEVELOPMENTAL HYPOTHESIS

Given enough stress, almost everyone will experience a traumatized
state of mind. Under "Post-traumatic Stress Disorder," the DSM-
III-R (American Psychiatric Association, 1987) includes events that
"would be markedly distressing to almost anyone, and is usually
experienced with intense fear, terror, and helplessness" (p. 247).
These events include a serious threat to one's life or physical
integrity, and a serious threat or harm to one's children, spouse, or
loved ones. Other traumas include rape or assault, natural disasters
(floods, earthquakes), airplane crashes, or the collapse of a building.
Deliberately inflicted disasters—bombing, torture, death camps—
tend to be more traumatic than naturally occurring disasters (p.
248). Even though these events would be traumatic to almost
everyone, preparation and training may help people cope with the
situation more effectively. This is the strategy behind fire drills,
earthquake preparedness drills, and training to help women deal
with attempted rape. Similarly, combat training helps people learn
to remain "cool under fire"; consequently, battle-tested troops are
much less panicked. The key element of this training is helping the
subjects to learn to stay in an integrated state of mind during
markedly stressful situations, thus allowing them to respond as
effectively as possible.

What we do not know is why some patients are prone to develop
panic attacks (or anxiety attacks) in situations that most people
would not find particularly stressful. For example, airplane travel,
driving on a freeway, or being in a crowded situation are often

implicated in triggering panic attacks; the thread that joins many of these situations is that a person may feel "out of control." After the first panic attack, the person begins to become apprehensive that, under similar circumstances, he will again panic. This apprehensiveness may lead him to begin to avoid the situations that are likely to precipitate the panic attacks, and agoraphobia ensues. Empirically, a wide range of treatments—medications, behavioral desensitization programs, and combinations of these—have all proved reasonably successful in alleviating the symptomatology. Even though we have empirically successful methods of treating panic disorders, we still lack a satisfactory explanation of their etiology. Even long-term exploratory treatment—with psychoanalysis being the paradigm—has not been successful in uncovering specific traumatic incidents that might be responsible for causing the problem. Neither has this type of treatment been particularly helpful in treating patients' symptoms, and whatever success that has occurred is probably the result of unsystematic desensitization.

What then do we know that may shed some light on the origins of panic attacks? We know that the mother's presence is particularly important in helping the infant master the feelings of fear—the misnamed "stranger anxiety"—that emerge at approximately eight months of age. From infant research experiments we also know that the neurophysiologic maturation that leads to stranger fear (stranger anxiety) is on a different developmental track from that which leads to "object permanence" (in Piaget's language). Usually these two events are synchronous, or functionally parallel, so that a permanent object representation is available to help the infant master the upsurge of frightening stimuli. Most of the hypothesizing about the consequences of stranger anxiety is in situations when the mother is physically absent or psychologically unavailable (e.g., severe depression, psychosis, or extreme narcissism). But hypothesizing that these two events are on separate developmental tracks opens up another interesting possibility. Suppose, for example, that the events are not quite synchronous and that the capacity to experience fear develops prior to object permanence; in this situation, *there would be no internal representation of the mother to help the infant master the emerging fear responses, except when the mother was physically present*. Hypothetically, this developmental asynchrony could lay the foundation for panic attacks.

There is some hint of this possibility in the work of Scarr and Salapatek (1970), who found that "at any given age, infants with precocious object concepts were not more fearful than those with a less well developed concept of object permanence. *If anything, the less precocious infants tended to be more fearful"* (p. 81, emphasis added). In other words, the lack of a permanent internal representation seemed to leave the infant less able to master the upsurge in fear; the net result was a more fearful infant. The question then arises as to what the legacy of this developmental asynchrony is. Does it simply fade away as the infant matures? This is certainly a possibility, but there is another. These early experiences may leave the infant with an inchoate fear of being overwhelmed, a fear that, when feelings of fear begin to emerge, he will not be able to handle them. This fear may remain hidden for years, like an invisible fracture line. Then, one day, fear does get out of hand, and the person experiences his first panic attack. In turn, his panic leads to a terror of experiencing fear, thus activating a vicious circle. The currently available data appears to be sufficient to hypothesize a possible etiologic link between "panic attacks" and a lag in the development of the capacity to form permanent representations of the mother. Admittedly, this hypothesis is speculative, and definitive proof would have to await careful developmental studies.

ANXIETY: THE BIRTH TRAUMA HYPOTHESIS

The centrality of anxiety in Freud's theorizing about affect emerged early in his career. In three early papers, Freud (1895b,c, 1898) brought forth what is known as the "toxic theory" of anxiety, in which he hypothesized that anxiety was undischarged sexual energy or transformed libido. This undischarged sexual energy formed the "actual neuroses." The actual neuroses, which included anxiety neurosis and neurasthenia, are conceptualized as neuroses *without neurotic conflict or symbolic content*. Phenomenologically, what Freud described as an anxiety neurosis would now be diagnosed as a panic disorder, with or without agoraphobia. Although Freud never repudiated the concept of the actual neuroses, interest in them declined as psychoanalysts deepened their knowledge of the psychoneuroses and, later, of the narcissistic neuroses. In recent years, there has been a marked resurgence of interest in the possible biologic origins of anxiety, particularly the panic disorders. At the present time, almost all this research has taken place within the framework of biologic psychiatry, and these findings have not been adequately integrated into psychoanalytic theory.

Over the years, Freud abandoned the "transformed libido" theory about the origins of anxiety.[1] He thus was left with an unresolved theoretical problem: how does one account for the origins of anxiety? In a brief footnote to the second edition of *The Interpretation of Dreams,* Freud (1900) stated his new theory: *"Moreover, the act of birth is the first experience of anxiety, and thus the source and prototype of the affect of anxiety"* (pp. 400–401). Freud (1916–1917) elaborated on this idea:

> We believe that it is in the *act of birth* that there comes about the combination of unpleasurable feelings, impulses of discharge and bodily sensations which has become the prototype of the effects of a mortal danger and has ever since been repeated by us as the state of anxiety. The immense increase of stimulation owing to the interruption of the renovation of the blood (internal respiration) was at the time the cause of the experience of anxiety; *the first anxiety was thus a toxic one* [emphasis added]. The name *"Angst"—"angustiae," "Enge"*—emphasizes the characteristic of restriction in breathing which was then present as a consequence of the real situation and is now almost invariably reinstated in the affect. We shall also recognize it as highly relevant that this first state of anxiety arose out of separation from the mother [pp. 396–397, emphasis added as noted].

In following the development of Freud's theory, he still considers anxiety as "toxic" (his word) but now traces its origins to the very beginnings of life, secondary to the traumatic separation from the mother.

The "birth trauma hypothesis" seemed to resolve several important theoretical issues. By being conceptualized as beginning at birth, anxiety could be viewed as the prototype of a generalized distress response, thus serving as the basic precursor for all negatively valenced affects (in the same way that contentment—Freud's "pleasure" or "satisfaction"—served as the precursor for all positively valenced affects). In the same paragraph, Freud states that he believes that the experience of birth was "toxic" and is "the prototype of the effects of a *mortal danger*" (p. 396, emphasis added). Thus, the birth trauma hypothesis served two very important functions in building a theory of affects: it combined a theory of normal affective development (birth → distress → negatively valenced "realistic" affects) with a theory of traumatic states of mind (birth → "mortal

---

[1] For an excellent summary of Freud's theories about anxiety, see Strachey (1959).

danger" → anxiety–panic). In terms of theory building, this type of neat, unifying solution is immensely appealing to us because of its elegance.

A major difficulty with the birth trauma hypothesis is that it does not adequately differentiate fear and anxiety–panic from the infant distress syndrome. As set forth in the previous chapter, the fear response manifested by what is called stranger anxiety does not develop until seven to nine months. In contrast, the infant distress syndrome is one of four moods that are present at birth and signals to both infant and caretaker that something is wrong. While external events, such as a loud noise, may trigger a distress response, there is no evidence that the neonate is worried about external danger; in all probability, the noise simply results in an uncomfortably high level of auditory stimulation, thus triggering a distress response. Cognitively, the neonate has not yet learned the inside/outside distinction that is embedded in the affect of fear. Commenting on the birth trauma hypothesis, Tomkins (1963) says:

> The crying response is the first response the human being makes upon being born. *The birth cry is a cry of distress.* It is not, as Freud supposed, the prototype of anxiety. It is a response of distress at the excessive level of stimulation to which the neonate is suddenly exposed upon being born [p. 3, emphasis added].

In differentiating distress from fear, Tomkins emphasizes how they differ in "toxicity" (pp. 9–18). He points out that the toxicity of distress has to be kept relatively low if it is to be biologically useful; the infant must be able to endure it until the mother has the time to fix it. In contrast, fear is a very toxic affect that evokes massive defensive strategies:

> Fear is a response which, psychologically, is very toxic even in small doses. Fear is an overly compelling persuader designed for emergency motivation of a life-and-death significance. In all animals such a response had the essential biological function of guaranteeing that the preservation of the life of the organism had a priority second to none. The biological price of such a response was also one of high toxicity. Physiological reserves are squandered recklessly under the press of fear, and the magnitude of the physiological debt which is invoked under such duress has only recently been appreciated to its full extent [p. 10].

There is every reason to believe that birth is a distressing event; after all, the infant leaves a place where his every need is provided for and enters a world where his needs are signaled by painful (but not toxic) distress signals. In contrast, fear, which comes on-line at approximately eight months of age, gives the infant a very strong danger signal and is potentially quite toxic. Therefore, if one accepts the research criteria for differentiating the infant distress response from fear, then it becomes very clear that birth is a distressing, but not frightening, event.

Part of the problem in defining anxiety is that, as used in ordinary English conversation, the word anxious has become a synonym for distress. For example, one might say, "I'm anxious about the test tomorrow"; in this sentence, "anxious" is a synonym for "apprehensive" or "worried about." Thus, the dictionary defines anxiety as a "concern or solicitude respecting some event, future or uncertain, which disturbs the mind and keeps it in a state of painful uneasiness." The synonyms for "anxiety" are "solicitude, care, foreboding, uneasiness, perplexity, disquietude, disquiet, watchfulness, restlessness." None of these words suggests much in the way of a powerful feeling connected with anxiety–panic; more important, they do not carry the connotation that the feeling is in any way disruptive, disorganizing, or pathological. A great deal of confusion has arisen because of the failure to adequately differentiate distress from what I have labeled anxiety–panic. I suspect that it was this difference that Strachey (1962b) was trying to describe in his distinction between "normal" and "pathological" anxiety (p. 116). In ordinary conversation, we are easily able to make the distinction, sometimes by labeling anxiety–panic as an anxiety attack and sometimes by describing the symptoms or by saying that we felt panicked. The confusion about anxiety illustrates the power of language: we assume that the usage of the same word—anxiety—to describe two different affective states means *that there must be a developmental connection between the two*. This is one of the ways in which language can—in Wittgenstein's (1945) words—bewitch us.

THEORY BUILDING

At this point, I think it is useful to take a half step backward and not simply review Freud's theories but briefly look at how theoreticians build theories. One hope—often implicit—is that we can discover a few deep, elegant, and inexorable laws that, if properly understood, will help us organize in our mind a seemingly incomprehensible amount of data. To do this, one hypothesizes an organizational structure and then tries to see if the data fits into the structure. Two major structures are used for this purpose: *trees* and *lattices*. Perhaps the best-known example of the tree model is the phylogenetic tree of Darwinian evolution. One starts with one-celled animals and, through the process of progressive differentiation, ends up with increasingly complex forms of life. After many eons, the first mammal appears; this differentiates into monkey; the great apes differentiate into man. Some of the branches—the Neanderthal—are dead ends, and simply disappear. The other organizational structure is the lattice, or grid. An excellent example of a lattice is the periodic table of elements. From this table, accurate predictions could be made about a number of undiscovered elements.

In proposing the birth trauma hypothesis, Freud was attempting to use a progressive differentiation (tree) model to work out a positive and negative developmental line for affects. (For an excellent historical summary, see Krystal, 1988, pp. 43–49.) In this model, pleasure (satisfaction or contentment) is the affect precursor for all positively valenced affects; distress ("anxiety") is the affect precursor for all negatively valenced affects. By labeling the birth experience as "anxiety" (contentless fear) rather than distress, Freud was able to ground both the negatively valenced affects of normal development and the affects associated with traumatic states into a progressive differentiation model of affect (the "anxiety plus" theory of negative affects).

SUMMARY

A large part of the problem in developing a psychoanalytic theory of affects has been that three distinct affective responses have been labeled anxiety: 1) infant distress syndrome (birth trauma); 2) fear (stranger anxiety); and 3) anxiety–panic (or anxiety attack). Distress, the infant distress syndrome, is one of four moods present at birth; there is good evidence that the experience of birth is physiologically distressing, perhaps extremely so, but certainly not terrifying. All our observations about the animal kingdom suggest that fearfulness, a very toxic affect, begins with hard-wired programs designed to protect the organism from *external* threats, such as fires, heights, and predators. In human infants, the onset of the fear response begins at eight months with the misnamed "stranger anxiety." At birth, the infant lacks the capability of knowing whether or not his life is in danger. Anxiety–panic is not intense distress, as

Freud's birth trauma hypothesis suggests; rather, anxiety–panic is a very specific signal that the mind—the report and control system of the human nervous system—is not able to function effectively. Hence, it is part of the phenomenology of traumatic states of mind.

Differentiating anxiety–panic from other affects should help us to understand better the phenomenology of traumatic states, one of the least understood areas of psychopathology. Until the distinctions among distress (birth trauma anxiety), fear (stranger anxiety), and anxiety–panic are clarified, it will be virtually impossible to understand anxiety, much less develop a comprehensive theory of affects.

7

Aggression and Rage

AGGRESSION

The subject of "aggression" has always been a confusing one, not just for psychoanalysts but for everyone. Part of the problem is that some of the terminology is confusing, leading us into a web of semantic difficulties. I suspect, though, that most of the confusion stems from our unconscious ambivalence about aggression and that the persistent disputes about the subject reflect differing views about the nature of human beings, who we are, and whom we ought to strive to become. Because these value-laden philosophical issues are rarely stated in a coherent, direct way, they tend to surface as difficult to understand questions about the "nature of aggression." Perhaps the most familiar form of the question is whether humans possess an innate aggressive drive or whether what is labeled aggression is primarily a reaction to frustration. As with many questions, finding the answer begins with semantic analysis: what do we mean when we use the word aggression?

The easiest place to begin is to try to understand what the term aggression means in everyday language. For most people, "aggression" or "aggressive" usually describes a type of behavior that is associated with the affect of anger, rage, or hate. The dictionary defines aggression as: "1) an unprovoked attack, or act of hostility, 2) the practice or habit of being aggressive." Similarly, the word aggressive is defined as "tending to aggress; starting fights or quarrels." These definitions more or less correspond to the psycho-analytic definition of aggression. Laplanche and Pontalis (1967) define aggression as the "tendency or cluster of tendencies finding expression in real or phantasy behaviour intended to harm other people, or to destroy, humiliate or constrain them, etc." (p. 17). As used in our everyday language, the word aggression usually defines the subjective state of the individual and the intention to do harm. The emphasis on the subjective state is clearly reflected in our legal system, where intent, rather than the consequences, partially deter-mines whether an action is considered a crime. Thus, in ordinary English, the word aggression is usually used to describe a type of behavior that is connected with the *intention* to harm or to destroy.

One of the difficulties in understanding aggression is that ethologists and behavioral scientists, rather than focusing on the inner state or affect, have tended to classify as aggression all behavior that inflicts damage on another creature. Emphasizing the effect on the victim, rather than intent, has had important and confusing consequences because it tends to classify together, and thus imply a similarity among, many types of behavior that are quite distinct. The problems that arise from this focus can be most clearly illustrated by a consideration of predation, a type of behavior that is often included with aggression. For example, the predatory behavior of the cats is normal, instinctive (wired in), and serves the obvious adaptive purpose of acquiring food.

> To get an idea of the magnitude of the problem [of defining aggres-sion], consider the following pattern of behavior. Many species in the cat family exhibit a sequence of predatory behaviors that are as close to constituting an instinctive sequence of motor action patterns as mammals are likely to get. It includes lying in wait, crouching, stalking, pouncing, seizing between the paws, and directing a "killing bite" quite specifically at the nape of the neck of the prey, where it will do mortal damage to the brain stem. A cat with no experience of prey will not do this properly at first, but with a few repeated opportunities, especially under conditions of playful excitement, the sequence "clicks into place" and it does so in a tiny fraction of the time required for cats to learn comparably complex sequences that do not draw on phylogenetic preparation [Konner, 1982, p. 184].

Although the carnivores' search for food may have fatal conse-quences for the prey, the classification of predatory behavior as aggression leads us to confuse two very different types of behavior.

Predatory behavior is simply a means of acquiring the necessary food to maintain an organism's physiologic requirements. There is no difference between a horse or cow grazing on grass, an owl grazing on field mice, or a bear picking berries from a bush or a salmon from a stream; these animals are simply getting their food. Furthermore, there is no real change when we move to the terrestrial carnivores, like lions, who may feed on larger prey, such as antelope or wildebeests. To consider predation (or predatory behavior) as aggression leaves us confused, with the net result that the term itself begins to lose any clear meaning (i.e., if getting food is aggression, then what isn't?).

The difficulties created by attempting to fit predatory behavior within the psychoanalytic concept of aggression is well illustrated by even a brief review of the literature. Stone (1971) called this *nonhostile, adaptive,* or *benign* aggression, and Rangell (1972) called it *constructive* aggression. In his book *The Development of Aggression in Early Childhood,* Parens (1979) opted for the label *nondestructive aggression,* noting "*nonaffective destructive discharges* (such as sucking or chewing) do evidence a trend deriving from *prey aggression,* a condition lucidly demonstrated in carnivores, which is not, in origin, influenced by an affective state and the aim of which is destruction of structure for the purpose of self-preservation" (p. 5). Terms such as "benign aggression," "constructive aggression," and "nondestructive aggression" are quite confusing because the qualifying adjectives benign, constructive, and nondestructive contradict what we usually think of as aggression.

An analysis in terms of motivational systems, which focuses on the affective monitors of experience rather than the behavior, helps to clarify this problem. As Konner (1982) points out, predatory behavior is usually carried out in a spirit of playful excitement. A good example of this type of playful excitement can be observed by watching a cat play with a mouse. From the mouse's point of view, this is clearly aggression; he will be toyed with, tortured if you will, painfully mutilated, finally killed, and possibly eaten. But the cat is playing in much the same way as he might play with a toy or a ball of yarn. For the cat, a mouse is little more than a small furry object that moves by itself and, as such, offers some interesting challenges. Predatory behavior, obviously adaptive in meeting an organism's nutritional needs, is monitored by the affect of playful excitement combined with the intensity of a skilled challenge. In short, predatory behavior clearly belongs within the competence/mastery system. In contrast, attack and fighting behaviors—which are the paradigm for aggression—belong within the competitive/territorial system.

Within the animal kingdom, aggression is most easily understood as fighting or, in many cases, the threat of fighting, accompanied by the affect of anger or rage. Rage is not a particularly difficult emotion to recognize, either in ourselves or in animals. For example, we are able to observe in a cat the widening of the eyes, growling and hissing, arching of the back, and the erection of the fur, all of which serve as a prelude to attack. This behavior is easily differentiated from the playful excitement associated with predatory behavior. These attacks, fighting, and the threat of attack serve a wide range of adaptive functions, primarily by establishing dominance hierarchies that allocate food, territory, mates, and other scarce resources. In the next chapter, I discuss how the emotions of contempt and shame serve as signals to communicate information about dominance hierarchies that accomplish, through psychological mechanisms, what aggression accomplishes through fighting: the first rights to scarce resources.

We know that, as with fear, there is an organic substrate to the rage response. (For a review of the neurophysiologic data, see Konner, 1982, pp. 175–207.) In terms of a process theory of affects, anger or rage acts as the signal that we are in a competitive/territorial dispute. The neurophysiology involved suggests that it is much too simplistic to assume that there is a single cause of aggressiveness. Rather, the evidence seems to indicate that the behaviors we label as aggressive represent instinctive, wired-in patterns of behavior that are substantially influenced by our neuroendocrine system (including hormones); this organic substrate can then be partially shaped in (recruited) or shaped out (extinguished) by learning.

Within the animal kingdom, aggression really is not difficult to understand if we keep one fact in mind: animals tend to take what they want unless prevented by force from doing so. As A. Phillip Randolph said, "At the banquet table of Nature, there are no reserved seats. You get what you can take. You keep what you can hold" (quoted in Davidson and Rees-Mogg, 1993, p. 52). When two animals compete for the same resources, an attack, a fight, or the threat of attack often ensues.

Threat, attack, and fighting can serve a wide range of adaptive functions: competition between individuals for mates, food, and other

scarce resources; play and exercise; enforcement of sexual intercourse, and defense against such enforcement; defense of the young;
elimination of the young, either one's own or those of others, for
purposes relating to the reduction of competition; competition between
groups for territory and other scarce resources; exploitation of prey
species, for the purpose of obtaining food; and action against members of another species, one's own species, even one's own family, for
purposes of self-defense [Konner, 1982, p. 185].

Essentially, fighting (or the threat of it) serves the adaptive purpose
of establishing dominance hierarchies. The emotion that usually
accompanies fighting is anger or rage. If we continue with our
exploration of the hypothesis that all important classes of behavior
have a specific affect as a monitor, then rage would be the monitor for
the class of behaviors that constitute aggression. If we translate this
hypothesis into the language of motivational systems, then aggression (the behavior) and anger–rage (the affective monitor) comprise
the key elements of the competitive/territorial system.

As is often the case, difficulties emerge when we try to determine
the exact definition of a concept. Playful fighting, or, more properly,
rough-and-tumble play, demonstrates the difficulty in defining the
concept of aggression. This type of behavior is universal among
young mammals and also occurs among many mammalian adults.
Konner comments:

It is not violent, it is usually not damaging, and it involves different
behaviors of threat, attack, defense, and especially expression from
those involved in real fighting. Nevertheless, it can sometimes grade
into real fighting, it provides exercise for real fighting, and it helps to
establish the dominance hierarchy that will regulate real fighting
[p. 185].

The skills developed in this type of play are the very ones used in
hunting (predation); however, as outlined earlier, predatory behavior usually takes place in a playful mood or a mood of skilled
challenge and is motivated by hunger and the need for food. These
fighting skills, when in adulthood are directed against members of
the animal's own species and are accompanied by the affect of rage,
closely approximate what most people mean by aggression. I suggest
that we have difficulty understanding the role of rough-and-tumble
play, not because aggression within the animal kingdom is difficult

to understand, but because we lack an adequate understanding of the adaptive function of play.

Animals are driven by their immediate biologic needs—food, water, sex, and the territory that controls access to these resources. If humans were *only* motivated by their competitive need to acquire these resources, the problem of aggression would be easy enough to understand (perhaps not easy to solve, but at least easy to understand). Like many competitive species, human beings form groups and tribes that compete for territory and resources. But unlike other animals, we also possess the capacity for symbolic thought, which, in turn, allows us to form a set of internalized goals and ideals for ourselves. Human beings compete not only for resources, but also for pride or, as Hegel put it, for glory. Consequently, aggression plays a substantially different role in human development than it does in other species; we react with rage, sometimes quite vigorously, not only to infringements on our territory, but to a vast number of symbolic injuries to our self-esteem. Psychoanalysts often use the term "narcissistic rage" to describe these injuries to self-esteem. As will be developed in the next chapter, a substantial amount of rage that adults experience is secondary to profound feelings of shame and mortification. Although the interrelationships are quite complex, the concept of narcissistic rage helps us distinguish the issues of individual psychopathology from the more broadly based cultural issues connected with aggression (e.g., wars of conquest).

In the animal kingdom, aggression is easy enough to define: you take what you want without regard to whether the other wants to give it to you. The affect of rage conveys a very clear message: "I want this and am willing to fight for it." As human beings are part of the animal kingdom, this is the innate biologic core of human aggression. Superimposed on this core, the process of socialization plays the major role in determining the behavioral patterns that we think of as aggressive. In animals, attack and fighting behaviors can be substantially diminished by the use of conditioning techniques; analogously, we can turn an ordinary dog into an attack or guard dog with relative ease. In human societies, aggressive behavior can also be shaped in or out, resulting in a spectrum from the relatively peaceful to the quite violent. Even in peaceful societies, however, such as the !Kung San of Botswana, homicide and other acts of violence do occur. What becomes clear through this type of cross-cultural study is that the learning of certain types of aggressive behavior is superimposed on an innate biologic core. While learning or education can help to shape in or shape out certain behaviors, there is no evidence whatsoever that aggression is due solely to cultural conditioning.

AGGRESSION: THE CULTURAL CONTEXT

It is our unresolved ambivalence, rather than neurophysiologic complexity, that creates so much confusion about aggression. This ambivalence is reflected in the two dictionary definitions of aggressiveness: "1) tending to aggress; starting fights or quarrels. 2) full of enterprise and initiative; bold and active; pushing." The first definition talks of aggressive (querulous) as contrasted to peaceful; the second talks about aggressive (assertive) as contrasted to passive or reticent (a sissy). At the present time, our society tends to value both being assertive *and* being peaceful; however, different individuals, groups, and cultures give different weightings as to which is most important. It is this conflict in our value system, rather than other issues, that leads to the seemingly endless debates about aggression. At the cultural level, the assertion that aggression is primarily a reaction to frustration is little more than the expression of the deeply felt wish that human beings should become more peaceful.

The evidence that *homo sapiens* is a fundamentally peaceful species is far from reassuring. Human history, more often than not, is the history of aggression and conquest. Within Western history, examples include Alexander's attempt to conquer the world, the formation of the Roman Empire, the overthrow of the Roman Empire by the Germanic tribes, and a series of European wars too numerous to mention. During the 17th and 18th centuries, France and England built great empires; the United States was formed by the conquest, with the accompanying slaughter of the indigenous Indian tribes (which, in turn, were at times at war with each other). These eruptions of aggressive conquest often seem to come about in specific bursts of energy that are largely unexplainable. At times, this may be connected with the emergence of specific leaders—the Mongols under Genghis Khan, the Swedes in the 17th century under Charles XII, the Russians under Peter the Great—but at other times a broad cultural dynamic seems to be at work. To dismiss most all of human history as a reaction to frustration simply trivializes the study of humankind.

A central concern, whether stated or not, in the study of aggression is to reduce the level of violence among human beings (assault, murder, rape, wars, genocide, etc.). There may be strategies for doing this, but first it is important to abolish some of the myths we have about aggression. One of these myths is that there are human societies where violence does not exist. This is much more than a faulty case of observation. The unstated premise of this myth is that *all* aggression is culturally learned rather than the product of innate aggressive tendencies. The problem with this argument is that "learning" is defined so broadly that it covers both instinctual and acquired learning; in other words, do we learn aggressive behavior the way we learn to walk (i.e., as the unfolding of a genetically determined program) or in the way that we learn physics?

A second, and related, myth is that humans are unique in the animal kingdom in that they kill members of their own species. The observation of chimpanzees—the primates most closely related to man—dispels this myth. At the Gombe reserve, Jane Goodall (1990) observed behavior that, in human beings, would be labeled murder, war, and genocide. During the years 1974 through 1978, a mother and daughter—Passion and Pom—worked together as an efficient killing team (pp. 77–80). They would seek out a mother and infant child within their own band at a time when males were absent. (A male might have come to the victim's rescue.) They would attack, take the child from its mother, and then eat the infant with great relish (as chimps normally eat their food). During the four-year period, only one infant survived. This apparently aberrant behavior both horrified and mystified Goodall and her staff: "Probably we shall never know why Passion and Pom behaved in this gruesome manner" (p. 79). The killings finally came to an end when Passion, and then Pom, became pregnant, which physically prevented them from functioning as a team. "After this the cannibalistic attacks came to an end and mothers, once again, could travel with their newborn infants without fear" (p. 80). The observations of serial killing (accompanied by cannibalism) within an apparently cohesive group have laid to rest the myth that human beings are the only animals that kill their own kind.

In the chapter entitled "War" (pp. 98–111), Goodall describes how the Kasakela chimpanzee community—containing 14 fully adult males and controlling approximately 25 square miles of territory—began to divide into two separate communities. Led by two powerful twin adult males—Hugh and Charlie—four other males, accompanied by females and children, formed a southern "Kahama community," interacting primarily with each other. Two years after the split began, the first attack occurred. The assault began when a Kasakela patrol of six adult males, accompanied by a highly sexual but sterile female, suddenly came upon a young male—Godi—feeding in a tree. One male pulled the fleeing Godi to the ground, and the others pummeled him and bit him; finally, one of the attackers threw a four-pound rock at the helpless Godi. "All of the chimpanzees were screaming loudly, Godi in terror and pain, the aggressors in a state of enraged frenzy" (p. 105). Godi was badly wounded, with great gashes on his face, one leg, and the right side of his chest. After 10 minutes, the attack stopped and the group left in a noisy, boisterous mood. Godi was left there on the ground; after the attack he disappeared and undoubtedly died of his injuries. Over the next four years, four more assaults of this type—three on males, one on a female—were witnessed by Goodall and her team. Of the remaining Kahama chimps, two adult males and two adult females disappeared from unknown causes, presumably killed by the Kasakela patrols, but possibly by members of the powerful Kalande community to the south. By 1978, the Kahama community had ceased to exist. Only the adolescent females were spared, returning to the Kasakela community, which reoccupied the Kahama territory. Similar intergroup assaults have been observed in the only other long-term study of chimpanzees in the field (Diamond, 1992, p. 293). These documented observations of intergroup "warfare"—unrelated to the need to control territory to secure an adequate food supply—have obvious parallels to the tribal warfare of human beings. Tribal warfare is endemic in the world, ranging from the Balkans in Europe to Africa, from the remnants of the Soviet empire to the streets of Los Angeles. The studies of chimpanzees convincingly demonstrate that the need for recognition as being "number one," and a willingness to fight for it, is not limited to human beings. Whatever it is that fuels this aggressive drive is part of our genetic inheritance.

We also know that aggressive behavior is partially mediated by hormones and neurotransmitters. The stress hormones—adrenaline from the central portion of the adrenal gland and cortisol from the outer portion—are secreted in abundance during a "fight or flight" situation. These stress hormones release energy from stored cellular to free blood forms and at the same time expand and constrict blood vessels selectively, in such a way that the blood flows from the viscera to the musculature, thereby bringing more oxygen and energy to the muscles when it is needed. More interestingly, we know that testosterone promotes aggressive behavior, certainly in males and possibly in females. This has been repeatedly demonstrated in experiments, where injections of testosterone in animals promotes aggressiveness in certain situations, while male castration can decrease it.

> Naturally occurring variations in testosterone level can accompany fighting behavior, and fighting can in turn affect that level. For example, in an experiment in which two groups of rhesus monkeys were made to fight, the losers experienced a large decrease after the fight (actually in two stages, the second perhaps corresponding to final acceptance of the loss), while the winner did not. In a similar study of members of the Harvard wrestling team, all men competing experienced a rise of testosterone level during the fight, but the winners experienced a significantly larger rise than did the losers, with those who fought to a draw having levels exactly in between [Konner, 1982, pp. 193–194].

The studies with testosterone have convincingly demonstrated that "male aggressiveness" is not simply learned but is partially the result of our hormonal endowment. More specifically, the studies clearly indicate that male hormones form part of the organic substrate that exerts an influence on groups of behaviors that we call aggressive. Male aggressiveness is not simply the result of cultural conditioning; it is part of the biologic given of being male.

THE SOCIALIZATION OF AGGRESSION

A study of the development of aggression and rage in human beings clarifies some of the core therapeutic issues. During the first few months of life, the infant reacts with frustration—the infant distress syndrome—when something goes wrong. This reaction is not, however, aggression; the infant's cognitive development does not yet allow him to connect his frustrated distress with the world. At some specific time during development, and the studies seem to indicate that it is around eight months of age, the infant makes a cognitive link: his distress is being caused by someone's failure. The exact developmental timetable is not the issue. This realization may occur earlier, as the Kleinians argue; it may occur at eight months; or it may be later. The point is that it does not exist at birth or during the neonatal period, and it most certainly does exist at two years. Now the infant is no longer merely enraged, but he is enraged at his mother for *her failure* to provide. In our affective vocabulary, anger adds a "because of . . ." to the more inchoate feelings of frustration or distress, and it signals the emergence of the competitive/territorial motivational system.

How the parents respond to normal rages (the process of socialization) will pretty much determine whether the individual grows up to become peaceful and content or whether he comes to live with a substantial amount of unresolved rage directed against himself, his internalized parents, or others. The optimal way for the parents to handle these rages seems to be to recognize that anger–rage is an important emotion for the infant to express; it is a communication that the infant is upset about something that is very important. A parent who can recognize this message should be able to figure out some kind of an adaptive response. Unfortunately, some parents interpret the child's rage as meaning that they have been bad parents (otherwise the child would not be angry), and they try to placate the child. Other parents may feel that anger is a "bad emotion" and that the child is bad for being angry; they may try to shame the child and/or make him feel guilty. Some parents may experience the child's anger as a personal attack, which, in turn, generates a parental counterattack. The response may be direct ("Yell at me and I'll beat the crap out of you") or more subtle, such as withdrawal of affection or love. These inappropriate responses to the child's rage often drive the angry feelings underground or displace them onto the wrong person. As most therapists recognize, this displacement leads to the necessity of mobilizing the negative transference. A discussion of the complexity of the therapeutic task is beyond the scope of this book, but the goals are straightforward: to help the patient be in touch with his hurt and angry feelings; to create an atmosphere where it is safe to feel them and communicate them; to explore their meaning with the patient; to uncover the accompanying phantasies that structuralize and perpetuate the problems; to help the patient be more assertive in directly stating his needs to the therapist; and, finally, to develop these skills to a point where the patient can effectively use them outside the therapist's office.

SUMMARY

Man is a territorial animal. Within the animal kingdom, the adaptive purpose of aggression is to secure first rights to scarce resources, such as food, water, mates, and territory. Anger–rage, the affect connected with aggression, gives a clear message: "This is mine!

You're in for a fight if you try to take it." In human beings, what we claim as territory has extended well beyond the biologic necessities of life (food, mates, territory) into areas of primarily symbolic significance. Consequently, we respond with what we label as narcissistic rage when we perceive someone as attacking something we have claimed or identified as "mine." If someone takes something from us—whether concrete or symbolic—we experience a drop in our self-esteem. These components—aggression (the behavior) and anger–rage (the affective monitor)—form what I have called the competitive/territorial motivational system. The next chapter presents the hypothesis that the presymbolic experience of shame signals surrender in a territorial dispute, thus avoiding a direct rival fight and leading to the establishment of dominance hierarchies.

8

The Prereflective Roots of Shame

In its diminished forms, perhaps a transient embarrassment or a barely noticed awkwardness, shame is a part of our everyday experience, so ubiquitous that we scarcely pay much attention to it. Along with fear and guilt, shame plays a prominent part in the raising of children, and I doubt that there are many children who haven't heard the phrase "Shame on you!" or "You ought to be ashamed of yourself." Shame is often experienced as being exposed or as a consciousness of being looked at. When we dream of shame, we often dream that we are caught in a condition of incomplete dress, or in night attire; quite literally, we are "caught with our pants down." Shame is often expressed as an impulse to hide, to bury one's face, to sink right then and there into the ground. These many experiences of shame, known to almost all of us, are part of "the psychopathology of everyday life."

Tomkins (1963) has painted an eloquent portrait of what it is like to experience intense shame, a feeling described by words such as humiliation or mortification.

> If distress is the affect of suffering, shame is the affect of indignity, of defeat, of transgression and of alienation. Though terror speaks to life and death and distress makes of the world a vale of tears, yet shame strikes deepest into the heart of man. While terror and distress hurt, they are wounds inflicted from outside which penetrate the smooth surface of the ego; but shame is felt as an inner torment, a sickness of the soul. It does not matter whether the humiliated one

137

has been shamed by derisive laughter or whether he mocks himself. In either event he feels himself naked, defeated, alienated, lacking in dignity or worth [p. 118].

As Erikson (1959) points out, intense feelings of shame can gradually lead to a paralyzing self-consciousness (p. 68). Humiliation may lead to anything from murder or suicide to war. What the newspapers luridly refer to as "crimes of passion" are more accurately described as crimes of humiliation, motivated not by love but by the desire to avenge an overwhelming sense of shame. The humiliation of the German people engendered by the Treaty of Versailles played a major role in bringing Adolf Hitler to power and thus, albeit indirectly, to World War II. Kohut (1977) eloquently points out the terrible effects of living with a chronic sense of shame:

The suicides of this period [young adulthood] are not the expression of a punitive superego, but a remedial act—the wish to wipe out the unbearable sense of mortification and nameless shame imposed by the ultimate recognition of a failure of all-encompassing magnitude [p. 241].

Despite the fact that shame often plays a major role in the lives of many of our patients, we still do not understand it very well. As Broucek (1982) says, "A psychology of the self demands that greater attention be paid to shame; shame is to self psychology what anxiety is to ego psychology—the keystone affect" (p. 369).

In the next section, we will briefly consider the relationship between shame and guilt. These two feelings are often confused, and many patients report "feeling guilty" when, in fact, they are feeling ashamed. Experientially, guilt has a different feel to it than shame, perhaps because fear of what will happen to us if we break the rules plays a much larger part in guilt than it does in shame. Obviously, punishment and, perhaps even more frightening, the constant fear of punishment have a different effect on the character than does shaming. The use of shaming, as opposed to direct coercion and punishment, varies from family to family and from culture to culture. Shame depends on contempt (or disgust or both) as the punitive affect; the threat is lack of stature in the eye of the beholder (which the Japanese call loss of face), ostracism, and the ultimate threat—banishment. Thus guilt threatens punishment—perhaps even death—but not exclusion from the community; shame threatens an end to the relationship.

As we mature, we come to a time in our life when we are able to adopt a set of inner standards of conduct for ourselves, rather than simply experiencing them as imposed from outside. This shift reduces the harshness of the superego demands and, in Freud's (1924b) words, produces a "dissolution of the Oedipus complex." As the boundary between shame and guilt diminishes, our behavior is regulated by our own inner standards. In David Riesmann's (1961) terms, we become "inner directed." Thus, in mature persons, the emotion of guilt (with its fear of punishment) virtually disappears; rather, we experience shame when "we let ourselves down."

PRIDE/SHAME: PSYCHOANALYTIC THEORIES

Perhaps the best place to begin the investigation of shame is with its opposite, the emotion of pride. As we can easily recognize from self-observation, we feel pride in ourselves when we attempt to live up to our ideals, and we feel shame when we don't. We do not have to succeed to feel proud of themselves; we can "die trying" and still feel that our lives have been a great success. When Nathan Hale said, "I only regret that I have but one life to lose for my country," it is hard to imagine that he felt anything but pride. It is in the power to be motivated by ideals that human beings differ from animals; as Hegel says, the quest for "glory" is the quintessential human enterprise. In contrast, animals can rather dully and reliably be predicted to attempt to do only what is necessary to survive; while they certainly do things such as fight to protect their young, they do so not because they are idealistic but because they are programmed for it.

The power of our ideals to motivate us is extremely strong, whether we are talking about a knight's crusade to the Holy Land or a scholar's effort to write the definitive treatise on some obscure subject. Although the word "ideal" certainly has connotations of some lofty and ethically uplifting enterprise, this is not always the case; the terrorist who blows himself up while on an aircraft is as "idealistic" as Joan of Arc. Nor are ideals necessarily a matter of great importance; even the Sunday golfer's struggle to shoot a round of golf at par is an attempt to reach the ideal. Ideals are the symbolically determined standards that we set for ourselves (or that we unconsciously adopt) and that can then guide our behavior. The human capacity to be motivated by ambitions or ideals does not form a separate motivational system; rather it operates in all motivational systems. Thus, one may try to form the best relationship possible (the affiliational system), become the best writer one can be (the competence/mastery system), enjoy the best romantic weekend (the sensual/sexual system), or possess the largest kingdom or fortune (the competitive/territorial system).

The relationship between our ideals and shame has long been recognized. Twenty-four hundred years ago, Aristotle said, "Shame is the mental picture of disgrace in which we shrink from the disgrace itself and not from its consequences" (*The Nicomachean Ethics,* IV, 5). Within the framework of psychoanalytic theory, ideals were first discussed in Freud's (1914) classic paper "On Narcissism," in which he outlined the concept of the ego ideal. He recognized that both internal and external sources contributed to the ego ideal, as represented by "admonitions of others and by the awakening of his own critical judgement" (p. 94). Freud explicitly related the ego ideal to self-regard and suggested that the inability to love, to invest oneself in the other, lowers self-esteem. At one point in the essay, Freud vigorously disputed Adler's concept of "organ inferiority," which hypothesized that a person will strive to remedy a sense of inferiority by overcompensating (e.g., a stutterer may end up as a great orator). As Andrew Morrison (1989) nicely points out in his book *Shame: The Underside of Narcissism,* a study of organ inferiority would inevitably have led to a psychology of shame. In retrospect, one can see that Freud's dispute with Adler may have played a major role in shifting psychoanalytic theory away from a significant study of shame and focusing, instead, on the emotion of guilt. As a consequence, the study of shame was more or less neglected for a substantial period of time.

Freud developed his psychology of guilt separately from his theorizing about shame.[1] In the 1917 paper "Mourning and Melancholia," he hypothesized that the ego contained within it a "critical agency, which is here split off from the ego," and is "the agency commonly called 'conscience'" (Freud, 1917a, p. 247). He described this critical agency as being formed through the process of identification (p. 249). In the 1923 monograph *The Ego and the Id,* Freud renamed this critical agency the superego. The close connection between guilt and shame might have led Freud to consider the idealizing function as part of the superego. He did not do so, however, and it was not until 1953 that Piers and Singer, writing within the framework of structural theory, pointed out that shame arises from the tension between the ego and ego ideal, not between the ego and

---

[1] For a full history and discussion of Freud's early ideas about guilt, see Strachey (1957b).

superego as with guilt. This tension generates an "awareness of 'inferiority' . . . most probably earlier than any guilt feelings can have developed" (p. 30).

As psychoanalytic theory has evolved, both the capacity for idealization and our prohibitions have come to be conceptualized as the core functions of the superego. The transgression of our internalized prohibitions (a set of no's) leads to the emotion of guilt. Thus, guilt is one of the first emotions that depends for its development on the capacity for symbolic thought. At first these no's come from our parents and family, later from friends, teachers, and society. Guilt is one of our first complex affects, a combination of the idea of no/bad blended with the affect of fear. Shame is much more difficult to understand because it too can be considered as a complex affect, evoked when we fail to live up to the ideals we set for ourselves (our internalized yeses). Shame, however, has deeper resonances, tapping powerful feelings that exist prior to the development of the capacity for symbolization. In the balance of this chapter, we will begin to explore the complex problem of the prereflective roots of shame.

COMPETENCE/MASTERY AND THE LINK TO SHAME

Freud (1900) described several embarrassing dreams of being naked and "a distressing feeling in the nature of shame and in the fact that one wishes to hide one's nakedness, as a rule by locomotion, but finds one is unable to do so" (p. 242). In this early discussion, shame was seen as a social-interpersonal affect, linked to being observed or found out. In 1905, Freud modified his views, now conceptualizing shame primarily as a defense against the drives. Although Freud returned to the issue of shame several times, he was never able to integrate it into his theoretical framework; consequently, his writings on the subject reflect a great deal of ambiguity.[2]

In *The Restoration of the Self*, Kohut (1977) conceptualized shame as the result of a lack of empathic responses and adequate mirroring by the selfobject during the "anal" phase of development. (Kohut put the term "anal" in quotes, emphasizing his dissatisfaction with the term.) He commented, "Healthy pride and healthy

---

[2] For an excellent review of Freud's views on shame, see Morrison, 1989, pp. 22–29.

assertiveness, I might add, are less easily formulated in drive-psychological terms than are the disintegration products of these wholesome basic experiences—shame and rage—that appear after the breakup of the primary psychological constellation" (p. 77). He suggested that two complementary theories were needed—"that of a conflict psychology and that of a psychology of the self " (p. 78)—to explain this phenomenon. By using the term "healthy assertive-ness," Kohut approached the problem of the origins of the prereflective sense of shame by focusing not on shame itself, but on the desirable alternative, "healthy assertiveness." Kohut was thus trying to describe the vast range of behavior that has to do with exploration, assertion, competence, and mastery. This range of activities, which has some-times been described simply as efficacy or competency, is difficult to fit within the framework of psychoanalytic theory.

In the *Three Essays on the Theory of Sexuality,* Freud (1905) mentioned an "instinct for mastery," but added "the fundamental psychological analysis of this instinct has, as we know, not yet been satisfactorily achieved" (p. 193). Fifteen years later, Freud (1920) again began to consider an "instinct for mastery" as a powerful force present in the repetition compulsion, but did not proceed to develop these ideas (p. 16). By his speculations about a drive for mastery, Freud was, in effect, saying that this is an important, albeit unre-solved, problem. In the early 1940s, Ives Hendrick (1942, 1943a, 1943b) wrote a series of papers on the "instinct to master," raising the possibility of a third drive whose function was to control the environment through action. In these papers, Hendrick was suggest-ing that this part of human behavior (i.e., mastery) was important enough to be considered as a separate drive. Translating this into the language of motivational systems, Hendrick was proposing that competence/mastery should be considered as a discrete motivational system.

The major effort to establish an observational-theoretical base for a competence/mastery motivational system can be said to have begun with Robert White's (1959) article, "Motivation Reconsidered: The Concept of Competence." In it, White concluded that compe-tence, the capacity to interact adaptively with the environment, cannot come "from sources of energy currently conceptualized as drives or instincts" (p. 297). In reviewing the work of animal psy-chologists, he noted that activities such as exploration and manipu-lation of the environment "might have to be assigned the status of independent motives" (p. 298). The experience of learning to interact effectively with the environment, White labeled as competence. He also recognized that the experience of competence was likely to have an affective monitor.

> Such activities in the ultimate service of competence must therefore be conceived to be motivated in their own right. It is proposed to designate this motivation by the term effectance, and to characterize the experience produced as a *feeling of efficacy* [p. 329].

These formulations—certainly compatible with the major thesis of this essay that each motivational system has its own affective monitor—powerfully influenced a number of investigators of infant development.

Almost 70 years ago, Karl Buehler (quoted in Piers and Singer, 1953) described this sense of efficacy as "'Funktionslust'—the pleasure experienced in and through one's own well-functioning" as the successful pursuit of what he called the "maturation drive" (p. 15). (Unfortunately, the English language does not seem to have a translation that captures the affective resonance of *Funktionslust*.) This type of experience becomes the foundation of the competence/ mastery system, where success in exercising contingent control is signaled by some kind of efficacy pleasure. Bower (1977) speculated that the interactive smiling responses with the mother give the infant a sense of mastery and control. This hypothesis was tested by his work with a blind infant, who at eight weeks of age did not smile at all.

> The baby had been blind from birth and so, of course, had been deprived of the visual stimuli that normally elicit smiling. However, when he was given an auditory mobile and contingent control over it, so that by kicking his legs he could produce a change of sound, he began to smile and coo. The smiles were vigorous and forceful. Normally at this age we cannot elicit smiling with sounds at all, particularly mechanical sounds of the sort we used in this experiment. Nonetheless, as soon as the baby had contingent control over this event in his external world, he began to smile. The stimulus objects in this case were small bells. Prior to the experiment the sound of these bells had not made the baby smile, and bells alone never produced a smile. Only when he was exercising control over the bells did we see smiling at this early age [p. 45].

In this situation, the baby did not smile when he passively heard the bells, but when he gained "contingent control over this event in his external world." This experiment strongly suggests that the ability to "make something happen" in the external world becomes linked with the ability to experience joy as indicated by the smiling response.

Broucek (1979), reviewing the work of White (1959), Bower (1977), Watson (1972), and the Papouseks (1975), forcefully argues that infants experience what he calls "effectance pleasure" in being able to control contingent events (p. 315). He ends the paper by saying, "I regard the sense of efficacy as the core of the developing sense of self and traumatic disturbances in the sense of efficacy as core narcissistic injuries which predispose to significant psychopathology in the course of development" (p. 315). In further developing this line of thought, Broucek (1982) theorizes that primitive shame experiences begin in the first 18 months of life as the result of "inefficacy experiences" (p. 376). Within the competence/mastery system, the infant experiences efficacy pleasure *(Funktionslust)* when he is successful, and a primitive sense of shame when he is not. Broucek was among the first theoreticians to develop specific hypotheses about the prereflective roots of shame in the experiences of inefficacy.

It is during what Margaret Mahler and her coworkers (1975) call the "practicing subphase," 9 to 18 months of age, that the flowering of the competence/mastery motivational system is most easily observable. Entrance into this phase begins with the subsidence of some of the fear that the infant is able to experience at approximately 8 months of age. During the early practicing subphase, the infant often uses the mother to help master some of the fear. The 8- to 10-month-old will crawl to the mother, touch her in some way, or just lean against her, a term Furer labeled "emotional refueling" (p. 69). As Mahler (1975) has commented, "It is easy to observe how the wilting and fatigued infant 'perks up' in the shortest time following such contact; then he quickly goes on with his explorations and once again becomes absorbed in his pleasure in functioning" (p. 69). The child's first upright steps mark the transition into the practicing subphase proper (p. 71). Greenacre (1957) described this phase as the child's "love affair with the world." During this period of time, the infant practices his motor skills and explores the environment, both animate and inanimate. As Mahler (1975) said, "We see a relatively great imperviousness to knocks and falls and other frustrations, such as a toy being grabbed by another child. Substitute familiar adults within the setup of our nursery are easily accepted (in contrast to what occurs during the next subphase of separation-individuation)" (p. 71).

I suggest that the infant's "love affair with the world" and relative imperviousness to the slings and arrows of misfortune are secondary to the development of competence in mastering the use of his body, skills that are accompanied by feelings of *Funktionslust*. This happy phase of development comes to an end with the arrival of the rapprochement crisis. Now the infant faces a new task: he must learn to think and become as competent in learning to use his mind as he was in learning to use his body.

CONTEMPT/SHAME: A DEVELOPMENTAL PERSPECTIVE

In reviewing their work, I see no important differences between Hendrick's instinct to master, White's concept of competence, Broucek's sense of efficacy, and Lichtenberg's exploratory/assertive motivational system. (However, I would not use the word *assertive* to describe the motivational system, as, imperceptibly, assertion shades into aggression, which I conceptualize as belonging to the competitive/territorial system.) In this essay, I have elected to call this system the competence/mastery system. In reviewing Lichtenberg's work and in discussing the matter with him personally, I very much agree with his hypothesis that the variety of functions variously conceptualized as mastery, competence, exploration, and efficacy is most usefully placed within a separate motivational system. In the beginning, success is monitored by some kind of pleasure in achievement *(Funktionslust)* and failure by a primitive sense of shame. These are important anlagen for what will eventually become a sense of self. The long evolution that begins with our feelings of enjoyment in efficacy/competence and eventually ends with the pride of achieving our aspirations/ideals is, however, not direct. These twists and turns in this line of development are what makes the understanding of shame difficult.

The thesis of this section is that the emotion of contempt is the "missing link" that allows us to complete the developmental history of pride and shame. The key observations involve determining what happens when competence is tested in the crucible of competition. As developed in the previous chapter on "Aggression and Rage," competitive/territorial species use fighting, or the threat of fighting, to determine how scarce commodities are allocated. In most species, dominance hierarchies (commonly called "pecking orders") achieve through psychological mechanisms what rival fights would achieve through physical contests. I suggest that the emotions of contempt and shame play a key role in establishing and maintaining these dominance hierarchies. Contempt, communicated through a complex set of rituals, says "I can beat you"; shame answers, "I know it. I concede. I won't fight." The residuals of these dominance hierarchies are easy enough to observe in humans: the swaggering gait, the insolent smile that dares a challenger; the averted eyes, the subtle flush of the skin that concedes. The message of contempt is clear: "I'm the boss; you're not." Shame concedes the point.

Tomkins (1963), one of the few theorists to seriously investigate the emotion of contempt, traced its origins to the affect of disgust. This hypothesis has had exceedingly important theoretical ramifications. From the adaptive point of view, disgust is one of the easiest of the emotions to understand: it protects against the ingestion of food that will be bad for us. Tomkins writes, "From an evolutionary standpoint, one would suppose that what was too noxious to be ingested with safety was information which came to be built into the mechanism of disgust and nausea" (p. 129). In speculating about the origins of contempt, Tomkins hypothesized that the disgust reaction generalized from its origins as a protection against noxious substances to persons or situations far removed from food. Following Tomkins's line of reasoning, Izard and Buechler (1980) stated, "Disgust can be a response to something either physically or *psychologically* deteriorated or spoiled" (p. 168, emphasis added). If used in the psychological sense, the distinction between disgust and contempt begins to disappear; they are both ways of devaluing another person. For example, if someone says, "You really make me sick, you piece of shit," the language is that of disgust but the meaning is contempt. In ordinary conversation, expressions of disgust or contempt for another person are virtually interchangeable.

One of the legacies of the disgust → contempt hypothesis is the classification of contempt as a negative affect, a classification that is simply wrong. If by negative we mean negatively valenced (and not morally reprehensible), *contempt is a positive affect*. This conclusion can be verified easily enough through simple introspection. Contempt certainly does not feel bad, in the way that anxiety, fear, shame, guilt, or depression do. No patient ever arrived at a psychotherapist's office complaining that he was "feeling contemptuous." At the very most, we may feel a little ashamed when we look down our noses at someone, but this is merely our ideals telling us that we shouldn't be so comfortable with our prejudices. In most cases, however, the contempt becomes embedded within the matrix of characterologic arrogance. Hence the chuckle, the sudden realization of a hidden truth, in the old psychoanalytic joke: "What do you get when you analyze a horse's ass? Answer: An analyzed horse's ass." Our difficulty in accepting contempt as a positive affect that bolsters self-esteem has played a major part in keeping us from understanding the prereflective roots of shame.

Contempt, or something close to it, is, I suggest, the key affect in what ethologists call dominance hierarchies. In competitive/territorial species, dominance hierarchies decide who gets first choice among scarce resources. If food is the scarce resource, the dominant male (and it usually is a male) eats first; then the less dominant have their turn; at the end of the chain, the least dominant gets the leftovers. In the selection of mates, the same principles apply. In tournament species, where a few dominant males impregnate large numbers of females, the less dominant males are left out; their genes simply vanish from the gene pool, leaving, as a result, males who are particularly large, strong, and aggressive. In species where territory is the prime resource, the results are approximately the same; the dominant individuals get the prime territory, the less dominant get less desirable territory, and so on. The adaptive usefulness of dominance hierarchies is that they settle disputes over resources without bloodshed.

The mechanisms for determining dominance are both complex and fascinating. Obviously, the simplest mechanism would be a straightforward rival fight; the winner emerges as the dominant one, and the loser is either killed or submits. However, such fights are dangerous to both participants. Therefore, in most of these situations, the confrontation does not lead to a fight, and the would-be loser signals his submission to the more dominant animal through what are known to ethologists as appeasement rituals. As Lorenz (1966) points out, this behavior fulfills "the most important function of the rival fight, namely to ascertain which partner is stronger, without hurting the weaker" (p. 105). In these rituals, the dominant animal signals his willingness to fight if necessary; he holds the weapon, whether it be teeth, beak, claws, or fist, "under the nose" of the opponent (p. 126). The appeasement maneuver is often made by offering the aggressor the most vulnerable part of the body. For example, in the dog or the wolf, it looks very much as if the supplicant is offering his neck veins to the victor, the very place a lethal bite would be made in a real fight (p. 127). Although the question of what an animal feels always involves difficult methodologic problems, the emotions of contempt and shame seem to play the same role in animals as they do in humans: to signal important information about dominance hierarchies.

In most dominance hierarchies, the principles are simple: might makes right; the stronger, more aggressive males dominate the weaker and more submissive. As we move up the scale of evolution, the situation becomes a little bit more complex. In the hope of understanding the leap from animal to human behavior, anthropologists Sherwood Washington and Irwin DeVore spent a considerable amount of time studying baboon troops living on the African savannah. Konner (1982) describes their findings as follows:

> In baboon troops living on the African savannah, the generation-to-generation social structure of the group depends for continuity on a solid core of closely related females. But on a day-to-day basis, the most prominent arbiters of social life are dominant males. One of the interesting things about savannah baboon-troop structure is that if you match males on a one-to-one basis—as DeVore did, instigating fights over food—you get a linear hierarchy of dominance, but it is different from the actual troop hierarchy observed in practice. DeVore showed that this discrepancy is explained by coalitions. At the top of a troop will be not a lone enduring tough, but a sort of troika in which the members reliably come to each other's defense. This enabled an elderly male who remained "politically" capable to exercise dominance over other males who could easily defeat him in individual combat. (Such coalitions have sometimes been observed to function in defense against predation, protecting females and young at the center of the troop, while younger males ["subdominants"] deployed themselves strategically at the periphery—but this aspect of the pattern is controversial) [pp. 39–40].

In the wild, a number of complex factors undoubtedly enter into the determination of "who is dominant." A number of simple observations can be made however: the big and strong tend to dominate the small and weak; males tend to dominate females; and as we move up the evolutionary scale, intelligence—which Konner describes as "political capability"—becomes a more important factor in determining dominance. The relevance of these ethologic observations to the structure of human society is fascinating because, without much doubt, dominance hierarchies are deeply embedded within our language, values, customs, and culture.

The part that gender plays in dominance hierarchies is also interesting. Consider, for a moment, the squirrel monkey's behavioral pattern known as a "genital display."

The monkey lifts its leg and spreads its thigh out to expose the genitals, while making a characteristic vocalization. It does this as a threat in aggressive encounters that may or may not lead to violence, and dominant animals are more likely to do it to submissive ones, even to the point of, as it were, sticking it in their faces. Males do it much more often than females in these dominance encounters, and also do it to females as a prelude to sexual intercourse. It is present in both sexes in essentially adult form from within a few days of birth, but the context is readily influenced by experience; one female who had a dominant position in a group exhibited it frequently, just as do males, although whether she had the anatomical analogue of the male phallic erection is not known [Konner, 1982, p. 149].

In more advanced species, such as baboons and macaques, a male shows his dominance over a lower ranking male and mounts him from behind, as he would a female for copulation (p. 289). These observations, illustrating the complex interweaving of sexuality and aggression, demonstrate the biologic anlagen of the war between the sexes. The embedded meaning of these gestures—"fuck you (if I want to)"—is so upsetting to our sensibilities that it has obscured an obvious fact: within the animal kingdom, contempt is one of the positive affects.

Man's dominance hierarchies, born in aggression and enforced through physical strength or psychological coercion, raise societal issues that are extremely discomfiting. In commenting on the male's domination over the female, Konner (1982) writes:

It is very far from my mind to suggest that such tendencies, however natural, are admirable, desirable, or unchangeable; but I must reiterate here my belief . . . that insistence upon the nonexistence of significant biological bases for the different behaviors we observe in the two genders can only obscure the path to understanding, amelioration, and justice. The truth may not be helpful, but the concealment of it cannot be [p. 290].

Until very recently, the male's domination over the female was taken for granted. The 19th amendment to the Constitution, guaranteeing women the right to vote, was not ratified until 1920, a scant 75 years ago. The biologic heritage of the male's domination of the female was reinforced (but certainly not created by) by our customs and culture. Only in the last 40 or 50 years have women begun to challenge and attempt to change our culture and work toward full equality. The truth about the biologic roots of the male's domination of the female may not be helpful to the process of change, but, as Konner (1982) says, "the concealment of it cannot be" (p. 290).

Contempt almost always arises within a relational context, and while it may be positive for the person who is feeling contemptuous, it is negative for the person on the receiving end. The net result is that the recipient is flooded with feelings of shame. After we form ideals and begin to think about the sort of society that we want, we identify ourselves with ideals that specifically reject this hierarchical view of human nature, especially the one that says "might is right." Our ideals lead us to think of contempt as a "bad" emotion to feel; our values lead us to label contempt as a "negative" affect. These unresolved ambivalences about human nature—contrasting our knowledge about the hierarchical structure of human society with our vision of the future—are among the primary impediments to developing an adequate theory of shame.

In working on this problem, Tomkins (1980) came to classify two distinct personality types: 1) the normatives, who favor the more hierarchical structure and 2) the humanists, who favor a more democratic structure. Not too surprisingly, contempt–disgust responses are much more acceptable within hierarchical societies than among humanists. In carrying out his psychological tests to distinguish the two groups, Tomkins found more than enough "humanistic" students among the college population, but not enough "normatives" (pp. 156–158). This data seems to indicate that better-educated persons tend to adopt ideals that lead them to suppress or repress their more hierarchical, elitist attitudes. The contempt response, however, does not disappear; we simply transform it into characterologic arrogance. These feelings of arrogance may become chronic, frozen into the facial musculature with a slight lift to the upper lip and nostrils, as though one were constantly in the presence of an offensive odor. The look of arrogance gives the face a perpetual smile of superiority (not the responsive smile of enjoyment).

In clinical practice, it is very important to be able to recognize, and help the patient identify, the feelings of shame that are reactive to being treated with contempt. In a child, parental contempt can trigger feelings of narcissistic rage and the wish to destroy the parent; these feelings become encoded in unconscious phantasies.

Simultaneously, the child recognizes that in the real world he lacks the power to hurt, much less destroy, the parent he so desperately needs. As a defense against this humiliation, he begins to develop feelings of contempt toward the parent (identification with the shaming person); then, as his character structure crystallizes, this may result in the emergence of feelings of arrogance and/or omnipotence. Any successful therapy needs to unravel the complexities of the contemptuous parent–shamed child relationship, as well as the various mechanisms employed to defend against it. Contempt emerging in the transference may be very difficult for the therapist to deal with if he lacks an adequate understanding of shame dynamics.

Melanie Klein conceptualized contempt as one of the three manic defenses against depression, the other two being control and triumph (see Segal, 1964, pp. 69–78). Control is a method of denying dependence on an object and, at the same time, compelling the object to fulfill a need for dependence; triumph involves the denial of depressive feelings. As Hanna Segal (1964) puts it:

> Contempt for the object is again a direct denial of valuing the object, which is so important in the depressive position, and it acts as a defence against the experience of loss and of *guilt*. An object of contempt is not an object worthy of guilt, and the contempt that is experienced in relation to such an object becomes a justification for further attacks on it [p. 71, emphasis added].

The problem with this formulation is that—based on Freud's dual-drive theory—it considers aggression (followed by guilt over aggression) as primary, and contempt as a defense against depression (which is secondary to the unacknowledged aggression). This is a standard formulation of guilt dynamics. In contrast, many people—I among them—regard the feeling of being shamed as primary, with narcissistic rage and aggression being a reaction to being shamed. The issue of which is primary—guilt dynamics or shame dynamics—is one of the many issues that tend to divide classical (and Kleinian) conceptualizations of psychopathology from self psychology.

Shame, more than any other emotion, touches on our unresolved assumptions about the nature of man. The essence of the problem is that the hierarchical structure of relationships, a legacy of a biologic heritage, conflicts with our ideals of equality. This ambivalence is reflected in the two primary dictionary definitions of the word "proud": "1) feeling pleasure or satisfaction over something regarded as highly honorable or creditable to oneself; 2) having, proceeded from, or showing a high opinion of one's own dignity, importance, or superiority." The synonyms for proud are particularly instructive. For the first definition, the synonyms are "contented, self satisfied," a way of saying that one is living up to one's standards (ideals) for oneself. The synonym for the second definition of proud draws the distinction sharply: "overbearing, self-important, disdainful, imperious, presumptuous" (*Random House Dictionary,* 1966). The dictionary goes on to say that proud, when used as a synonym for arrogant or haughty, implies "a consciousness of, or a belief in, one's superiority in some respect." In this sense of the word proud, belief in one's superiority incorporates within itself contempt for one's inferiors (i.e., those we can force to submit). Whenever we use the word proud, we can feel the duality: are we using it as a term of respect, reserved for someone who has earned the right to feel good about himself, or are we using it as a way of describing some arrogant son of a bitch? This ambivalence, perhaps more than any other factor, is responsible for our difficulties in understanding the prereflective roots of shame.

SUMMARY

The beginnings of shame are found in the competence/mastery system. We feel good about ourselves when we do well—we take "pleasure in efficacy"—and feel the beginnings of shame when we do not. Thus, the first phase of the evolution of shame begins with efficacy pleasure/primitive shame. The second phase of the development of shame begins when our competence is tested in the crucible of competition. As developed in the previous chapter, aggression (the behavior) and rage–anger (the affect) are key elements of any competitive/territorial species. The rules of territorial species are not especially complicated: take what you want until you meet someone who can stop you (i.e., "might makes right"). In order to avoid the bodily injury connected with direct rival fights, dominance hierarchies emerge that determine who gets first rights to the disputed resource (e.g., food, mates, or territory). Who is dominant is communicated through an elaborate signaling system; contempt says, "I can beat you"; prereflective shame says, "I surrender, I won't fight you." At this stage of development, contempt is a positive affect. Thus, the evolutionary purpose of contempt is to maintain the dominance hierarchy without the necessity of a rival fight.

Human beings have simply extended the process of fighting over the bare necessities of life to include a multiplicity of issues that relate to power and privilege. Even a cursory study of human history demonstrates that society has always been organized by hierarchies of sex, race, ethnic group, religious affiliation, and class. This hierarchical organization, subtly communicated by feelings of contempt (or arrogance) and acknowledged by shame (or deference), reflects the biologic origins of man as a competitive/territorial animal. These responses are strongly reinforced by those in power through cultural conditioning. The third stage in the evolution of shame begins with the formation of ideals; in this stage, we feel pride when we live up to our ideals and shame when we do not.

The argument about whether society should be democratically or hierarchically organized is certainly not resolved. As Tomkins (1980) demonstrates, the "normative" personality type more or less accepts the hierarchical, or elitist, organization of society. "Humanists" do not. The derivatives of this struggle between the normative/hierarchialists and the humanist/democratic "ideo-affective" postures can easily be seen in many of the political struggles of today, such as those over racism, feminism, civil rights, multiculturalism, and so on. Thus, an investigation of the origins of contempt and shame leads us not only to important clinical issues, but also to larger issues about society and how we believe it ought to be organized.

9

Presymbolic Character Structure

In the first eight chapters of this essay, we explored how affects serve as the experiential representation of a nonsymbolic information-processing system. A cross-comparison of the affective intensity from competing motivational systems gives us a simple, effective method of prioritizing information; a response to the "loudest signal" then initiates a course of action. Affective information processing—an analogic system—is what we share with the rest of the animal kingdom. Bodily sensations convey information about physiologic needs: physical pain (bodily damage occurring); hunger (need food); smothering (need air immediately!); tiredness (need sleep); and so on. Four neonatal moods—interest, surprise, distress, and contentment—begin to synthesize this information with information about the world. After the biobehavioral reorganization that occurs at approximately eight weeks, the information that the affect conveys becomes much more specific. Many of these affects convey information about the world-out-there: disgust (bad food); fear (danger! protect yourself); affection (stay close to this person); rage (mine!). When animals (nonhumans) reach sexual maturity, several new affects emerge that have to do with reproduction, the raising of the young, and territoriality (with associated dominance hierarchies). If primary process means the first information-processing system to come on-line, then affects are our real "primary process."

The fundamental concepts that help us understand presymbolic behavior—innate behavior patterns, stimulus releasers, behavioral shaping, and control systems theory—are well known and not particularly controversial. Although the specific details of this developmental unfolding are endlessly complex and fascinating, the fundamental challenge of understanding animal behavior has been resolved. In this chapter, we examine how behavioral shaping leads to relatively stable and predictable behavioral response patterns (which we call character organization or character structure); in turn, this structure is represented affectively by what I will call "complex moods." Simple moods are the direct response to a single environmental event; in contrast, complex moods begin to emerge that summarize the results of numerous events. As a result of this synthesizing process, complex moods become the affective representations of presymbolic character structure.

The final task in constructing a model of the presymbolic infant is to understand how the infant's experience with the environment is stored and retrieved. Necessarily, this leads to discussion of memory and how the internalized models of the world-out-there—which Piaget calls schema—are constructed. One major problem for psychoanalytic theorists is that there is no commonly accepted term that specifically describes and differentiates these presymbolic working models of the world from the later-acquired world of concepts. (Piaget's "schema" is not yet a comfortable term for most psychoanalysts.) The problem centers on trying to find an agreed-upon definition of the term representation, which has sharply differing connotations in Piagetian developmental psychology than it does for most English-speaking writers. These issues are explored in the section of this chapter called Memory, Schema, and the Concept of Representation.

COMPLEX MOODS

Moods, the affective signals of the reptilian brain, are our first central information-processing affect. During the first eight weeks of life, four simple moods—interest, surprise, distress, and contentment—act as the primary organizing affects for the waking infant, allowing him to sort and classify information both about his body and about the world. Each mood has a very specific and easily decipherable message: interest (let's learn); surprise (new information coming); distress (something's wrong); and contentment (everything is OK). The interrelationship of these primary moods can be easily understood if one sees it as a matrix with two coordinates:

inner–outer and good–bad. The inner–outer axis of the matrix describes the focus of our attention. Interest and surprise tend to focus us toward the outer world; contentment focuses us inward; distress can be either. The other coordinate of the matrix—good–bad—adds a qualitative assessment to the experience. Contentment and interest are positive; distress is negative; surprise may be either good or bad, depending on the context. These four primary moods (interest, surprise, distress, contentment) play a major role in organizing, and thus structuralizing, the infant's experience.

Let us examine how this system works. The special senses— sight, touch, hearing, smell—bring the infant information about the outside world. In addition, specific sensations such as hunger, thirst, tiredness, or physical pain act as analogic monitors of physiologic processes that give the child information about his body. If one of these monitors flashes an alarm (e.g., hungry!), the neonate responds with the cries of the global distress syndrome. This distress response, which easily fits the definition of a mood, serves two specific purposes: 1) the crying summons the caretaker with the preemptive message, "Fix what's wrong"; and 2) the distressed mood serves as an indicator *to the neonate himself* that his body needs attention in some way. At the present time, most of the developmental literature emphasizes the communicative function of the infant's distress cries (his helplessness) but deemphasizes how distress helps him begin to learn about his body. These distress sensations, affective representations of information about the body, form the core of a motivational system that assesses and regulates the infant's physiologic requirements. During the first eight weeks of life, this motivational system is of primary importance; the mother is certainly important, but primarily as the caretaker of the infant's physiologic needs.

At approximately eight weeks of age, the infant undergoes a biobehavioral reorganization that, as Stern (1985) says, is almost as clear a boundary as birth itself. The infant begins to make direct eye contact; shortly thereafter, he begins to smile more frequently and also more responsively and infectiously. With the possibility of shared joyfulness between the mother and infant, the relationship itself becomes more important than physiologic needs. Neurophysiologically, this biobehavioral reorganization correlates with a shift of dominance from the reptilian brain to the old mammalian brain. This means that the infant is able to experience "discrete emotions," as well as moods.

Basically, the discreteness of the response is a direct result of the improved neurophysiologic processing secondary to the development of the limbic circuitry of the old mammalian brain. As a consequence, the minute-to-minute reaction of the infant to the environment can be registered either by simple moods (e.g., interest, surprise, distress) or by discrete emotions (e.g., joy, fear, rage). This change allows moods to assume a new, and very important, function. Prior to this reorganization, moods served as the sole central-processing affect. Subsequent to the reorganization, there are two semi-independent systems for processing affect (the reptilian brain plus the old mammalian brain), which create the possibility for an interaction between the two systems. This, in turn, allows moods to assume a new function: not only do simple moods (e.g., surprise) reflect a direct response to a single environmental event, complex moods begin to emerge that summarize the results of numerous events. As a result of this synthesizing process, complex moods become the affective representation of presymbolic character patterns.

During infancy (approximately 2 months to 18 months), one of the important tasks of the mother is to facilitate the infant's involvement both with her and with the world. How well the mother accomplishes this task can be tracked by observing the infant's positive affects, such as interest and joy. The absence of these affects usually indicates that something is going wrong. For example, in the course of their effort to extend Tomkins's (1962, 1963) work to infant observation, Demos and Kaplan (1986) describe the case of infant Cathy; the mother mistook Cathy's prolonged gaze at her face (interest) as "boredom" and would turn away or attempt to give her toys as a substitute for the relationship with her.

> Our observations of Cathy's responses suggested a gradual dampening of affective intensity, particularly of the affects interest and joy. Cathy would begin each new exchange with her mother in a moderately intense state of interest and enjoyment. Then, as her mother turned away, either to substitute a toy for her face, or to attend to her son, the animation on Cathy's face would fade as she would look at the toy with only mild interest, or would look away with a somewhat blank expression [p. 191].

Thus, the mother's misreading of Cathy's affective communication resulted in partial interruption of the affective interchange between them. While it is not entirely possible to know what Cathy felt when she looked away "with a somewhat blank expression," it is not unreasonable to assume she had learned that the appearance of mother did not lead to an increase in excitement or joy (the usual result of an affective interchange between mother and infant).

Consequently, she may have felt something akin to distress or disappointment and thus tried to avoid the disappointment by averting her gaze, thereby interrupting the visual communication with her mother. (A straightforward learning or conditioning paradigm would be sufficient to explain these behaviors.) Furthermore, one can assume that the blank expression represents feelings of mild distress or boredom, perhaps the anlage of depressive symptomatology. These feelings—complex moods—are the affective representation of what Cathy had learned about the relationship with her mother.

At approximately eight months of age, the infant experiences a sudden upsurge in the capacity to experience fear, easily observed as the onset of what is often called "stranger anxiety" (and might better be called "stranger fear"). This upsurge in fear increases the infant's need for the mother as a soothing presence to deal with this fear. Another important emotion that emerges is anger; the infant needs to learn that he can become enraged at his mother without causing her to withdraw or to retaliate. Cathy's mother had difficulty in coping with the emergence of fear and anger in her infant. She saw them as something to be gotten rid of, rather than mastered. Consequently, viewing herself primarily as a "nurser, soother, and comforter" (p. 215), she did not allow Cathy to cry during the early months. The results were not promising:

> Cathy's early experiences of distress were extremely mild and fore-shortened, so that her capacity to make a connection between a felt need and the remedy offered was not facilitated. In other words, there was little opportunity for her to learn that her inner experience of distress and her efforts to cope had anything to do with what happened to her. We also suggested that this general pattern of muted affect may have contributed to the rarity of anger in Cathy's experience, and thus to the lack of opportunities for her to learn to cope with or modulate her anger. Her later expressions of distress and anger did not have a communicative signal quality to them, nor the expectation that any help was on the way. . . . However, Cathy's distress, anger, and fear seemed to be increasing over time, and since her expressions did not often result in helpful interventions, she tended to retreat and to fall back on repetitive play [pp. 214–215].

Basically, the mother made the critical mistake of intervening too quickly to eliminate negative affects, thus depriving Cathy of the opportunity of developing the capacity for "self-soothing, self-regulation, and modulation" (p. 215). The acquisition of the ability to self-soothe plays an extremely important part in the infant's development of a sense of competence, a belief that he can "make it" in the world. Anger plays a critical role at this juncture, because the infant needs to learn that he can become furious with the mother without causing her to withdraw or retaliate. If the mother reacts in those ways in response to the infant's anger, the infant will conclude that anger is too dangerous an emotion to express.

Clearly, the key tasks for the mother in affective interchanges with the infant at this stage are to: 1) *facilitate* the development of the positive affects of interest and joyfulness; 2) *protect* the infant from being overwhelmed by fear and provide a "background of safety"; and 3) *absorb* the infant's inevitable anger and rage without either withdrawing or retaliating.

The mother's success or failure at these tasks will be reflected by the valence of the complex, background mood that emerges. If the mother is successful, the child experiences a sense of well-being that is manifested by what Erikson (1959) describes as a sense of "basic trust" toward the world. (In describing his "sense of trust," Erikson draws a parallel with what Therese Benedek called "confidence," p. 61.) Basic trust is a good example of a complex, background mood state that persists despite intermittent emotional ups and downs in the relationship with mother such as transient grief due to mother's absence, the smiles at her return, disappointments, rages, and fears. This mood synthesizes, and thus organizes, a general response toward the world. If in the aggregate, however, things are not "good enough," the infant may develop a sense of mistrust. As Erikson (1959) says, "It must be said that the *amount of trust* derived from earliest infantile experience does not seem to depend on absolute *quantities of food or demonstrations of love* but rather on the *quality* of the maternal relationship" (p. 63).

Erik Erikson's well-known monograph *Identity and the Life Cycle* (1959) sketches out a theory of complex moods—healthy as contrasted to the pathologic—that predominate at certain phases of the life cycle. In describing the first of his stages, "Basic Trust versus Basic Mistrust," Erikson says:

> In describing this growth and its crises as a development of a series of alternative basic attitudes, we take recourse to the term "*a sense of.*" Like a "sense of health" or a "sense of not being well," such "senses" pervade surface and depth, consciousness and the unconscious. They are ways of conscious *experience*, accessible to introspection (where it develops); ways of *behaving*, observable by others; and unconscious *inner states* determinable by test and analysis. It is important to keep these three dimensions in mind, as we proceed [p. 56].

Erikson's description of a "basic attitude" fits Jacobson's (1957), as well as my, definition of a mood rather well. It is to be hoped that this essay will help supply the theoretical foundations for a deeper understanding, as well as a long-overdue appreciation, of the theory of complex mood states described by Erikson.

If the relationship with the mother is "good enough," then the infant will experience Erikson's sense of "basic trust." This sense of basic trust originates in the relationship with the mother, but generalizes into a global assessment about life. If the assessment is, on balance, negative, the infant experiences a sense of mistrust. The factors that may lead to developing of a sense of mistrust include the following: 1) physical abuse by either parent; 2) the prolonged physical absence of the mother; 3) the psychological unavailability of the mother (e.g., psychosis, severe depression, severe narcissism); 4) murderous phantasies toward the child that the infant intuitively senses; and 5) a lack of affective attunement to the developmental needs of the infant (e.g., Cathy). Each of these experiences would evoke a specific affective response such as boredom, fear, grief, distress, or depression. If these negative experiences are, on balance, painful enough, they will lead to new, relatively stable behavioral patterns designed to minimize the impact of the negative affects; in turn, these emerging behavior patterns are represented by the complex mood we call mistrust.

Moods such as trust or mistrust, then, reflect the quality of the relationship with the mother, which, in turn, generalizes into an attitude toward life itself. The cognitive content of the sense of mistrust might be phrased as follows: "Shut down the affiliational system as much as possible. Get rid of the affects, too. They're not safe!" If this mood persists into adulthood, the person may develop a schizoid personality. The DSM-III-R (American Psychiatric Association, 1987) describes the schizoid personality disorder as follows: "The essential feature of this disorder is a pervasive pattern of indifference to social relationships and a restricted range of emotional experience and expression, beginning by early adulthood and present in a variety of contexts" (p. 339). The schizoid personality represents the behavioral response to the sense of mistrust; there is the attempt to do without, or to minimize, to the extent possible, all affiliational ties. Accompanying this response is a sort of global shutdown of all affective life, leaving the individual suffering from this condition with a pervasive sense of emptiness (which may, in turn, lead to what is called schizoid depression). Within the framework being explored here, the schizoid personality represents what I would characterize as one of the mood disorders that can begin to evolve prior to the emergence of the ability to use symbols.

In some cases, the pervasive sense of mistrust becomes elaborated by phantasy, resulting in the paranoid personality. As described in the DSM-III-R: "The essential feature of this disorder is a pervasive and unwarranted tendency, beginning by early adulthood and present in a variety of contexts, to interpret the actions of people as deliberately demeaning or threatening. . . . Almost invariably there is a general expectation of being exploited or harmed by others in some way. Frequently a person with this disorder will question, without justification, the loyalty or trustworthiness of friends or associates. Often the person is pathologically jealous, questioning without justification the fidelity of his or her spouse or sexual partner" (p. 337).

The schizoid and paranoid mood disorders trace their origins to the failure to find enough gratification within the relationship (i.e., the affiliation) with the mother. This failure, signaled by the persistent mood of mistrust, generates two basic coping strategies, flight or fight. Schizoid withdrawal represents the flight response, the avoidance of relationships accompanied by an avoidance of affects. In contrast, the paranoid response moves toward the fight end of the spectrum; the willingness to fight serves the important purpose of maintaining a sense of affective aliveness but at the price of alienating others.

Both the schizoid and the paranoid responses are based on the assumption that the infant is able to locate the source of his difficulties in the failed mother–infant relationship. In effect, the infant recognizes that "Mother isn't doing a good-enough job." The infant may not, however, always recognize this relationship deficit. During the neonatal period, the most important motivational system deals with the infant's physiologic needs. After the biobehavioral reorganization at eight weeks, the relationship with the mother becomes important in and of itself; however, a great deal of the mother's interaction with the infant remains centered on taking care of his physiologic needs (nursing, comforting, diapering, etc.). This interaction not only teaches the infant something about the quality of the caretaking, but also, at a more subtle level, forms the basis of how, at a much later stage in life, the person will relate to his body. If the caretaker is successful in her ministrations, the infant will experience global feelings of contentment that say, "Life is OK"; and a secondary message says, "My body is OK." If things do not go well during the "oral phase" of development, the infant may be left with chronic, low-grade feelings of distress that are difficult for him to localize—"Does the problem lie with my mother or with my body?" In some cases, he may conclude that the problem is with his body and believe that, if only his body were feeling better, everything would be OK. It is not difficult to imagine a number of circumstances—difficulties in nursing; being given a bottle to soothe him whenever he is distressed; having a particularly sensitive digestive system—that would push him toward this conclusion. The belief that "I'll be OK if my body is OK" forms the anlage of addictive disorders. If these premises are correct, then addictive disorders represent a regression to the phase of development when the predominant motivational system is the one that takes care of the body's physiologic needs.

MEMORY, SCHEMA, AND THE CONCEPT OF REPRESENTATION

Until well into the 20th century, the predominant theory of memory, of which Freud's is an exemplar, was that a memory is basically a *stored sense impression*. This theory of memory dates back at least as far as Plato, who in *Theaetetus* compared memory to an impression on a wax tablet.[1] In his *Confessions* (X, 13), St. Augustine describes "the great core of memory," where images are stored until they are "brought forth when there is a need of them." In *An Essay Concerning Human Understanding*, Locke described memory as "the store-house of our ideas," adding, in the second edition, that "this laying up of our ideas in the repository of the memory signifies no more but this—that the mind has a power in many cases to revive perceptions which it has once had, with this additional perception annexed to them; that *it has had them before.*" This viewpoint characterizes perception as a passive experience; metaphorically, Plato's writing on a wax tablet, or, in more modern terms, like the lens of a camera. As Schimek (1975) has pointed out in his trenchant analysis of this viewpoint, "This means that perception is uninfluenced by past experience and not subject to a developmental and learning process" (p. 172). Philosophically this is sometimes known as the "copy" theory of knowledge, or, more lightheartedly, as "the doctrine of immaculate perception."

---

[1] This summary of Plato and the summary and quotations from St. Augustine and Locke that follow are taken from *The Encyclopedia of Philosophy* (1967), "Memory" section.

We now know that the "copy" theory of knowledge is simply wrong and that what we call memory is much more than a stored sense impression. From the moment of birth on, all mammals, not just humans, possess the capacity to learn from experience. The world, as well as the body in it, is represented by concrete, schematic models that are continually being updated through the acquisition of new experience. These internalized models (Piaget's schema) are not "remembered sense impressions"; rather, they are schematic models that synthesize perceptual experience. The workings of this process are easy enough to observe in our pets; if you move into a new house with a cat, the cat will explore its new surroundings until it really knows its new home. As there is absolutely no evidence that human beings process perceptual experience in ways that are different from those of other sentient species (those capable of paying attention), one would conclude that human infants begin life with this capacity to construct this concrete, schematic working map of the world. It is part of our presymbolic heritage.

One of the most important steps in constructing a schematic working map of the world is the achievement of what Piaget and Inhelder (1969) define as "object permanence." In simple language, object permanence is achieved when out of sight is no longer out of mind. Before reaching object permanence:

> The universe of the young baby is a world without objects, consisting only of shifting and unsubstantial "tableaux" which appear and are then totally reabsorbed, either without returning, or reappearing in a modified or analogous form. At about five to seven months (Stage 3 of Infancy), when the child is about to seize an object and you cover it with a cloth or move it behind a screen, the child simply withdraws his already extended hand or, in the case of an object of special interest (his bottle, for example), begins to cry or scream with disappointment. He reacts, therefore, as if the object had been reabsorbed [p. 14].

After reaching the stage of object permanence, the infant will actively search for a missing object after it has disappeared from sight. In Piaget's terminology, this retained image is usually called the "permanent object" (Piaget and Inhelder, 1969, pp. 32–33). The acquisition of object permanence is an important developmental step, for now the infant has learned that an object (the phenomenologic object that is part of the shifting "tableaux" of the infant's experience) has an existence that is independent of his perception of it. The question—one with hidden metaphysical connotations—is whether or not this working map of the world should be called a "representation."

In ordinary English, the word "representation" is defined as a "likeness or image" that gives an impression of the original; philosophically, this definition is a derivative of the English empiricist tradition (Locke, Hume), which traces the origins of knowledge to perceptual experience. Thus, images were faint copies of perceptual experience, while ideas were "superfaint copies"; the difference between an idea and an image was merely in the degree of acuity (Furth, 1969, p. 71). As Furth says, "In the English language today representational thinking means distinctly thinking in images, of whatever type" (p. 71). In contrast, within the French Cartesian tradition, the expression "l'idée representative" became part of the French philosophical vocabulary, thus linking the concept of representation with symbolic capacity (Furth, 1969).[2] Following this usage, Piaget and Inhelder (1969) described sensorimotor intelligence as occurring "without the intervention of *representation* or thought" (p. 4, emphasis added). For an English reader, this statement is extremely confusing unless one understands that Piaget is writing within the French philosophic tradition that equates representation with thought (which is radically different from the common English language definition of representation as "a-picture-in-the-head"). For Piaget, a representation might best be considered as a (re)presentation, accomplished through symbolic mechanisms.

Problems begin to surface when one attempts to translate into English the observations and descriptions of Piaget about the cognitive development of the child. For example, in their well-known paper "The Concept of the Representational World," Sandler and Rosenblatt (1962) say:

> A representation can be considered to have a more or less enduring existence as an organization or schema which is constructed out of a multitude of impressions. . . .
> The development of these representations has been studied in detail by Piaget, who has shown that an enduring representation (as distinct from image) cannot be said to be well established before about the sixteenth month of life [p. 133].

Inasmuch as Sandler and Rosenblatt adopt the more restrictive Piagetian definition of representation that holds that "an enduring

---

[2] For a detailed exploration of the influence of Descartes upon Piaget and how it influences the concept of representation, see Furth's (1969) excellent chapter on "Piaget's Theory of Knowledge: The Nature of Representation and Interiorization."

representation (as distinct from image)" does not begin until the advent of symbol usage, the presymbolic synthesis of experience—Piaget's schema—cannot be called a representation. Consequently, the "representational world" as defined by Sandler and Rosenblatt does not take shape until the infant is able to use symbols (i.e., at about 16 months). This definition, a legacy of the French Cartesian tradition, creates a number of difficulties as we attempt to arrive at an agreed-upon vocabulary to describe the mind of an infant.

The difficulty with the term representation is well illustrated by the definition in *Psychoanalytic Terms and Concepts* (1990), published by the American Psychoanalytic Association: "A *psychic representation* is a more or less consistent reproduction within the mind of a perception of a meaningful thing or object" (p. 166). This definition is consistent with the premises of the English empiricist tradition, which traces the origins of knowledge to perception. The ambiguity emerges when we note that the "representational world," as defined by Sandler and Rosenblatt, does not consist of "psychic representations," as defined by the American Psychoanalytic Association. The absurdity of this is highlighted by the fact that this dictionary cites the Sandler and Rosenblatt article as one of only two references used to define "psychic representation." As I have tried to show, these ambiguities are not simply the result of carelessness or sloppy thinking; they trace their origins to unresolved issues about how human beings acquire knowledge (the subject matter of what philosophers call epistemology). As a result of these contradictory and confusing definitions, the concept of "representation" has lost much of its usefulness as a psychoanalytic term.

This brings us back to the problem of trying to define the concept of "representation." We know that all sentient animals form schematic working models of external reality inside their head. At the present time, there is no agreed-upon term to label these working maps of the world-out-there, primarily because the terminology becomes a vehicle for covert metaphysical debate. My own suggestion is to label these working maps of experience as "presymbolic schematic representations," an accurate, if lengthy, description; the word "presymbolic" defines the age of onset and the adjective "schematic" defines the process as an active, not passive, one. This usage would allow the word representation to eventually free itself from the philosophic connotations of the French Cartesian tradition and thus become a user-friendly term to describe the presymbolic working maps of experience. Serendipitously, this usage would also more or less coincide with the definition of psychic representation in the dictionary of the American Psychoanalytic Association. It is hoped that the term representational world will gradually fade away, to be replaced by a term that clearly differentiates the working map of presymbolic experience (what I would call representations) from the later-acquired network of concepts that the infant develops to describe that experience.

SUMMARY

Infants, like all organisms, are influenced by their experience and organize schematic models of the world that partially determine future behavior; affects (sometimes in a complex form such as moods of mistrust) represent how that experience is organized. Infants develop a working map of the world-out-there, which Piaget calls a schema and I recommend calling a presymbolic schematic representation. In short, presymbolic infants are simply little animals, governed by the same behavioral control systems that regulate other animals. Complex theoretical assumptions—drives, phantasies, identifications, internal objects, the dynamic unconscious, the self— are not needed to adequately describe and account for the infant's development. One does not need to hypothesize the ability for symbolic functioning to explain the "oral" phantasies that illustrate the important elements of this phase of development; rather, one can assume that the prereflective organization of experience becomes embedded in stable behavioral patterns (represented affectively by complex moods), which are then retrospectively encoded into phantasy at the time when the ability to use symbols comes "on-line."

The next chapter discusses how the emergence of the ability to use symbols leads to the fork in the road when human beings become a very different kind of animal. In turn, the use of symbols leads to a new type of affects that transcend their origins as affective signals through their ability to incorporate ideas. Love, hatred, envy, sadness, and guilt are good examples of affects that acquire symbolic meaning and thus become more easily "displaceable." In turn, this displaceability leads to the formation of phantasies that form the core of the dynamic unconscious. The complex interweave between affects and symbol usage is the subject matter of the balance of this book.

10

The Development of Thought

At some specific point in time, perhaps as early as eight to ten months of age, perhaps somewhat later, the program that will eventually lead to speech is activated. The exact timing of when humans make the symbolic turn is not critical to the hypotheses of this essay; suffice it to say that there is no proof (and, perhaps more important, not even a plausible argument) that symbol usage begins at birth. Consequently, symbolic functioning—what we usually call thinking—must be layered upon and eventually integrated into the smooth, presymbolic affective information processing of infancy. These two discrete ways of processing information form the experiential substrate of the "divided mind"; the necessity of integrating them results in the rapprochement crisis, the second biobehavioral reorganization (to be dealt with in the the next chapter).

NAMES, CATEGORIES, AND SYMBOLIC LOGIC

The evolution of the capacity for thought irrevocably changed the nature of man. In response to this change, his affective spectrum expanded far beyond that found in other animals. This change is magnificently illustrated by a quotation from the autobiography of Helen Keller (1902):

> One day, while I was playing with my new doll, Miss Sullivan put my big rag doll into my lap also, spelled "d-o-l-l" and tried to make me

169

understand that "d-o-l-l" applied to both. Earlier in the day we had a tussle over the words "m-u-g" and "w-a-t-e-r." Miss Sullivan had tried to impress it upon me that "m-u-g" is mug and that "w-a-t-e-r" is water, but I persisted in confounding the two. In despair she had dropped the subject for the time, only to renew it at the first opportunity. I became impatient at her repeated attempts and, seizing the new doll, I dashed it upon the floor. I was keenly delighted when I felt the fragments of the broken doll at my feet. Neither sorrow nor regret followed my passionate outburst. I had not loved the doll. In the still, dark world in which I lived there was no strong sentiment or tenderness. . . .

We walked down the path to the well-house, attracted by the fragrance of the honeysuckle with which it was covered. Someone was drawing water and my teacher placed my hand under the spout. As the cool stream gushed over one hand she spelled into the other the word water, first slowly, then rapidly. I stood still, my whole attention fixed upon the motions of her fingers. Suddenly I felt a misty consciousness as of something forgotten—a thrill of returning thought; and somehow the mystery of language was revealed to me. I knew then that "w-a-t-e-r" meant the wonderful cool something that was flowing over my hand. That living word awakened my soul, gave it light, hope, joy, set it free! There were barriers still, it is true, but barriers that could in time be swept away.

I left the well-house eager to learn. Everything had a name, and each name gave birth to a new thought. As we returned to the house every object which I touched seemed to quiver with life. That was because I saw everything with the strange, new sight that had come to me. On entering the door, I remembered the doll I had broken. I felt my way to the hearth and picked up the pieces. I tried vainly to put them together. Then my eyes filled with tears; for I realized what I had done, and for the first time I felt repentance and sorrow [pp. 35–37].

This poignant record reveals how Helen Keller, with the help of her gifted teacher, Anne Sullivan, discovered "the mystery of language." The experience of Keller, an experiment by nature unlikely to be repeated, offers unique testimony to the transforming power of symbolic thought on our affective life, for it compresses years of incremental changes into a few dramatic moments. Two new emotions emerge, love and sorrow. "I had not loved the doll [for love did not exist]. . . . my eyes filled with tears; for I realized what I had done, and for the first time I felt repentance and sorrow." In this transforming moment, Helen Keller became a human being.

As Keller points out, "Everything had a name, and each name gave birth to a new thought." Naming—the ability to attach a word/symbol to a discrete part of our experience—gives birth to the ability to think. With words, we can draw lines through the Heraclitean world of flux. Consequently, for a very long period of time people drew an obvious, but incorrect, conclusion that equated intelligence with the ability to speak. As Oliver Sacks—whose book *Seeing Voices* (1989) is an excellent introduction into the world of the deaf— has said, "Perhaps indeed this passionate misperception, or prejudice, went back to biblical days: the subhuman status of mutes was part of the Mosaic code, and it was reinforced by the biblical exaltation of the voice and ear as the one and true way in which man and God could speak. ('In the beginning was the Word')" (p. 15). The easy equation between linguistic/verbal means of representation and the ability to use symbols has been a major hindrance to the development of an adequate theory of mind.

These prejudices are deeply embedded in our language in phrases such as "deaf and dumb," where the word "dumb" has the twin meanings of "mute" and "stupid." These "common-sense" assumptions led to frightening consequences for the prelingually deaf, who were treated as little more than "dumb" animals. Sacks paints this moving portrait:

> The situation of the prelingually deaf, prior to 1750, was indeed a calamity: unable to acquire speech, hence "dumb" or "mute"; unable to enjoy free communication with even their parents and families; confined to a few rudimentary signs and gestures; cut off, except in large cities, even from the community of their own kind; deprived of literacy and education, all knowledge of the world; forced to do the most menial work; living alone, often close to destitution; treated by the law and society as little better than imbeciles—the lot of the deaf was manifestly dreadful [pp. 13–14].

It wasn't until the mid-18th century that things began to change. In France, the deplorable status of the deaf aroused the curiosity and the compassion of the *philosophes*. In response to their plight, Abbé Sicard asked the key questions:

> *Why* is the uneducated deaf person isolated in nature and unable to communicate with other men? *Why* is he reduced to this state of imbecility? Does his biological constitution differ from ours? Does he

not have everything he needs for having sensations, acquiring ideas, and combining them to do everything that we do? Does he not get sensory impressions from objects as we do? Are these not, as with us, the occasion of the mind's sensations and its acquired ideas? *Why* then does the deaf person remain stupid while we become intelligent? [quoted in Sacks, 1989, pp. 14–15, quoting Lane].

As is often the case, to formulate the question clearly is to grasp the answer, to understand that the problem lies in the lack of access to a symbolic means of communication. Sicard theorized that the deaf person has "no symbols for fixing and combining ideas . . . that there is a total communication-gap between him and other people" (Sacks, 1989, p. 15).

In response to these ideas, Abbé de l'Epée began to study the indigenous sign language of the poor deaf who roamed Paris. As Sacks suggests, perhaps the vocation of the Abbé powerfully influenced him to undertake this pioneering study: he "could not bear to think of the souls of the deaf-mute living and dying unshriven, deprived of the Catechism, the Scriptures, the Word of God" (p. 16). Approaching the problem with a different attitude, he began by acquiring their language, something that rarely had been done before; then, by associating signs with pictures and written words, he taught them to read. This system of "methodical signs"—a combination of their own sign language and signed French grammar—enabled deaf students to read and write French and thus acquire an education. By the time of his death in 1789, he was instrumental in establishing 21 schools for the deaf throughout France and Europe.

Most people think of a sign language as something rudimentary and primitive, perhaps akin to our attempts at pantomime when we play the game of charades. As a result of the unconscious equation of verbal speech with symbol usage, it is profoundly counterintuitive to imagine that a language can exist totally without words. Thus, even de l'Epée did not understand that Sign—in and of itself—could be a complete language; hence, his "methodical signs" were an intermediate step between French and Sign. ("Sign" is the generic name for all indigenously arising sign languages.) It was not until 60 years later that Sicard's pupil, Roch-Ambriose Bébian, recognized that Sign was a complete language with its own grammar, syntax, and semantics, and threw out the "methodical signs" and their imported French grammar (Sacks, 1989, p. 20). If prelingually deaf children are encouraged to learn Sign language—which, in practice, means that they are raised with adults and other children fluent in Sign—then they are able to reach their full intellectual potential.

With access to Sign, the deaf often develop a powerful hunger for names. The example of Jean Massieu, one of Sicard's first and best-known students, is illustrative. Deaf from birth, Massieu had virtually no education until he was almost 14. Sicard's description of Massieu's education is fascinating. He started by drawing pictures of objects and then asked Massieu to do the same. Then, to introduce him to language, Sicard wrote the name of the object under the picture. At first, Massieu was "utterly mystified. He had no idea how lines that did not appear to picture anything could function as an image for objects and represent them with such accuracy and speed" (Sacks, 1989, p. 47). Then, in an experience very similar to that of Helen Keller, Massieu understood that an object or an image might be represented by a *name*. As a result, he acquired a tremendous hunger for names. Sicard gives a moving description of how, as the two took walks together, Massieu demanded to know the names of everything:

> We visited an orchard to name all the fruits. We went into a woods to distinguish the oak from the elm . . . the willow from the poplar, eventually all the other inhabitants. . . . He didn't have enough tablets and pencils for all the names with which I filled his dictionary, and his soul seemed to expand and grow with these innumerable denominations. . . . Massieu's visits were those of a landowner seeing his rich domain for the first time [quoted in Sacks, 1989, p. 47].

With the acquisition of names, Sicard felt there was a radical change in Massieu's relationship to the world. He had become like Adam: "This newcomer to earth was a stranger on his own estates, which were being restored to him as he learned their names" (quoted in Sacks, 1989, p. 47).

The experiences of Jean Massieu and Helen Keller are remarkably similar. As Helen Keller (1902) put it in a single dramatic insight, "the mystery of language was revealed to me. . . . Everything had a name, and each name gave birth to a new thought." Why is naming so important? Naming allows an individual to move from the concrete—the realm of perception, sensations, objects, and images—to the world of concepts, which can then be manipulated through the process of symbolic logic. (In all probability, symbolic logic codifies what Chomsky, 1957, refers to as "deep structure.") As Vygotsky

(1934) points out, "A word does not refer to a single object, but to a group or to a class of objects. *Each word is therefore already a generalization*. Generalization is a verbal act of thought and reflects reality in quite another way than sensation and perception reflect it" (p. 6, emphasis added). Thus, naming is the behavioral manifestation of the internal process Vygotsky calls "generalization."

The process of generalization is most easily observed in the everyday nouns we use as categories, words such as cat, dog, baby, boy, and girl. For example, what do we mean when we use the word cat? An animal is a cat, or so it would seem, because it in some way participates in something common to the nature of all cats. This implicit recognition of the generalization process is the basis of Plato's theory of "forms" or "ideas." He hypothesized that the word cat means a certain ideal cat, *the cat,* created by God and unique (Russell, 1945, p. 121). Any particular cat participates in the nature of the cat, but more or less imperfectly. It is only because of these imperfections that there can be so many of them. *The cat* is real; the particular cats, your cat, my cat, the cat next door, are only apparent (Russell, 1945, p. 122). Generalization carried to its logical conclusion results in idealization. Although Plato's doctrine of forms may be flawed by his assumption that the ideal cat exists somewhere in the universe, as an observation about the capacity for generalization that is present in our ordinary language, his doctrine powerfully states one of the key problems we must solve if we hope to understand the mystery of language.

The example of deaf mutes who acquire language—there are dozens of examples—proves a simple point: the capacity for symbol usage is independent of the means of representation. This hypothesis has been powerfully reinforced by the work of Petitto and Marentette (1991), who found that deaf babies of deaf parents "babble" with their hands in the same rhythmic, repetitive fashion that hearing infants babble vocally. Just as hearing infants experiment with a few key phrases such as "mamamamama" or "dadadadada," so deaf infants use the same motion over and over, including one that looks like the gesture "O.K." All children (barring the neurologically impaired) pass in stepwise fashion through the same developmental sequence, beginning with simple cooing at approximately five to seven months. Structured babbling emerges at eight to ten months, and the first words are spoken at twelve to fifteen months. The acquisition of language requires a special combination of capacity plus experience. It is impossible to acquire language without the hard-wired program that contains its rules (Chomsky's deep structure), but the ability to use the program can be activated only by another person who already possesses linguistic power and competence. It is only through this transaction (Vygotsky, 1934, would say "negotiation") that language can be achieved.

There are compelling reasons to believe that the first words that we acquire are "no" and "yes." The importance of no and yes was emphasized by Spitz (1967), who hypothesized that the head shaking "no" of 15 months was the first use of symbolic speech, a concrete manifestation of the ability to think:

> The word "No" implies no comparison with an existing representation. It is what logicians call an algorithmic symbol, just like the minus sign in mathematics. Algorithmic symbols, such as the "symbol of negation," are specifically reserved for interindividual communication [p. 87].

The ability to use the word "no" is of critical importance in the development of language, for it heralds the arrival of yes/no coding, which is the key element in using symbolic processes. As Spitz says, yes and no operate as algorithmic symbols, similar to the plus and minus signs of mathematics. These two words, the verbal equivalent of pointing with a finger, allow us to create categories through the process of generalization: "*Yes*, it fits into the category; *No*, it doesn't." Thus, no and yes are not categories themselves but are the method for forming categories, the invisible markers that enable us to draw lines through the Heraclitean world of flux.

DRIVE THEORY RECONSIDERED

Stripped to its essentials, Freud's theory of instinctual drive *(Trieb)* attempts to account for the origin of what we call phantasies. Most psychoanalytic theorists would hold that drive theory reached its final form in 1923, when Freud incorporated the drives into the tripartite (ego-id-superego) model of the mind. I strongly disagree. I believe that his 1925 paper "Negation" provided the key that clarifies the internal logic of his theory of drive. In that paper, only five pages long but reading with the terse elegance of a mathematical proof, Freud writes:

> The antithesis between subjective and objective does not exist from the first. It only comes into being from the fact that thinking

possesses the capacity to bring before the mind once more something that has once been perceived, by reproducing it as a presentation without the external object having still to be there [p. 237].

In other words, thinking frees us from the immediacy of the situation. Freud then discusses the importance of the "symbol of negation" and the word "no." In the last paragraphs of this paper, he says,

> The study of judgement affords us, perhaps for the first time, an insight into the origin of an intellectual function from the interplay of the primary instinctual impulses. Judging is a continuation, along lines of expediency, of the original process by which the ego took things into itself or expelled them from itself, according to the pleasure principle. The polarity of judgement appears to correspond to the opposition of the two groups of instincts which we have supposed to exist. Affirmation—as a substitute for uniting—belongs to Eros; negation—the successor to expulsion—belongs to the instinct of destruction. . . . But the performance of the function of judgement is not made possible until the creation of the symbol of negation has endowed thinking with a first measure of freedom from the consequences of repression and, with it, from the compulsion of the pleasure principle.
>   This view of negation fits in very well with the fact that in analysis we never discover a 'no' in the unconscious and that recognition of the unconscious on the part of the ego is expressed in a negative formula [pp. 238–239].

If I am interpreting Freud correctly, he seems to be saying that thought does not exist at the beginning of life. He says, "With the help of the symbol of negation [i.e., no], *thinking* frees itself from the restrictions of repression and enriches itself with material that is indispensable for its proper functioning" (p. 236, emphasis added). In the final paragraph, he adds, "This view of negation fits in very well with the fact that in analysis we never discover a 'no' in the unconscious" (p. 239). In other words, drives, now reconceptualized as affirmation and negation, lead to secondary process. The key intermediate step is the word "no," the symbol of negation. If the paper "Negation" represents the culmination of Freud's thinking about the theory of drives, then *Trieb* can be most usefully conceptualized as an attempt to account for the origins of thought. It is these beginnings of thought that lead to the formation of phantasies and the dynamic unconscious.

Freud did not give the same attention to the word yes that he gave to no. They are, however, of equal importance. The connection between love, excitement, sexuality, and yes may be less obvious, but it is beautifully captured in the closing lines of Molly's interior monologue, the final chapter of James Joyce's *Ulysses:*

> . . . and the night we missed the boat at Algeciras and the watchman going about serene with his lamp and O that awful deepdown torrent O and the sea the sea crimson sometimes like fire and the glorious sunsets and the figtrees in the Alameda gardens yes and all the queer little streets and pink and blue and yellow houses and the rosegardens and the jessamine and geraniums and cactuses and Gibraltar as a girl where I was a Flower of the mountain yes when I put the rose in my hair like the Andalusian girls used or shall I wear a red yes and how he kissed me under the Moorish wall and I thought well as well him as another and then I asked him with my eyes to ask again yes and then he asked me would I yes to say yes my mountain flower and first I put my arms around him yes and drew him down to me so he could feel my breasts all perfume yes and his heart was going like mad and yes I said yes I will Yes [1922, pp. 643–644].

In this superbly crafted passage, one can palpably feel the linkages of affirmation, sexuality, and yes. The algorithmic symbols "yes" and "no" not only allow us to draw lines through the world of inchoate experience, but also, at a very deep level, form the ground for our primary adjectival categories, good and bad. Idealizing love and enduring hatred acquire their absoluteness from the absoluteness of the yes/no dichotomy.

In the paper "Negation," Freud (1925) began a line of inquiry that *could* have led him to clarify the distinction between drive and affects. Inevitably, this would have resulted in a revision of his theory of affects. One might begin by thinking of "the drives" as the moving force behind the second biobehavioral reorganization. Defined this way, the term drive becomes an important conceptual tool in describing the epigenetic push toward the divided-mind organization of affects *and* thought. With this as a starting point—and admittedly this is highly speculative—one could hypothesize that the negative quality of the negative affects (disgust, anger, fear) gradually becomes differentiated from the affect itself, until eventually it emerges as the first word: No! In other words, we get to "no" through the process of distilling the negative quality (i.e., negation) from the embedded content of the negative affects. Similarly, the valence of the positive affects (excitement, joy) would differentiate through affirmation to "yes." I suggest that this process could be described with reasonable accuracy as *affective polarization*. If this hypothesis is correct, then thought would begin to emerge through the differentiation of the positive and negative valence of the affect to form the no/yes algorithm that is fundamental to the process of categorization. This formulation would bridge what I take to be the fundamental thrust of Freud's late theory of drives as implied in the paper on "Negation" and the more recent work in cognitive psychology.

SYMBOLS AND MEANING

Meaning is not a feature of the world itself but a property of the complex matrix of thought that we construct to parallel reality. This process is illustrated by what philosophers call truth tables and what psycholinguists call a Distinctive Feature Matrix. These tables show how words create meaning:

	Woman	Girl	Boy	Man
Animate	+	+	+	+
Human	+	+	+	+
Adult	+	−	−	+
Female	+	+	−	−
Male	−	−	+	+

Thus, the meaning of the word boy may be expressed as: animate, human, not adult, male. One of the appeals of the matrix is that it demonstrates the interrelationships of our word knowledge; for example, that "man" and "boy" are closer in meaning than "man" and "girl." Psycholinguists have found that a child usually does not learn a complete meaning all at once; rather, the child learns the definition piecemeal (Sharpless, 1985). Evidence for this incremental learning is found in the phenomenon of *overgeneralization*, in which a word is too broadly defined because only some of its defining features are discerned (Clark, 1973). For example, a child may apply the word "dog" to all quadrupeds because only the defining features of animate, nonhuman, and four-legged have been learned; the specific characteristics that allow dogs to be differentiated from other quadrupeds may take additional time.

In trying to understand the "meaning of meaning," one should note that the word meaning is widely—and incorrectly—used to describe any event to which we attribute causal significance. For example, when a chick scurries for cover at the sight of a hawk, the hawk does not "mean" danger to the chick; rather, the hawk is a behavioral signal that activates a preprogrammed (i.e., instinctive) sequence of behavior. When a Pavlovian-conditioned dog cowers at the sound of a bell in anticipation of an electric shock, the bell does not mean that "a shock is coming" to the dog; rather, the bell acts as a *signal,* and the dog has learned that a painful event will follow. (Technically, the bell has significance, not meaning.) When a five-month-old infant recognizes his mother and becomes excited in anticipation of being fed, does mother's presence have "meaning" for the infant? Again, the answer is no; the mother's presence is a signal that certain, in this case pleasurable, sequences of behavior are likely to follow her appearance. These are all examples of cause-and-effect sequences about which we are likely to think and talk in terms of meaning. Unfortunately, this tendency to overgeneralize the definition of meaning leaves us very confused if we are trying to construct a theory to account for the origins of thought.

Let us return to the word "symbol." Laplanche and Pontalis (1967) point out that:

> The etymological sense of "symbol" is well known: for the Greeks the όύμβολον was a means of identification (between two members of the same sect, for example) consisting of the two halves of a broken object that can be fitted back together. The notion that it is the *link* that creates the meaning is thus already present in the original conception [p. 445].

As originally used, linking was inherent in the term symbol. Usefully defined, the word "meaning" should be limited to describing the link between the symbol and its referent.

Language—the naming process—creates the categories with which we think; then we manipulate these categories through the process of symbolic logic. The father of symbolic logic was George Boole, an English philosopher who created what is known as a logical calculus. The true importance of Boole's logical calculus, or the algebra of classes as it came to be known, was unappreciated until it was pointed out in 1910 by Bertrand Russell and Alfred North Whitehead. They argued that "symbols" can be defined specifically as a shorthand way of talking about classes that are formed by our language; once formed, these classes can be manipulated by the processes of symbolic logic. Fortunately, symbolic logic is not nearly as difficult as it may seem; basically, it deals primarily with how categories can be manipulated by the connective words of our

180   *II.   Affects as Process*

language. Stripped of its mystery, symbolic logic illustrates how categories, once formed, can be added ("and"), subtracted ("but not"), and sequenced ("if-then") by these connective words. John Venn, a British logician, described how these logical ideas could be put into visual forms, which now bear the name of Venn diagrams. Analytic philosophers have demonstrated how these relationships can be arranged in truth tables. In the early 1940s, Claude Shannon demonstrated how electrical circuitry could best be described by Boolean logic. As one might expect, the true/false system of Boolean logic exactly parallels the on/off switches of electrical circuitry. This discovery laid the groundwork for the invention of the digital computer, the foundation of the "information revolution" of today (Halacy, 1962, p. 106). The processes of symbolic logic, then, can be represented mathematically by the formulas of Boolean algebra, by the truth tables of philosophers, pictorially by Venn diagrams, linguistically by no/yes, and electrically by off/on.

SUMMARY

Thinking is best defined as a specific process that uses the no/yes coding pattern to form categories. Behaviorally, the emergence of the infant's capacity to think is demonstrated most dramatically by his ability to talk, to begin to attach names to objects. Once these categories are formed, he learns to manipulate them through the process of symbolic logic. The process of forming categories (naming) and then manipulating them through the process of symbolic logic is a basic description of what we call thinking.

11

Rapprochement

Margaret Mahler and her coworkers (1975) proposed a theory that attempts to synthesize Freud's drive theory and the development of the sense of self. During the first five months of life—which Mahler calls the autistic and symbiotic phases—the sense of self does not exist but is first fused with, and then in a symbiotic relationship with, the self of the mother.[1] Borrowing Freud's "egg within a protective shell" metaphor, Mahler conceptualizes the self as "hatching" at approximately five months of age. This event—manifested by a permanently alert sensorium while the child is awake (pp. 53–54)—leads to the name of the book, *The Psychological Birth of the Human Infant*. The first phase of separation and individuation—approximately five to nine months—is called the differentiation phase. With the subsidence of the fear response ("stranger anxiety") at eight to nine months, the infant enters into what Mahler calls the "practicing subphase." During this period of time, the "precious" few months between the decline of stranger anxiety and rapprochement crisis, the child is quite resilient to adversity (p. 71). If things have gone "well enough" (paraphrasing Winnicott's concept of the good-enough mother), "the world is the junior toddler's oyster," and the child seems relatively impervious to "knocks and falls and other frustrations, such as a toy being grabbed by another child" (p. 71).

---

[1] Contemporary researchers have criticized Mahler's conception of the "autistic" phase and have insisted that even the neonate readily distinguishes self from other.

The practicing subphase marks the flowering of the presymbolic phase of development. At 18 to 20 months, the child enters the psychological turmoil of the rapprochement crisis, which lasts for 4 to 6 months. When the rapprochement crisis is resolved, it is followed by an integrative phase, which Mahler describes as "on the road to object constancy" (circa 24–36 months).

The thesis of this chapter is that the rapprochement crisis is triggered by the emergence of the capacity for symbolic thought. This phase of development is limited to human beings; it does not occur elsewhere in the animal kingdom, even among the higher primates. The uniqueness of the rapprochement crisis was recognized by Mahler, who commented, "The rapprochement struggle has its origin in the *species-specific* human dilemma that arises out of the fact that, on the one hand, the toddler is obliged, by the rapid maturation of his ego, to recognize his separateness, while, on the other hand, he is as yet unable to stand alone and will continue to need his parents for many years to come" (p. 229). She added, "At that time, from about the fifteenth to sixteenth month, there develops in the toddler the *definite awareness of his own separateness*" (p. 228, emphasis added). This "*awareness* of . . . separateness," I would emphasize, cannot refer to the simple fact of physical separateness. From a very early age, all mammals recognize that they are physically separate from their mothers; if they did not, it would be impossible for them to learn to control their own bodies. To continue the comparison, we can also note the following: all mammals are born, are nursed and cared for, acquire physical skills and stamina, hone various coping mechanisms, and then strike out on their own. Although the trajectory is not always smooth—the young are sometimes ejected from the nest despite their vigorous protest—there are no significant signs of *internal* turmoil. Therefore, in seeking the origins of the rapprochement crisis, one must look to the acquisition of the ability to form concepts, which, in turn, leads to an increased awareness of one's own separateness. Mahler points out that the infant is struggling with the "*realization* that mother's wishes seemed to be by no means always identical with his own—or contrariwise, that his own wishes did not always coincide with mother's" (p. 90, emphasis added). In this formulation, the word "realization" carries hidden metaphysical weight because it carries the implication that *the infant is recognizing in a new way* the importance of something that he already knows. This change in awareness comes from thinking; it is this *conceptual differentiation* from the mother that leads to the rapprochement crisis.

The "crisis" begins at approximately 15 to 18 months of age with a subtle change in the quality of the child's relationship with his mother. Mahler comments:

> During the practicing period as described, mother was the "home base" to which the child returned often in times of need—need for food, need for comforting, or need for "refueling" when tired or bored. But during this period mother did not seem to have been recognized as a separate person in her own right. Somewhere around 15 months, mother was no longer just "home base"; she seemed to be turning into a person with whom the toddler wished to share his ever-widening discoveries of the world [p. 90].

As the child begins to think and recognizes that mother is a separate human being with thoughts and ideas of her own, this, in turn, catalyzes a number of other changes. One is a subtle shift in the affective response of the infant to loss of the mother. Before the rapprochement crisis, the mother's absence led to a kind of wilting or "low-keyedness" in the infant. After the child begins to think, the realization of his separateness leads to sadness, which requires a great deal of strength to bear (Zetzel, 1965).

In terms of affects, the initiation of symbolic functioning serves to catalyze the change in the infant's reaction to mother's loss from a mild grief response (a mood) to the new emotion of sadness. This leads to an interesting question: how does thinking enlarge our affective range generally? An exploration of this question may throw some light on the differences in symbolic and nonsymbolic processing. Without symbols, life is experienced like a motion picture, an ever-shifting tableau of perceptions, sensations, feelings, and memories. Heraclitus, the ancient Greek philosopher, described this as a "world of flux." The use of a symbol freezes a moment in time, similar to a still photograph, allowing us to focus our attention on what previously was transient. This ability to "stop the process" is what makes humans different. For however brief a moment in time, the infant is forced by the mechanism of thought to reexperience the importance of mother. Thus, sadness is not simply grief, but *grief plus the added knowledge of how important the loss of mother would be*. Through the process of what Freud called "trial action"—running through a sequence of events without actually doing them—one can imagine the loss, even though it has not taken place. Returning to Mahler's theorizing about the origins of the rapprochement crisis, one could add that it is not the separateness, but the necessity of translating the fact of separateness into conceptual terms, that catalyzes the rapprochement crisis.

Another change initiated by the rapprochement phase is a sudden increase in interest in the father (Abelin, 1971; Mahler et al., 1975, p. 91). Prior to this time, the father may have been somewhat important, but as Mahler says, "from very early on [the father] belongs to an entirely different category of love objects from mother" (p. 91). The increase in importance of the father initiates what Mahler calls the "widening of the emotional range and the beginning of empathy" (p. 97). I suggest that there is a direct connection between the onset of the use of symbols and this widening of the emotional range. As the infant begins to think, he begins to become aware of the distinction between the mother who fulfills a caretaker function and the mother who gradually becomes an individual in her own right. It is this ability to respond to the mother *as an individual* that allows for the possibility of the "widening of the emotional range and the beginning of empathy." Thus, if the relationship with the mother is "good enough," then the child is encouraged to form a relationship with the father. From there the child will then progressively branch out to form friendships with siblings, neighborhood companions, and others. But if the relationship with the mother is experienced as too painful, not "good enough," then the infant will adopt mechanisms that protect against further hurt. Thus, the infant's ability to form a reasonably good relationship with the father is a fairly good predictor of whether the child will continue to develop emotionally.

The observations that led Mahler to describe the rapprochement crisis have been verified by dozens, if not hundreds, of researchers. The difficulty is in trying to account for it theoretically. In her introduction to her discussion of the rapprochement phase of development, Mahler mentions Piaget's finding that representational intelligence, culminating in symbolic play and speech, begins at the same time (p. 76). Rather than pursuing the obvious lead that the rapprochement crisis is secondary to this cognitive development, she attempts—unsuccessfully—to harmonize her work with Freud's theory of drives. For example, she assumes that the relative ease of the practicing subphase is secondary to the child's "narcissism" (p. 71) or "delusion of omnipotence" (p. 228). If this assumption is correct, then Mahler is abandoning Piaget's timetable concerning the onset of symbolic usage and assuming a capacity for omnipotent phantasies during the 9-to-15-month age range. A more reasonable assumption is that the practicing subphase is simply the result of the increasing confidence that accompanies the growth of physical skills and psychological maturation absent the capacity for phantasies; this smooth developmental unfolding is interrupted by the rapprochement crisis, which is secondary to the turmoil caused by the ability to think, thereby catalyzing the formation of unconscious phantasies. Thus, the rapprochement crisis is not caused by any upsurge of any specific phantasies; rather, it is caused by the emergence of the capacity for phantasy itself, including omnipotent, aggressive, and castration phantasies.

SUMMARY

If one compares human beings with other mammals, one can observe that their development is functionally parallel until approximately the end of the practicing subphase. At this point, human infants enter the rapprochement crisis, and their development begins to significantly deviate from that of the other mammals. For all practical purposes, the psychological development of mammals can be viewed as simply a continuation of the practicing subphase with the later additions of motivational systems associated with dominance hierarchies, reproduction, and caring for the young. As the rapprochement crisis brings an end to the practicing subphase, the human infant begins to think and enters the phase of development that is quite different from that of the rest of the animal kingdom. Not only must human infants become competent at using their bodies (the challenge of the practicing subphase), they must become competent in using their minds. On the evolutionary path, the rapprochement crisis (18–24 months) is the fork in the road, where humans take a separate path from the rest of the animal kingdom.

12

Object Relations and Object Constancy

The rapprochement crisis is the behavioral manifestation of the second biobehavioral reorganization, the psychological turmoil that results from the struggle to integrate symbolic thought onto the previous organization of core emotions and motivational systems. This reorganization is followed by the stage that Mahler and her colleagues (1975) call "consolidation of individuality and the beginnings of emotional object constancy," which takes place between 24 and 36 months (p. 109). According to Mahler's observations and developmental timetable, the achievement of "object constancy" (what Mahler calls "emotional object constancy" and what Fraiberg, 1969, calls "libidinal object constancy") is part of the consolidation subphase of development that follows the turmoil of the rapprochement crisis. The difficulty in trying to understand this phase of development ("on the road to object constancy") is that it depends on having agreed-upon definitions to work with: what is an "object," and what do we mean when we say that a person has achieved "object constancy"? Without agreement on what these terms mean, it is next to impossible to even begin to understand the extraordinary complex changes that are taking place.

As used in the psychoanalytic literature, the term "object" is vague, confusing and, at times, contradictory. The depth of the problem can be understood by reviewing the definition of the term object in *Psychoanalytic Terms and Concepts* (1990). Under the heading "object," the editors list the following concepts: internal object; object representation; object relations; object relationship; part object; libidinal object; object cathexis; object libido; object

187

choice; idealized object; object loss; transitional object; good object/ bad object; and object constancy. At the present time, there are no commonly accepted definitions for *any* of these terms; one author may use a term in a way that is quite different from another. Consequently, the meaning of these terms must be determined by their context and usage, which may not be immediately apparent from the reading of a specific passage but requires a working familiarity with the entire corpus of an author's work. The major reason for this confusion is because the term "object" is seldom used as a specific concept with an agreed-upon referent; rather, it is usually used as a code word—a linguistic banner—to identify a body of psychoanalytic theory known as object relations.

Part of the difficulty in arriving at a clear conception of object constancy derives from the tendency to confuse object permanence with object constancy.[1] Although these two terms appear to be similar, in fact they belong to two different vocabularies, with subtle, often unrecognized, differences between them. Object permanence, a concept derived from developmental psychology, especially Piaget, refers to a specific maturational step that occurs at approximately eight months of age. In contrast, object constancy is a traditional psychoanalytic term, first introduced by Hartmann (1952), that refers to the ability of the child to maintain an image that endures and remains stable "independent of the state of needs" (Hartmann, 1953, p. 181). (This is usually couched in the language of drive theory.)

Object constancy clearly presupposes the capacity for object permanence; consequently, it *must* reflect a later developmental achievement. Trying to specify the achievement of object constancy is very difficult because the critical terms used to describe this phase of development—object, internal object, object relations, and inner world—are themselves vague and confusing. Consequently, we begin with an effort to define these terms. Only then can we try to understand the developmental achievement which is known as "object constancy."

OBJECTS AND OBJECT RELATIONS

Long before Freud began to elaborate his theory of drives, the word object had a number of meanings. The first, and clearly the most

---

[1] For an excellent review tracing the historical roots of the term object constancy and the interweave with Piagetian developmental psychology, see Fraiberg (1969).

general, dictionary definition is "anything that is visible or tangible and is stable in form" (*Random House Dictionary,* 1966). In this usage of the term, the knowing subject is contrasted with the perceived object. Linguistically, this usage of the term object corresponds to the formation of a category; the part of speech used to identify the category is usually a noun. This sorting of experience into what might be called phenomenologic objects—a dog, a table, a mountain—is familiar to us and does not cause any particular difficulty. Another closely related usage of the term object has the word as a synonym for the word target, as in "the object of my affection." This usage is also well captured in the dictionary definition: "a thing, person, or matter to which thought or action is directed." In many ways, this usage is similar to the first, but it adds a qualitative dimension that now the object has special importance. In the paper "Instincts and Their Vicissitudes," Freud (1915a) used the term object in this way, as one of the four defining characteristics of a drive; the drive object was the person or thing that satisfied the instinctual need. Thus, the object (target) of the instincts of self-preservation could be the ingestion of food or some other substance that satisfied a bodily need; the object of the libidinal drive was the mother. Within this theoretical framework, the object, now more restrictively defined as a "drive object," is conceptualized as "the target for or releasor of an instinctual trend" (Panel, 1985, p. 168). As Freud (1915a) first used the term, a drive object is not particularly difficult to understand; basically, it is little more than a phenomenologic object of special importance (i.e., an object as target). Used in this way, the term phenomenologic object and drive object are simply part of the vocabulary describing things of special importance in the world-out-there.

This brings us to the key issue of this chapter: what is the meaning of the term object, particularly as used in phrases such as internal object and object relations? As these concepts play an exceedingly important role in what is known as object relations theory, let us examine the matter in greater detail. At four months of age (if not before), the infant knows his mother, as manifested by increased excitement when she comes into the room. At approximately eight months of age, the infant reaches the stage of object permanence, which means that the infant can keep the mother in mind even though she is out of the room. I call this working map of the world a presymbolic schematic representation (see chapter 9). At approximately 18 months of age, the infant can go further and think (and fantasize) about the mother, not only in her absence but also in contradistinction to any experience he has ever had with her. This, to me, properly demarcates the era during which the infant can begin to have "internal objects." If the concept is to have any useful meaning, *then internal object must refer to symbolic constructs.* (Otherwise, the term internal object would simply point out the trivial and obvious: that everything that is important to the infant is recreated in his head in some kind of working model.) Simply stated, internal objects must refer to our first concepts, the infant's first attempts to categorize and conceptualize what is important in his world. Following this definition, object relations are certainly not the infant's first experience with relationships, *but his first attempts to symbolize or conceptualize that experience.* Using these definitions, what is usually referred to as object relations theory (from Melanie Klein to Otto Kernberg) is an elaborate theory about the development of thought, how the capability for symbolic usage reorganizes experience and creates new experience, and the therapeutic ramifications that flow from the ability to process information in two different ways.

Unfortunately, the term object relations is routinely used to describe *both* the relationship between the subject and another person and the symbolic encoding of this relationship, thus blurring the distinction between the two. Until this distinction is clarified, it is hard to imagine that we will make much progress in building an adequate theory of thought formation.

THE INNER AND OUTER WORLD

Although it might not be readily apparent on first reading, the difference between the outer (or external) world and the inner (or internal) world corresponds to the same distinction between presymbolic and postsymbolic functioning. We know for a certainty that all sentient animals (those capable of paying attention) begin, at the moment of birth, to construct a working map of their world that roughly corresponds to their experience with the external environment. Consequently, we usually do not draw a distinction between the inner and outer world when we talk about animals; we simply assume that the inner mother is little more than the synthesized experience of the outer mother. If the inner world of an animal should interest us at all, it would very likely be for what it could tell us about neurophysiological functioning. With people, however, the distinction between the inner world and the outer world does not contrast the outer world of external reality with the inner world of neurophysiologic processing. Rather, this distinction refers to the fact that human beings have a hidden inner life that cannot be easily accounted for by direct experience with outer reality. This is the inner world of imagination.

One of the best examples of the discrepancy between outer and inner was Freud's discovery that some of his patients' "memories" were not memories at all, but phantasies. As a consequence of this discovery, psychoanalysts began to develop a working vocabulary to describe this inner world as well as a set of theories to account for its origins. This task set the metaphysical agenda for psychoanalytic theory. Many of the original psychoanalytic terms—*in*ternalization, *in*trojection/*in*troject,*in*corporation—stronglysuggestthisinner/outer distinction. This journey inward was followed further by Melanie Klein, who began to talk about the *in*ner world, *in*ternal objects, and *in*ternal object relations. Thus we are led to the key question: what is the process that catalyzes the development of this inner world? There is only one reasonable answer to this question. As the infant begins to develop the ability to think and use symbols, he inevitably begins to translate all the important information of his experience— both perceptive and affective—into symbolic form. Consequently, an inner world of symbols must arise as the infant struggles to develop a network of concepts that parallels the concrete working map (what I have called a presymbolic schematic representation) of the world that has formed as the result of an interaction with it. Thus, the words inner (and internal) and outer (and external) become unrecognized code words for talking about how symbolic processing begins to construct a network of concepts that parallels the world of direct experience.

OBJECT CONSTANCY

In the same way that a child cannot be said to walk when he takes his first step, so he cannot be described as being able to use symbols when he thinks his first thought or says his first word. The child's first concepts, like his first steps, are not likely to be particularly stable; this is particularly so because they cannot be defined by other concepts. Let me invoke a spatial metaphor. If an explorer discovers a new land, he must begin by charting the territory, a task that is not accomplished all at once. (Remember the early maps of America, with the land to the west simply labeled "unknown" or "unexplored.") The infant's initial charting of experience must be similar, with large areas of experience that cannot be conceptualized. For example, anyone reading this book has a vocabulary of thousands of words (and each word is itself a concept). Therefore, it would not be particularly difficult for any reader to come up with a working definition of the word mother that is a reasonable approximation of the dictionary definition: "1) a woman who has borne a child. 2) the female parent of a plant or animal. 3) that which gives birth to something . . . or nurtures in the manner of a mother." This definition depends on a working knowledge of other words/concepts— woman, child, parent, female, birth/borne, nurture—which the reader already knows. A child who is just learning to think, however, has not yet mastered any of these terms; therefore, he cannot use them to hold onto as he struggles to *create for the first time* the concept "mother."

In terms of cognitive development, what is called object constancy describes the phase of symbol development and usage when the child has achieved useful and reliable conceptual stability. To use a specific example, object constancy occurs when the *concept* of mother becomes stabilized enough that it can be reliably evoked when the access code, the word or thought "mother," brings the concept to mind with all the accompanying cognitive and affective colorations. If we return to the assumption that the rapprochement crisis is the behavioral manifestation of the ability to use symbols, then object constancy describes the consolidation phase of this process, when the newly acquired concepts are firmly connected with their specific referents. This serves to frame the key question: what is the connection between the infant's affective state and conceptual stability?

As will be developed in the next chapter, the advent of symbol usage catalyzes the development of a new type of affect, emotions that have acquired meaning. Specifically, now the infant can love (and idealize) his mother; in addition, he can also hate her. (As will be elaborated, rage plus the idea of badness leads to the formation of hatred.) The development of affects with meaning allows us to sharpen the question: what happens when the infant, perhaps only transiently, hates his mother? McDevitt (1972) suggests that in an 18- to 20-month-old infant, "the mental representation of the mother may be so buffeted by violent and angry feelings that the stability of this image, at least from the libidinal as opposed to the cognitive side, is disrupted" (quoted in Mahler et al., 1975, p. 111). In other words, high-intensity negative affects—hatred is the paradigm case— leads to a breakdown of conceptual stability. This assumption parallels our everyday observations about ourselves and others; we experience greater difficulty in maintaining our integrated state—"keeping our shit together"—when experiencing intense negative affects. This allows us to arrive at an operational definition of object constancy: object constancy in the developmental sense occurs when the infant achieves the ability to maintain a consistently available concept of the mother in the face of high-intensity negative affects such as rage and hatred. If development is satisfactory, this achievement occurs at the end of the consolidation phase of separation-individuation, which Mahler places at approximately 36 months of age.

SUMMARY

At somewhere around 10 to 12 months, the infant *begins* to acquire the ability to use symbols, a process crowned by the first spoken words at approximately 18 months; the ability to attach names to things leads to the formation of concepts. Nouns are the first type of speech the infant uses; typically, they describe phenomenologic objects in the world-out-there (Mama, Daddy, cat, etc.). As used in the psychoanalytic literature, the term internal object *must* refer to these first concepts; otherwise the term is simply redundant for a presymbolic schematic representation or it has no meaning at all. Similarly, the term object relations does not refer to the infant's first experience of relationship, but, rather, to his first attempts to symbolize or conceptualize that experience. If one holds to this definition of object, object constancy occurs when the infant achieves the ability to maintain the *concept* of his mother in his mind even when experiencing high-intensity negative affects—rage and hatred— directed toward her. In other words, object constancy (or its equivalents, libidinal object constancy and emotional object constancy) implies conceptual stability despite the presence of intense affectivity. The lack of clear, consistent definitions of these terms is unfortunate, because it prevents us from looking closely at a truly remarkable phenomenon: the birth of the process of thought.

13

Love, Hate, and the Dynamic Unconscious

In chapter 10, we began to investigate how the infant learns to use and manipulate symbols, a process we usually refer to as thinking. The necessity of integrating these two ways of processing information—affective and symbolic—leads to the turmoil of the rapprochement crisis, the second biobehavioral reorganization. The first part of speech the infant uses is nouns, attaching a name or a label to an object in the world-out-there. Consequently, it is not surprising that these first attempts at conceptualization are referred to as "internal objects." (The ambiguities surrounding the terms "object" and "object relations" are the subject matter of chapter 12.)

After learning to use nouns, the infant acquires the ability to use verbs and adjectives. Through the naming process, many sensations (hungry, thirsty, tired) and easily recognizable core emotions such as disgust (yucky) and fear (scary) acquire names. This process of attaching a name to an affect gives that affect *meaning*. It is important to recognize that, in the beginning, all affects function as adjectives (the hungry child, the yucky food, the scary dog). Consequently, the affective valence of these core affects becomes connected to the object that first evoked it. The necessary process of differentiating the stimulus from the evoked affect appears to be an important step in learning to think.

In this essay, the term "meaning" is used to define the relationship between the symbol (usually a word) and its referent. Within this definition, our core affects do not possess meaning as they are presymbolic signals. At first reading, this distinction may seem difficult to understand, primarily because we are used to describing all important events as "meaningful." Yet, when a chick sees a hawk in the sky, this does not "mean" danger; rather, the sight of the hawk serves as a specific signal that the chick is in a dangerous situation, thus activating prewired protective programs. The hawk is not a symbol, but, rather, activates a signaling system; technically, the sight of the hawk has significance, not meaning. While this distinction may seem pedantic, it is extremely important to remember that not all information is communicated by symbols that carry meaning.

LOVE AND HATE

The growth of the capacity for thought leads to the acquisition of a network of concepts that parallels the presymbolic world of experience. This adds a level of complexity to affective life far beyond that found in other animals and catalyzes the emergence of a set of new feelings that transcend their origins as affective signals through their ability to incorporate ideas and thus acquire meaning. Sometimes, this difference is phrased as the distinction between our core emotions (in place *prior* to our acquiring the ability to think) and complex emotions (which can only occur *after* we have learned to think). Love and hatred, which incorporate the ideas of "good" and "bad," are excellent examples of the process of forming complex emotions. As love and hatred play such an important role in psychoanalytic theory, let us review their development in some detail.

The infant and mother are reciprocally programmed to form a powerful attachment (a behavioral description) with one another. The adaptive purpose of attachment is to provide a mechanism that guarantees that the mother will try to take care of the infant and that the infant will attempt to stay with the mother. This attachment is monitored by feelings of affection; grief signals the loss of the attachment. In the background, more subtle feelings, which I have labeled as complex moods, begin to emerge that describe the *quality* of the relationship with the mother. Erikson (1959) described the background mood of the first 18 months as "trust versus mistrust." A feeling of trust signals that the relationship with the mother, and indirectly with life itself, is "good enough"; conversely, a feeling of mistrust indicates that it is "not good enough." Thus, the history of the relationship with the mother is concretely recorded in the subtle interweave of this complex affective tapestry. The ability to think is superimposed on this presymbolic character structure. The key concepts that lead to the formation of love and hatred are the ideas of "good" and "bad." Quite simply, love begins with the infant's affection for the mother but is transformed through the incorporation of the idea of idealized goodness into the complex affect we think of as "Love." Thus, the affect of love endows the beloved (the "object") with the *quality* of goodness.

Although it is easy enough to recognize the idealizing aspect of love, we sometimes forget that hatred depends on idealization in the same way that love does. The fundamental difference between rage and hatred is an extremely important one. Virtually all territorial species experience rage, but only man hates; only in a storybook does "an elephant never forget" (i.e., bear a grudge). In real life, animals do not brood or plot revenge. The capability for hatred emerges only with the acquisition of the power of symbolization, which allows the target of rage to be connected with the quality of badness. As love is affection *plus* the idea of goodness, hatred is rage *plus* the idea of badness.

Where do the categories of "good" and "bad" come from? It seems fairly reasonable that "good" begins with what the infant experiences as "good for me," and "bad" begins with what is "bad for me," a distinction that is made presymbolically by affective valencing. Thus, our "good" feelings would include the excitement at the prospect of being fed, the joyousness of play, and a more persistent, but subtle, feeling connected with a background of safety; our "bad" feelings would include frustration, disgust, fear, anger, and shame. Thus, it is highly likely that our hard-wired affective valencing— what Henry Krystal (1988) calls "hedonic tone"—forms the experiential substrate that is transformed into our first adjectival categories, good and bad. Inasmuch as our first noun categories are likely to emerge from the dyadic mother–child interaction, the combination of these categories makes it a virtual certainty that love and hatred are the first affects to incorporate ideas within them. Consequently, they are equally likely to be the first affects with meaning. The ability to combine ideas with presymbolic affects quickly leads to the emergence of a set of affects with meaning. These new affects include not only love and hatred, but also sadness (which is different from grief), envy, and guilt.

During this stage of development, the capacity for symbolization has emerged, but the distinction between the symbol itself and the symbolized is still incomplete; this intermediate stage has been characterized by Melanie Klein as the paranoid–schizoid position (Segal, 1964). During this phase, the phenomenon of splitting is of particular importance; splitting does not represent psychopathology but is a normal phase of development. As Ogden (1986) says, "Splitting is the binomial ordering of experience, i.e., a dividing of experience into categories of pleasure and unpleasure, danger and safety, hunger and satiation, love and hate, me and not-me, and so on" (p. 47). In attempting to understand splitting, one should note that love and hate belong to different motivational systems: love is part of the affiliational system, whereas hate, in contrast, is part of the competitive/territorial system. If the development of the capacity to think is inhibited, then affective information processing will tend to remain in the ascendancy; if this happens, it is reasonable to assume that the loved and hated aspects of "the object" remain relatively unintegrated, as their motivational systems are independent of one another. A current debate about the phenomenology of splitting in adolescent or adult patients has to do with whether the persistence of "distinct objects" (i.e., loved and hated) represents the persistence of traumatically heightened affective information processing from childhood, or whether it represents a defensive retreat from higher levels of symbolic processing and integration in response to frustration. A better understanding of the development of the process of thought should help us answer these questions.

In Kleinian terminology, the resolution of the splitting leads to the achievement of the depressive position. Conceptual thought—primarily through its specific ability to direct our attention toward or away from selected aspects of experience—is ideally suited to implement these defensive functions. Thus, splitting catalyzes the evolution of behavioral coping mechanisms (such as avoidance) into increasingly sophisticated psychological defenses (such as denial, displacement, and repression).

DISPLACEABLE AFFECTS

With the unfolding of symbolic capacity and the formation of complex affects, our emotional life takes on a new richness and plasticity. One very important feature of this plasticity is that affects now become displaceable. As the displaceability of affect plays such an important part in Freud's theorizing, I think that it is important to review his formulations of this issue. In *Studies on Hysteria* Breuer and Freud (1895) point out that helping patients reconnect themselves with painful, buried memories leads to the amelioration of hysterical symptomatology. As any good clinician would, Freud wondered about how this change was accomplished. In his major theoretical paper "The Neuro-Psychoses of Defence," Freud (1894) arrived at his answer: *displaceable affects*.

> The task which the ego, in its defensive attitude, sets itself of treating the incompatible idea as *"non arrivée"* simply cannot be fulfilled by it. Both the memory-trace and the affect which is attached to the idea are there once and for all and cannot be eradicated. But it amounts to an approximate fulfilment of the task if the ego succeeds in *turning this powerful idea into a weak one*, in robbing it of the affect—the sum of excitation—with which it is loaded. The weak idea will then have virtually no demands to make on the work of association. *But the sum of excitation which has been detached from it must be put to another use.*
>
> . . . In hysteria, the incompatible idea is rendered innocuous by its *sum of excitation* being *transformed into something somatic*. For this I should like to propose the name of *conversion* [pp. 48–49].

In the footnote, Strachey points out that this is the first use of the term "conversion." This term makes the assumption that the affective intensity originally connected with the repressed memory is displaced, that is, "converted," onto the body. In the remainder of this paper and in the followup paper "Further Remarks on the Neuro-Psychoses of Defence," Freud (1896) uses the idea of displaceable affects to begin to understand psychopathology: phobias are affects displaced from something inside onto the outside world; obsessions are affects displaced onto ideas. Thus, in the case of Little Hans, Freud (1909) concluded that Hans's fear of horses was a displacement of a fear of his father. Today, the theory of displaceable affects sets the core agenda for any dynamically oriented therapist dealing with a phobia: *what is the patient really afraid of?* At the clinical level, the hypothesis of displaceable affects continues to have great utility. At the theoretical level, displaceability is much more difficult to explain.

As the first step in constructing a theory of displaceable affects, Freud (1895b) hypothesized that anxiety was an undifferentiated negative affect.

> We may perhaps say that here a *quantum of anxiety in a freely floating state* is present, which, where there is expectation, controls the choice of ideas and is always ready to link itself with any suitable ideational content [p. 93].

Although Freud was to change his opinion about the origins of anxiety, his conceptualization of anxiety as a free-floating negative affect state to which ideas are attached remained a cornerstone of his thought. Then, the cognitive content (an "idea") is added to what he labels as "floating anxiety" to create an affect with meaning. Twenty years later, in a lecture on "Anxiety," Freud (1916–1917) says: "In the first place we find a general apprehensiveness, a kind of freely floating anxiety which is ready to *attach itself to any idea* that is in any way suitable" (p. 398, emphasis added). A few pages later, he adds: "Anxiety is therefore the universally current coinage for which *any* affective impulse is or can be exchanged if the ideational content attached to it is subjected to repression" (pp. 403–404). These hypotheses lead to the conclusion that all negatively valenced affects can be understood as anxiety plus the ideational or symbolic content. Inevitably, these assumptions lead to the conceptualization that affects are composites and that some type of primitive thought (i.e., ideas) is necessary to account for the cognitive content of the affect. In this lecture, he repeats this conclusion: "And what is an affect in the dynamic sense? It is in any case something *highly composite*" (p. 395, emphasis added). This conclusion can be conceptualized as the "anxiety plus" theory of affects.

If affects are composites, then their displaceability seems to make sense because we assume that they are assembled from more basic components or building blocks (anxiety + idea = a negative affect). Using the building-block model, we can arrive at a theory of displaceable affects by assuming that we switch one block (idea A) with another (idea B), thus resulting in the possibility of displaceability. This model of affect is clearly what Freud had in mind when he says, "Anxiety is therefore the universally current coinage for which *any* affective impulse is or can be exchanged if the ideational content attached to it is subjected to repression" (pp. 403–404). The problem with this theory is that it presupposes that affects possess meaning (i.e., an attached idea) from the beginning. As I have tried to show, the acquisition of meaning by an affect is the end result of a complex developmental process that depends on symbolic competence. In summary, *presymbolic* affects are not composites but are embedded, concrete signals conveying specific information; in contrast, complex emotions, achieved through a synthesis of core affects and symbolization, *are* composites.

Fear is a good example of how affects acquire meaning. Fear of heights is not the experience of distress or danger *plus* the idea that heights are dangerous because you may fall and hurt yourself. Similarly, the fear of predators is not danger *plus* the idea that predators may kill and eat you. Rather, the exposure to threats to bodily integrity activates a preprogrammed maneuver to protect the life of the organism. Thus, affects are the signals of a presymbolic behavioral program. It is only with the advent of symbol usage that the presymbolic significance of affects—their concrete, embedded message—begins to change. Through this process, affects acquire names and thus meaning, which partially frees them from their embedded content. Linguistically, there is a shift from the use of adjectives to indicate affective response to the use of verbs that link subject and object in a transactive relationship. With the further development of language, we no longer have simple, specific fears of heights, predators, fire, or being separated from the mother; we have "fear" as the transitive verb that encompasses a whole range of objects. Consider the following sentences:

> "I fear you."
> "You fear me."
> "I fear Daddy."
> "I fear horses."
> "I fear God."
> "I fear small spaces."

In each of these sentences, fear is the verb linking the subject with a concept. Some of these concepts are very specific (Daddy); some are abstract (God). If we hear a child say, "I fear Daddy," observations of how the two interact might give clues as to why the child fears Daddy (maybe he beats up Mommy; maybe he threatens the child). Observation, however, may not tell us why a child fears small spaces. An understanding of how the child came to fear his father is based on the assumption that the fear of small spaces is actually a displacement of a fear of something else. As Freud (1909) so brilliantly pointed out, Little Hans's fear of horses was a displacement of a fear of his father. The important thing to understand is displaceable affects are not present at the beginning of life; *displaceability can begin only after affects acquire meaning*. Thus, fear becomes displaceable when we can begin to think of "fear" by itself, disconnected from the embedded fear of any specific situation.

PHANTASY, REPRESSION, AND THE DYNAMIC UNCONSCIOUS

Let us retrace our steps and review what we know about the beginnings of concept formation. We shall use as an example the concept of mother. The concept begins with the infant's experience with the mother, which is stored as a nonsymbolic, internalized model (what Piaget called a schema). As the infant struggles to form his first concepts, the original presymbolic schematic representation is going to be modified not only by new experiences, but by *what he believes, feels, and imagines about her*. The drawings of young children give us tantalizing hints about the power of symbols. When a child draws hands emerging from a shoulder, he is not drawing what he sees, *but what he knows* about humans (that humans have two hands). From these drawings, we can infer that, at times, conceptual knowledge can override perceptual experience. This single fact, in and of itself, is why we differentiate an inner world of concepts from the outer world of direct experience. Internal objects must be our first concepts; consequently, "object relations" are not the child's first experience with the mother, *but the first attempt to try to conceptualize that experience*.

Prior to the emergence of the capacity to think, the infant has a great deal of experience with his mother and easily recognizes her. Perhaps in the beginning, the word "Mommy" may be used simply to designate his own, particular mother (i.e., a name). But, as Vygotsky (1934) says, "A word does not refer to a single object, but to a group or to a class of objects. Each word is therefore already a generalization" (p. 6). Thus, as Vygotsky points out, language gives us more than the ability to name, it gives us the capacity to create the category "mother." At a somewhat later time, we also begin to use the adjectives that describe the *qualities* of that category. In all probability, the terms "good" and "bad" are our first adjectival categories. This virtually guarantees that the concepts of "good mother"/"bad mother" and "good me"/"bad me" will, at least briefly, come into the infant's mind. Then, because the relationship with the mother is the most important relationship in the infant's life, some type of *imagined* relationship between the two will be generated. The quality of the relationship between the infant and mother will be symbolically represented by the affect linking the two: love, hate, fear, envy, sadness (secondary to loss). These briefly imagined scenarios of a "good me" sucking (loving) the breast of a "good mother" or a "bad me" attacking (hating) a "good mother" or a "bad mother" are the anlage of phantasies. In these scenarios, what have been called internal objects serve as nouns; affects, which now have acquired meaning, serve as transitive verbs linking the two. In effect, what we call phantasies are one- or two-sentence stories, formed at the time we are just acquiring the ability to symbolize and use concepts, our legacy from the period of thought formation.

Perhaps most controversial is the extent to which the infant's actual experience with his mother (external reality) influences the content of the phantasies. If we begin with a set of empiricist assumptions that the mind is a tabula rasa, then we can conclude that these phantasies fairly accurately record and thus reflect the observed relationship between the infant and mother. (If one assumes this, then phantasies are not particularly important.) At the other end of the spectrum, the Kleinians assume that these phantasies are relatively independent of the quality of the mothering. At the present time, we still know very little about the beginnings of the process of concept formation, and, admittedly, accurate data is going to be difficult to come by.

A related issue, also difficult to investigate scientifically, is to try to explain how these phantasies—often at odds with the realities of everyday experience—are repressed. Conceivably, one avenue of understanding would be through the study of the processes of attention, and especially selective inattention. Although symbols do many things, perhaps their most powerful effect is to allow us to focus our attention selectively on something and to ignore other things. Prior to the emergence of symbol usage, our attention is reactive to the environment, with the stimulus generating the most intense affect capturing our attention. Later, we can use symbols to focus our attention *despite* what we feel, a process usually referred to as will or will power. For example, we can study for an examination even though we really don't want to. This ability to direct our attention and scan and screen selective parts of our experience is an extremely sophisticated mechanism. It is likely that the use of symbolic thought allows us not only to pay attention, *but also, selectively, not to pay attention* to certain stimuli. As a result, we can learn not to pay attention to those experiences, thoughts, and feelings that we fear will be too painful; when we have learned to do this automatically and are no longer aware of doing it, we have learned the process we know as repression.

Repressed phantasies, forming the core of the dynamic unconscious, become a semipermanent structure that shapes one's character and influences how one lives one's life. I would submit that it is the process of experience becoming translated into concepts that creates "structure." As used in the psychoanalytic literature, the word structure carries a set of connotations beyond the simple definition as biological organization. The ability to think and form concepts *adds* what we call structure to organization, primarily because ideas and concepts, particularly when we are unaware of them, create patterns of behavior that are no longer simply amenable to behavioral shaping. In summary, the ability of human beings to use symbols catalyzes the change from organization to structure. To think, and thereby create phantasies, has the power to transform the presymbolic character organization into a complex structure anchored by the dynamic unconscious.

As affects are one of the key features of the mind, it follows that many of our phantasies focus on the nature of affect. In the case of hysterics or those with a hysterical personality style—Freud's original clinical population—strong, unpleasant emotions are often treated as toxic substances that need to be gotten rid of. Thus, hysterical vomiting is the somatic concretization of an unconscious phantasy about affect, in effect getting rid of—discharging—the toxic affect. As Jonathan Lear (1990) says, "The hysteric is tyrannized not by his unconscious desire, *but by his values which treat the desire as unacceptable*" (p. 66, emphasis added). To summarize Lear's major point, the "theory" of cathartic discharge is one of the core phantasies of the hysterical state of mind, which experiences affects as toxic substances that must be gotten rid of. With this as a background, Freud's success with the cathartic method can be understood as a type of emotional reeducation, helping his patients reorient their perspective on their repressed desires.

These observations well illustrate the close relationship between theory and technique. If one were forced to formulate one, and only one, simple rule as a guideline for those just beginning to learn the craft of psychotherapy, it would probably be this: *Follow the affect.* This rule would seem to apply equally to practitioners of many theoretical persuasions. The thesis of this chapter is that unconscious phantasies about affects powerfully influence both the patient and the therapist. As virtually every therapist knows, the reluctance to experience powerful affects forms a major resistance to treatment, particularly when these feelings are mobilized within the transference. Conscious reasons for not voicing our feelings include considerations of tact, a sense of propriety, and a sensitivity to the feelings of others; unconscious reasons include feelings of guilt, shame, and fears of retaliation. The fears about the emergence of powerful, particularly repressed, feelings are often expressed in such familiar phrases as, "I'm afraid that I'm breaking down" and "I can't cope anymore. I'm losing it." These phrases should not be heard as simply an expressive way of the patient saying that he is feeling bad, but as a derivative of unconscious phantasies about the destructive impact of strong affects.

SUMMARY

With the coming on-line of the "old mammalian brain," emotions convey more specific information than the global moods. This maturational step, both neurophysiologically and cognitively, allows for a greater flexibility of response. At this stage of development, however, the message that the affects convey is still quite specific; adaptively, it would be difficult to imagine any usefulness for displaceable affects within the animal kingdom. These hypotheses suggest that what Freud called the dynamic unconscious is not present at birth but emerges secondary to the ability to use symbols. This is a three-step process. The first step leads to the formation of primitive concepts, internal objects. The second step creates new affects with meaning, such as love, hate, envy, and guilt; in addition, our presymbolic affects acquire meaning through the process of acquiring names. After affects acquire meaning, they become displaceable. Once internal objects and affects acquire meaning (names), they can then be rearranged as easily as words in a sentence. Quite simply, internal objects are the nouns; affects function as transitive verbs linking two concepts. Once we have acquired this level of symbol usage, we can create phantasies, the core of the dynamic unconscious. The third, and last, step is to repress the phantasies, which is accomplished through the process of selective inattention (i.e., repression). These steps lead to the formation of the dynamic unconscious.

Compared to other mammals, the affective palette of human beings is extraordinarily rich and complex. In addition to the sensations that signal us about bodily needs (hunger, thirst, sleepiness) and the core affects that serve as monitors of motivational systems (fear, interest, prereflective shame), the capacity for thought leads to the expansion of our affective range far beyond that found in other animals. For example, love is a combination of affection plus the *idea* of goodness; hatred equals anger plus the *idea* of badness; futility equals distress and/or grief plus the *idea* that this feeling will go on forever. In many ways, this ability to add or subtract ideas to our core affects is similar to the painter's ability to create literally thousands of colors through the process of tinting (adding white) or toning (adding black or brown) to the primary colors. The composition of some of these complex affects—love, hatred, futility—is relatively easy to figure out; however, others—compassion and serenity—have a much more complicated mix and depend on a high level of affective and intellectual development. Whether explicitly stated or not, one of the goals of any type of uncovering therapy is the expansion, both in breadth and in depth, of the affective palette.

14

Thought Dysfunctions

We are only now beginning to understand the origins of thought, how the child learns to isolate a specific part of his experience, mentally draw a line around it to create a category, and then manipulate these categories through the process of symbolic logic. Although we do not know exactly when this type of processing begins, the ability to use language, perhaps the best example of thought in action, takes place at approximately 15 to 18 months. The necessity of integrating these two quite different modes of information processing—the smooth, analogic, waves of affective functioning versus the discrete, yes/no, of symbolic functioning—leads to the turmoil of the rapprochement crisis. These two events, the use of language and the onset of the rapprochement crisis, are very specific markers of the arrival of the capacity for thought.

With the onset of the capacity to think, the infant moves into a new phase of development during which his primary task is to develop a "mind of his own." This development brings the competence/ mastery motivational system into the foreground. This does not mean, however, that the relationship with the parents becomes less important; if anything, the opposite is true because the task of developing a mind of one's own can take place only within a rela- tional matrix. If the infant is allowed to learn and use his capacity to think, then he acquires, in Erikson's (1959) terms, "a sense of autonomy." Autonomy is a complex mood that gradually evolves as the infant becomes confident in the use of his mind. As Erikson

207

points out, how the infant does in this phase of development depends on success in the preceding stage.

> To develop autonomy, a firmly developed and a convincingly contin-
> ued stage of early trust is necessary. The infant must come to feel
> that basic faith in himself and in the world (which is the lasting
> treasure saved from the conflicts of the oral stage) will not be
> jeopardized by this sudden violent wish to have a choice, to appropri-
> ate demandingly, and to eliminate stubbornly [p. 68].

The major developmental task of this period is for the parents to communicate effectively that they value the infant's autonomy. The growth of this autonomy is markedly facilitated when the parents clearly indicate that they treasure the child's independence of mind, even (one should say particularly) when they have to frustrate his acting upon his wishes.

One of Freud's lasting contributions was to point out how strug- gles for autonomy are likely (perhaps destined) to become embedded in phantasies concerning defecation. In the classic paper "Character and Anal Erotism" (1908), he was able to illustrate how these phantasies, and the reaction formations against them, influence the formation of character. As time has passed, we have come to realize that the battleground does not have to be over toilet training; although this was the specific issue that was important at the time Freud was writing, the contest can be over any issue—food, bedtime, don't touch . . . , cleaning the room—that the parents choose to make important.

What is easily apparent to all observers is the unequal contest of wills. If push comes to shove, the parents can usually win any contest, if "win" means to get the child to do as they wish. They can literally force the child into submission by using physical punish- ment or the threat of physical punishment or, more sophisticatedly, by threatening the child with a loss of love. Two of the possible outcomes of this struggle—rebellious defiance and defensive compliance—are described .at length in the psychoanalytic litera- ture, and I will not go into them any further. I would, however, like to call attention to another consequence that is not so well known: the infant's ability to use his capacity to think may be severely compro- mised. Psychological impairments in the ability to think—cognitive developmental arrests—are what I would describe as *thought dysfunctions*. A compromised ability to think is accompanied, as Erikson (1959) says, by feelings of shame and doubt. These feelings of shame and doubt are unrelated to any specific thoughts or acts but signal a sense of defectiveness in not being an autonomous, thinking human being.

THOUGHT DYSFUNCTIONS

Thought dysfunctions stand in the same relationship to thought disorders as sexual dysfunctions do to sexual disorders. Basically, the term sexual dysfunction was introduced to make it easier to discriminate between physical problems that interfere with sexual functioning and psychologically determined inhibitions. A number of sexual disorders have an organic basis; for example, Peyronie's disease, in which compromised blood flow to the penis prevents an erection, or endocrine disorders that prevent vaginal lubrication. In addition to these organic disorders, there are a number of sexual dysfunctions—premature ejaculation, anorgasmia, frigidity—in which the physical equipment is in working order but the ability to use it has been compromised by psychological factors. Analogously, there are number of thought dysfunctions in which the capacity to use the symbolic process has been compromised through the formation of dynamically determined mechanisms that inhibit or seriously interfere with the capacity to think.

As a beginning, thought dysfunctions need to be distinguished from the more severe, organically determined thought disorders. Twenty years ago, most, if not all, thought disorders were lumped together under the wastebasket diagnosis of schizophrenia. Today, we are beginning to understand that what we called schizophrenia then is quite probably the result of a number of specific information-processing deficits. (Consequently, it makes more sense to talk of "the schizophrenias" rather than of schizophrenia.) From what we know about how the brain (as well as the body) works, we can assume that each specific step of the complex information-processing mechanism is monitored or catalyzed by an enzyme or by neurotransmitters. If this is true, then we can also assume that in some part of the population that enzyme is either absent or impaired as a result of some kind of genetic deficit. The population affected may be so small that it is insignificant, or, as with sickle cell anemia, a significant part of the population may be affected. Over the next quarter century, one of the major items on the brain science agenda will be the effort to pinpoint the exact deficiencies (the enzymes and neurotransmitters) that are responsible for the problems in information processing that we call thought disorders, that is, *organically determined* impairments in the capacity to think.

In contrast to thought disorders stands a broad class of dynamically induced difficulties in self-reliant thinking, which I have labeled thought dysfunctions. In most cases, the primary dynamic is that the child's independent use of his mind triggers a parental attack. The classic injunction against children's daring to think is contained in the well-known phrase, "Children should be seen and not heard." It is not the noise the parents object to; it is the idea that children possess minds of their own and dare to use those minds without permission. Independent thinking becomes an affront, an act to be punished. The injunction may be direct ("Don't you dare contradict me; I'm your father!") or it may be exquisitely subtle (the ever-so-slight sigh of the narcissistic mother that always occurs at the first signs of disagreement). The net result is the same: a signal that communicates withdrawal of love as punishment for having an independent thought. However the message is delivered, a sustained parental attack on the child's attempt to think independently produces a not unexpected result: a profound disturbance in the ability to use the symbolic process.

Perhaps the easiest thought dysfunction to understand is the collection of symptoms that goes by the name "dependent personality disorder." Basically, these symptoms are caused by a dynamic inhibition against using the process of thought. The diagnostic criteria of the DSM-III-R (American Psychiatric Association, 1987) provides an excellent phenomenologic description of the problem. The patient

> (1) is unable to make everyday decisions without an excessive amount of advice or reassurance from others; (2) allows others to make most of his or her important decisions, e.g., where to live, what job to take; (3) agrees with people when he or she believes they are wrong, because of fear of being rejected; (4) has difficulty initiating projects or doing things on his or her own; (5) volunteers to do things that are unpleasant or demeaning in order to get other people to like him or her; (6) feels uncomfortable or helpless when alone, or goes to great lengths to avoid being alone; (7) feels devastated or helpless when close relationships end; (8) is frequently preoccupied with fears of being abandoned; (9) is easily hurt by criticism or disapproval [p. 354].

This is a vivid portrait of what happens when people cannot use their capacity to make decisions: they tend to rely excessively on others to think for them and become frightened, if not terrified, when placed in a position where they are forced to decide for themselves.

Consequently, they attempt to become dependent (ingratiating would be a more descriptive term) in an effort to get others to take care of them; they unconsciously enact their fear that they are unable to cope with the world. (If you can't think, the world *is* a frightening place.) A person with dependent personality disorder is one who habitually depends on and, failing that, attempts to coerce others to think for him.

IMPULSE DISORDERS

The dynamics of impulsive action—another type of thought dysfunction—are much more complicated. Impulsive actions include binge drinking, anorexic and bulimic behavior, compulsive gambling, impulsive heterosexual or homosexual activity, wrist slashing, overdosing, and bouts of blaming in conflict-ridden marriages. This group of symptoms does not coincide with any particular psychiatric diagnosis, but patients who display them are frequently diagnosed as impulsive characters, psychopaths, addicts, and alcoholics. Let us consider David Shapiro's (1965) excellent description of impulsive action:

> If we consider the formal characteristics of impulsive action, certain ones easily come to mind. For example, I have mentioned that impulsive action is speedy; it is typically quick in execution, and, more important, it is speedy in the sense that the period between thought and execution is usually short. To mention another, it is usually abrupt or discontinuous in contrast to normal activity, which ordinarily seems to follow from avowed or at least perceptible aims or visible preparations. To these two characteristics, we may add a third, perhaps more basic one. Impulsive action is action that is unplanned. This is not to say that it is necessarily unanticipated; the drinker may very well anticipate his next binge. But anticipation, such as anticipation of the next snowfall, is by no means the same as planning. Each of these characteristics—speediness, abruptness, and lack of planning—seems to reflect a deficiency in certain mental processes that are normally involved in the translation of incipient motives into actions. The translation here of motive or inclination into action seems to "short-circuit" certain active mental processes. What are these processes? May we attribute to the deficiency or "short-circuiting" of them the impairment of subjective sense of deliberateness and intention that also characterizes these people? [pp. 139–140].

This "short circuit," often described as a lack of ego strength, is a very specific bypassing of the process of reflective thought. In everyday terms, we label as impulsive someone who acts on his feelings without reflecting on or thinking through the consequences of his actions.

Before attempting to understand the dynamics of impulsive action, let us review the concept of impulse. As discussed in this essay, specific affective signals serve as the central control mechanisms for the organism. These affects—whether sensations, such as hunger and thirst, or feelings, such as lust and fear—serve as the signals that activate or inactivate complex behavioral patterns. Let us use food intake as an example of this process. Every species of animal has innate programs that determine its feeding patterns. These programs work something like this: feelings of hunger activate the basic feeding program, which is organized around specific behaviors; if hungry, grazing animals will begin to graze, browsing animals will begin to browse, and hunting animals will begin to hunt. After eating, feelings of satiety "turn off" the feeding program unless some variation on the program tells the animal to store up enough food for the winter. The program may be fairly simple or quite complex in terms of the organization of behavior; for example, an animal that hunts may spend hours looking for a suitable meal, stalk its prey, lie in wait, kill in a very specific way, and bring part of the food back to its young. Impulses—the affective signals that control the body—are the sole mechanism for initiating, guiding, and regulating behavior prior to the development of thought.

The development of the capacity for thought adds a second method for regulating behavior. We can do not only what we feel like doing (the impulse), but what we *think* we should do. For example, we can avoid tasty foods (e.g., a nicely marbled steak, Häagen-Dazs ice cream) because we believe they are "bad for us," eat tasteless foods (tofu, oat bran) because we believe they are "good for us," try really exotic foods out of curiosity (snails, raw sea cucumber intestine), fast on fast days, and feast on feast days. These homely examples illustrate how thinking can alter the basic biological "feeding program" that says, "If it tastes good, eat it" and "If you feel disgust, don't eat it." When thought acts as a brake on our impulses (I wanted to eat the Häagen-Dazs but didn't), we tend to label the exercise good judgment or will power.

This everyday experience of conflict between impulse and being held in check by our better judgment or will power provides the experiential substrate for the "divided mind" and leads to the common-sense explanation of impulsive actions: people act impulsively because they lack the will power to restrain themselves. After all, there is a certain plausibility to thinking that people eat because they are hungry, have intercourse because they are sexually aroused, quarrel with a spouse because they are angry, and slash themselves out of despair. But things are really much more complicated than that. As Melvin Lansky (1992) says:

> Compulsive eaters seldom feel hunger, binge drinkers are usually not addicted to alcohol, compulsively promiscuous women often feel no desire and do not reach orgasm during compulsive sexual episodes. Very often patients will say as much, but therapists may discredit their statements as evasive or defensive attempts to disown both unacceptable activities and the parts of themselves that engage in such activities [p. 94].

After working with impulse-driven patients for a number of years, I very much agree with Lansky's conclusions: impulsive actions cannot be explained by a surfeit of drive or desire or by a lack of ego strength or will power.

Lansky describes a three-phase sequence of impulsive action: 1) the prodromal phase; 2) the impulsive act; and 3) the reaction to the act. During the prodromal phase, the patient experiences feelings "of disorganization, of dissociation, of emptiness, or of disintegration [which] is often felt as the presence of persecution" (p. 100). Lansky goes on to say:

> The prodrome includes the registration of the precipitating event, but is most difficult to identify from the patient's account of what transpired. Since the experience is entirely subjective, it is impossible to know about except from the patient's report. In the patient's recollections of his conscious experience, it is often unlocatable, indescribable, obscured so much by what precedes and what follows, and so foreign to the usual capacities of language, that all or part of it may not be conceptualized or even registered in conscious experience [pp. 100–101].

I submit that the prodromal symptoms as described by Lansky are secondary to a dynamically determined inhibition in the ability to think. When a person is faced with a situation that, potentially at least, calls for a decision between affectively driven and symbolically chosen courses of action, he does not experience "conflict," but is flooded with feelings of shame and panic; the impulsive act serves as a way of masking these intense feelings of shame.

The impulse disorder, and the feelings of shame that accompany it, develop in a very specific way. As the child learns to think, he is forced to deal with the fact that, at times, he will not be able to act upon his wishes. Mother won't let him! How the mother handles these inevitable conflicts will determine if the child grows up feeling that he has a mind of his own. The major issue is how the mother experiences the infant's demands. Ideally, she will experience them as simply part of growing up; then she will say "Yes" when she can and "No" when she must, and work out compromises whenever possible. The mother, however, may experience the infant's demands as trying to "control her" or feel that she is engaged in a power struggle or a contest of wills. (If this happens, the mother is probably reenacting her own developmental history, identifying with her own parent and placing the child in her role.) As this struggle unfolds, she may very well come to see the child—consciously or unconsciously or both—as an adversary. The child's struggle with this mother, which includes not only reacting to what the mother says and does but also intuitively tapping into her unconscious phantasies, leaves the child with the sense that his mind is under attack. This attack generates not only feelings of fear and anger, but intense feelings of shame. These feelings of shame have two etiologies: 1) the prereflective signal conceding dominance in a territorial struggle; and 2) the difficulty in living up to one's own expectations of being a thinking human being. It is the two sets of differing dynamics connected with the same affective signal—shame—that makes impulse disorders so difficult to treat.

One way for the child to handle the mother's attack—the solution for the dependent personality—is to surrender, to get someone else to do his thinking for him. (If confrontation leads to the choice of "fight or flight," this is the flight response.) This psychological surrender, although never explicitly acknowledged or even conceptualized by either party, is accompanied by intense feelings of prereflective shame conceding dominance in a territorial struggle. But another solution would be to push on and fight, even though the ability to think is seriously compromised by feelings of shame and panic. In much of the psychoanalytic literature, these feelings are often described as fragmentation, which is the experience of *affective flooding* with feelings of shame and panic, reciprocally reinforcing each other, making effective action extremely difficult. Labeling this experience of disorganization as fragmentation is reasonably descriptive, as the affective–symbolic connections are being ruptured because of the intensity of the affects. Despite this affective flooding, the person may attempt to act anyway, which gives the action a mindless, "not thinking it through," quality. This quality of impulsive action is nicely captured by David Shapiro. Shapiro (1965) asks a patient after a gambling binge why he did it; the patient responds, "I just *did* it—I don't know why." In describing the patient's experience, Shapiro goes on to say:

> This patient probably means to say, "I didn't really mean to do it," or "I didn't intend to do it." Some such statement as, "I just *did* it—I don't know why," is often made by impulsive people, sometimes regretfully and guiltily and sometimes not. . . .
>
> It is an experience of having executed a significant action, not a trivial one, without a clear and complete sense of motivation, decision, or sustained wish. It is an experience of an action, in other words, that does not feel completely deliberate or fully intended. Yet, these are not experiences of external compulsion or of submission to moral principle. They are experiences of wanting, of wish, or even of decision; but they are experiences of exceedingly abrupt, transient, and partial wish, wish that is so attenuated as to be hardly comparable to the normal experience of wanting or deciding and so attenuated as to make possible or even plausible a plea of, "Guilty but without premeditation." The experience seems, in some respects, to approximate the normal experience of whim [p. 136].

As Shapiro says, this type of action is fairly close to what we think of as a whim. According to Lansky (1992), the impulsive act itself is "usually accompanied by a discharge in tension and a sense of relief" (p. 103). As Lansky, citing Sperling, says, the relief caused by the impulsive action has an "enigmatic, fetish-like component" that is not amenable to explanation by traditional psychoanalytic theory. Subsequent to the impulsive act, the individual is very likely to be flooded with feelings of shame and humiliation; in turn, these feelings are often defended against through the use of powerful character defenses (p. 105).

If the hypotheses presented in this chapter are correct, impulsive actions can be understood and interpreted as the result of the *child's willingness to fight* to protect his autonomy of mind by taking action even when flooded by feelings of shame and panic. The psychodynamics are this: if the patient doesn't act, he is flooded by feelings of prereflective shame and humiliation because the inhibition of action has the unconscious meaning of conceding dominance—control over his mind—to a powerful rival (i.e., his parent). As a consequence, impulsive actions—bingeing, addictions, gambling, compulsive sexuality—often appear to be particularly shameless. This is not an accident, because the impulsive action is a classic reaction formation designed to mask the humiliation caused by not being able to think and then act. Instead, the person simply acts impulsively, often in a particularly flamboyant way. By acting impulsively, the patient converts the prereflective shame that concedes dominance in a relationship into the postreflective shame of failing to live up to our cultural ideals that say you should think things through before you act.

The difficulty in treating patients with symptoms of impulsivity stems from the fact that the shame has two sources, which leaves a patient "damned (shamed) if he does (act impulsively), and damned (shamed) if he doesn't (act at all)." The impulsive patient chooses to act; for him, it is better to be a jerk than a coward. The therapist's recognition and explicit acknowledgment of the patient's courage in fighting, even in the face of overwhelming odds, has the effect of reducing the amount of surrender shame that drives the impulsive behavior. If this specific dynamic is not sufficiently appreciated by the therapist, his interpretations are very likely to be understood by the patient to mean, "Stop doing these impulsive things so that we can understand what is really going on." This seemingly rational approach recreates in the transference the very situation that gave rise to the thought dysfunction, because the patient experiences inaction—or the therapist's request for it—as a surrender to the internalized parent/therapist. If the therapist can help the patient differentiate these two sources of shame, he has a much better chance of helping the patient who acts impulsively. The key, however, is not in technique but in the therapist's deep understanding of the patient's predicament: impulsive actions often represent an act of courage, the willingness to try to continue fighting, even if in a traumatized or fragmented state of mind.

THOUGHT DYSFUNCTIONS
AND ANALYTIC NEUTRALITY

Among the major tasks facing contemporary psychoanalysis is to understand the mechanisms that underlie thought dysfunctions and to help develop specific treatment modalities designed to help treat the problems. The dependent personality syndrome and the impulsive personality represent two very specific types of thought dysfunction. They do not, however, exhaust the list. For example, hysterical personalities tend toward affective processing, while obsessive personalities attempt to ignore or isolate affect; both of these character types present difficulties in integrating thought with affect. The borderline personality organization represents what appears to be the most severe of the pure thought dysfunctions (i.e., before one gets into the thought disorders of schizophrenia).[1] The basic problem is that the borderline personality appears to have serious difficulties in achieving what is often described as object constancy but what is more usefully thought of as conceptual stability. Conceptual instability may be the result of hatred toward the mother. Without a world of stable internal concepts, the thoughts, feelings, and behavior of the borderline become chaotic. As a result of this thought dysfunction, borderline personalities are extremely difficult to treat.

The first step in treating thought dysfunctions is to recognize them for what they are: dynamically determined inhibitions that compromise the patient's ability to think. Even if we recognize the problem, however, a number of covert prohibitions often prevent a therapist from commenting directly on how the patient thinks. This reluctance to talk about the patient's thought processing raises very specific questions concerning analytic neutrality. The purpose of the analyst's neutrality is to facilitate the emergence, recognition, and interpretation of the transference neurosis and to minimize the distortions that must be introduced if the analyst attempts to "educate, advise, or impose values upon the patient" (*Psychoanalytic Terms and Concepts,* 1990, p. 127). Freud's recommendations for accomplishing a neutral stance led to some of his most dogmatic and controversial statements. In some of his "Papers on Technique," he recommended that the analyst adopt the article of the surgeon (1912, p. 115), that he be only a mirror to the analysand (pp. 117–118), and that he enforce abstinence (1915d, p. 165). These statements, although directed toward a whole set of issues describing the quality of the relationship between the patient and the analyst, seemed to be designed by Freud primarily to protect both the patient *and* the analyst from the analyst's temptation to do the patient's thinking for him.

---

[1] Whether or not there is a substantial number of functional psychoses is an exceedingly difficult question. At the present time, we are simply unable to differentiate adequately the psychoses that result from the normal brain's trying to process the information from a crazy environment (e.g., the double messages) and those that follow from subtle organic deficits (e.g., missing enzymes or neurotransmitters) that cause specific difficulties, which, in turn, cause symptoms. Attempting to distinguish the organically driven from the psychologically determined psychosis—seemingly a prerequisite to a rational treatment choice—is an immensely difficult job. In all probability, we will find that there are both organic and functional psychoses, as well as a number of combinations.

Over the years, there has been an increasing recognition that the analyst's values cannot be kept secret from the patient. Furthermore, those values of the analyst that emphasize the search for truth, knowledge, and understanding form the framework within which the analytic work can take place and affect the therapy in complex ways that we are only beginning to understand. Today there is a much greater diversity of opinion regarding the "correct" emotional attitude of the analyst, especially concerning such qualities as "distance," emotional responsiveness, sympathy, and encouragement. The primary difficulty with the metaphors that Freud chose to describe the analytic relationship—surgery, mirrors, abstinence—is that they all suggest a coldness or remoteness in the relationship between the patient and therapist. (Although Freud did not follow his own advice, some of his followers did.) One of the obvious difficulties with this approach is that a patient is highly unlikely to reveal himself, to "spill his guts," to an analyst he experiences as distant and cold. If the patient reacts negatively to this situation, it is not the manifestation of transference, but simply a healthy reaction to a current situation that, unfortunately, may very well recapitulate the milieu in which the patient grew up. The recognition of some of the deleterious effects of neutrality has led to a movement to rethink and to redefine the optimal relationship between the therapist and patient.

The challenge of devising effective methods of treating thought dysfunctions may help in reaching the goal of optimal therapeutic responsiveness. Psychoanalysis and psychotherapy do reasonably well with certain types of thought dysfunctions, such as hysteria and the dependent personality syndrome, in which the capacity for reflective thought is intact but underdeveloped. Within the supportive environment of the therapeutic setting, the central problem will emerge in the form of the patient's attempting to get the therapist to take charge of his life. Inasmuch as the basic rules of analytic neutrality that say "Don't give advice" and "Don't do the patient's thinking for him" are both well understood and followed by most well-trained therapists, the core dynamic—usually a parent attacking the child for having "a mind of his own"—becomes manifest in the transference, where it can be worked on. Consequently, patients with hysterical and dependent personality organizations do reasonably well in psychotherapy, a fact reflected in the research statistics.

In contrast, obsessive patients, impulsive patients, and borderlines do not do nearly so well, primarily because these patients have already learned to think in ways that are particularly maladaptive. These maladaptive thinking patterns create a particular quandary for the therapist: how do you talk with the patient about *how* he is thinking without, at the same time, telling him *what* to think? This is the challenge facing the therapist. I suggest that the most effective method of treating thought dysfunctions is for the therapist to place this issue—how the patient thinks—at the center of the therapeutic work. The therapist is often reluctant to delve into the process of how the person is thinking, because he fears that inquiries along this line will be interpreted, by the patient and by his internalized analytic conscience, as an attempt to tell the patient what to think. Ideally, a therapist should be able to discuss the specifics of how a patient thinks with the same ease and frankness that a sex therapist has in discussing sexual dysfunctions.

A major obstacle in reaching this goal is that we are only now beginning to understand how the process of thought develops; consequently, we lack an agreed-upon set of terms to help us distinguish process (how a person thinks) from content (what he thinks). A study of the development of thought should help us understand what happens when development goes awry, thus leading to the dynamically determined inhibitions in the capacity to think that I have called thought dysfunctions.

SUMMARY

The failure to consider thinking as a specific skill that needs to be developed has caused psychoanalytic theorists considerable difficulty, particularly in attempting to devise effective therapeutic methods for some of the severe thought dysfunctions. Psychoanalysis and psychotherapy are, or rather should be, goal-directed activities. For me, two of the goals of the therapeutic process are very specific: 1) to help the patient expand, in both breadth and depth, his affective range; and 2) to help the patient develop the ability to think, culminating in the achievement of a certain type of mindfulness that leads to a deeply felt appreciation of life, including its tragic aspects. Honed by education, discipline, and practice, the ability to think well becomes a subtle art, one of an individual's proudest achievements. Helping the patient learn *how* to think, however, is radically different from telling him *what* to think. The notion of the therapist as neutral or nondirective is the somewhat clumsy attempt to draw this distinction. What is critical is that the analyst, in his heart, truly value the independent mind of the patient. If he does this, then the technique will probably follow; if he doesn't, then no amount of silence can possibly hide the fact and salvage the analysis.

15

Psychosexual Development and Motivational Systems

Freud's theory of psychosexual development proposes a specific sequential unfolding of *unconscious phantasy*. The first three stages of development—oral (birth to 18 months); anal (18 to 36 months); oedipal (three to six years)—all refer to unconscious phantasies and their derivatives that organize experience during each phase of development. At the end of the oedipal period, these phantasies are partially repressed and are much less amenable to observation; consequently, Freud named this the "latency" period (six years to puberty). With "the transformations of puberty," the child enters the genital phase of development; the ability to access phantasy re-emerges and, given optimal development, is directed toward a person of the opposite sex. In summary, Freud's theory of psychosexual development describes five phases of development, each defined by a specific type of phantasy or by the fact that phantasies are absent (i.e., latency).

In this chapter, I attempt to demonstrate two points: 1) that during each of Freud's stages of psychosexual development a different motivational system, as described by Lichtenberg (1989) (but with the addition of a competitive/territorial system), comes into the foreground; and 2) that the success or failure of the primary development task of each stage is reflected in a complex mood, as described by Erikson (1959). During adolescence, all this material has to be synthesized into what is often called "a cohesive sense of self."

PREOEDIPAL DEVELOPMENT

In addition to the stages of development outlined by Freud and Erikson, I consider the neonatal period (from quickening to eight weeks) to be a separate phase of development. Distinguishing the neonatal period from infancy proper (8 weeks to 18 months) highlights the biobehavioral reorganization that takes place at approximately 8 weeks. During the neonatal period, physiologic concerns such as eating and sleeping, the motivational system that deals with physiologic self-regulation, occupy most of the infant's time. Although bodily functions can be used as the phantasy language to encode subsequent phases of development, the neonatal period is not the subject matter of a specific type of phantasy.

Between 8 weeks and 18 months, the infant begins to learn the most important lesson of his life: about relationships with other people. Everything the mother does or fails to do contributes to this lesson. How well the mother facilitates the infant's ability to interact with others can be monitored by tracking the infant's affective responses; the mother needs to reinforce the positive affects of interest and joy, help the child master the fear that emerges at eight months, and absorb the infant's anger and rage without withdrawing or retaliating. The infant's experience of relationships will be summarized into a complex background mood, Erikson's (1959) "trust versus mistrust." As Erikson points out, the infant's experience with his first relationship(s) generalizes into an attitude toward the world. If, on balance, the infant's experience is negative, then he may very well take steps to protect himself against all relationships through mechanisms that form the anlage of a schizoid or paranoid character structure. Alternatively, the failure of the relationship may set the stage for a regression to the neonatal phase of development, where the primary emphasis is on the body. This emphasis on bodily function leads to the unconscious premise that "if my body feels good, then everything is okay" (a belief that helps lay the foundation for substance abuse, addictive disorders, or both). The capacity for unconscious phantasy does not have to be present during the oral phase of development; rather, the *quality* of the mother–infant relationship can be easily encoded into stable affective patterns (trust versus mistrust), which can then be converted into unconscious phantasy once this capacity emerges. As a substantial part of the interaction between mother and infant will still center on meeting the infant's physiological needs (i.e., food, sleep, etc.), it is not surprising that the quality of the relationship is later encoded in phantasies that relate to feeding.

The anal phase of development—18 to 36 months—begins with the rapprochement crisis (the beginnings of thought) and ends with emotional object constancy (conceptual stability). The primary goal of this period is for the child to develop a mind of his own. This requires a subtle shift in emphasis to *how* the mother interacts with the child; rather than simply performing general caretaking functions for the child, she needs to help him specifically to develop confidence in using his mind. With this shift in emphasis to *how* the toddler uses his mind, there is a parallel shift from the affiliational system to the competence/mastery system. If the child is successful in developing a mind of his own, he experiences a sense of accomplishment manifested by feelings of pride *(Funktionslust)*. If the child is unsuccessful in this task, he may develop a thought dysfunction, a difficulty in thinking that leaves him with a profound sense of incompetence, often experienced as powerful feelings of shame and doubt. Consequently, Erikson characterizes the complex moods that represent this phase of development as "autonomy versus shame and doubt." In passing, I would note that the term "autonomy" makes sense only when applied to human beings, where symbolic thought gives rise to the ability to choose between affectively driven and symbolically chosen courses of action. As the quality of the mother–child relationship is encoded into phantasies concerned with feeding, so the struggles of the child with the parent for autonomy are easily encoded into phantasies related to control of bowel and bladder functioning.

THE OEDIPAL PHASE

Having developed a mind of his own, the child of four or five now must decide *what kind* of person he is going to be. As Erikson (1959) said: "here he hitches his wagon to nothing less than a star: he wants to be like his parents, who to him appear very powerful and very beautiful, although quite unreasonably dangerous. He 'identifies with them,' he plays with the idea of how it would be to be them" (p. 74). Recognizing that a simple learning paradigm is insufficient to show how these identifications arise, psychoanalytic theorists have proposed a number of explanatory mechanisms that postulate a world of inner reality: *in*ternalization, *in*corporation, *in*trojection, *i*dentification, *i*dealization, and *int*ernal object. While it is virtually impossible to sort out the conflicting usages of these terms, it is important to note that all of them implicitly assume a capacity for symbolization. Thus, these *in*-words describe a type of learning that is substantially different from presymbolic learning. The inner/outer dichotomy does not really contrast what is inside the head with external reality; rather, it contrasts an inner world of thought and unconscious phantasies (which are secondary to the beginnings of thought) with the reasonably accurate presymbolic schematic representation of the world-out-there.

The beginning of this third phase of development is marked by the formation of sexual phantasies. As Erikson points out, "This is . . . the stage of infantile sexual curiosity, genital excitability, and occasional preoccupation and overconcern with sexual matters" (p. 76). (The term infantile sexuality is something of a misnomer, as infancy is the term usually used to describe the first two years of life, and these phantasies begin to emerge at least a year after that.) As Erikson (1959) says, "Psychoanalysis verifies the simple conclusion that boys attach their first genital affection to the maternal adults who have otherwise given comfort to their bodies and that they develop their first sexual rivalry against the persons who are the sexual owners of those maternal persons" (p. 77). If conceptualized in terms of motivational systems, the onset of the oedipal phase of development marks a shift from the preeminence of the competence/ mastery system to the sensual/sexual system. During this period, the child consolidates his ideas of who he is, and dreams (and fantasies) about the kind of man or woman he would like to be.

The basic accuracy of the observations about infantile sexuality has been verified by clinicians the world over, but sometimes lost in this widespread agreement is the sense of mystery about the biphasic nature of human sexuality. *Why* is it that humans have sexual phantasies far before they can act on them? From a biologically adaptive point of view, this is a difficult and puzzling question. In seeking an answer to this question, Freud, primarily because part of his hidden philosophic agenda was to reestablish the "bond of community between him and the animal kingdom," never really emphasized how very different humans are from the rest of the animal kingdom in this respect. In his explanations of the "why?" of infantile sexuality, Erikson says:

> Three strong developments help at this stage, yet also serve to bring the child closer to his crisis: (1) he learns to *move around* more freely

and more violently and therefore establishes a wider and, so it seems to him, an unlimited radius of goals; (2) his sense of *language* becomes perfected to the point where he understands and can ask about many things just enough to misunderstand them thoroughly; and (3) both language and locomotion permit him to expand his *imagination* over so many things that he cannot avoid frightening himself with what he himself has dreamed and thought up. Nevertheless, out of all this he must emerge with a sense of *unbroken initiative* as a basis for a high and yet realistic sense of ambition and independence [pp. 74–75].

To summarize Erikson's reasoning, factors one (physical maturation) plus two (language) lead to factor three (imagination). As a matter of fact, most mammals have many more physical skills than human beings but no animal demonstrates biphasic sexual development. Consequently, physical maturation appears to be a secondary factor in the development of imagination, and hence of sexual phantasies. The only reasonable conclusion, then, is that the biphasic nature of human sexuality is secondary to the power of conceptual thought (Erikson's factor number two, language), which creates the potential to imagine events beyond direct experience.

As Freud (1905) pointed out, two questions that are of great interest to children are "Where babies come from" and the differences between males and females (pp. 194–197). Therefore, the child's imagination (unless constrained by the prohibitions of the superego) allows him to focus his attention and interest on sexual questions long before he is physically able to carry these thoughts and phantasies into action. As Erikson (1959) says:

This "genitality" is, of course, rudimentary, a mere promise of things to come; often it is not particularly noticeable as such. If not specifically provoked into precocious manifestation by especially strict and pointed prohibitions ("if you touch it, the doctor will cut it off") or special customs (such as sex play in groups), it is apt to lead to no more than a series of fascinating experiences which soon become frightening and pointless enough to be repressed [pp. 76–77].

Perhaps we should struggle harder to retain a sense of surprise that sexual interest and curiosity can generate genital excitement even though the child lacks the physical capacity to carry these fantasies into action. Evolutionarily, it appears that the biphasic nature of human sexuality is a consequence of the capacity for symbolic thought, which allows for the imaginative exploration of sexual thoughts, feelings, and possible scenarios far before the onset of the physical maturity that would allow them to be acted upon. These sexual thoughts and feelings, stimulated by the child's speculations about what it would be like to be mother and father, lead to the formation of the oedipal phantasies so characteristic of this phase of development.

An analysis in terms of motivational systems clarifies the developmental task of the oedipal period and illustrates how the results are signaled by specific background affects. The primary developmental task of the anal phase is to learn to think (the competence/mastery system). As the child moves into the oedipal phase, the question now is whether he will be allowed to think specifically sexual thoughts and feel sexual feelings (the sensual/sexual system). How the child navigates the oedipal period depends on his parents' toleration and understanding. If the child is allowed to experience and explore his sexual phantasies, he will develop the character trait that Erikson calls initiative. Initiative—although phrased in the context of behavior—is an excellent example of a complex mood, a blend of curiosity, a lively imagination, and a zest for life *(joie de vivre)*. On the other hand, if the parents are afraid of their own sexuality and unconscious phantasies, they will inevitably communicate this fear to the child. This message will usually take these forms: 1) sex is frightening (because it means loss of control), and/or 2) sex is bad. As Freud (1923) pointed out, these prohibitions are generated by the superego and are signaled by feelings of guilt, that is, by the fear of punishment. As a result of these prohibitions, the child may learn to deny himself access to these sexual feelings and phantasies, and a closed-in or restricted personality ensues. Thus, Erikson (1959) characterizes the oedipal stage of development as "initiative versus guilt."

LATENCY

The end of the oedipal period is marked by a subsiding of sexual phantasies; this leads to the phase of development that Freud calls latency. In almost every culture in the world, the subsidence of the phantasies of the oedipal period at approximately six years of age corresponds with going to school. In literate cultures, beginning school usually means entering some sort of formal educational setting to begin to learn the fundamentals of literacy; in preliterate cultures, the child begins to learn how to handle the animals, utensils, tools, or weapons that are used by adults. During the latency phase, the child must begin to learn the difference between work and play. In sketching out the development of the sense of identity, Erikson suggests that this stage crystallizes around the shift from "I am what I can imagine I will be" to "I am what I learn." Rather straightforwardly, the sense of "I am what I learn" then evolves into a sense of "I am what I do." According to Erikson, if the schooling process goes reasonably well, the child develops a positive identification with those who know things and know how to do things, and he acquires a sense of "industry"; if he fails, he is left with a sense of "inferiority." Erikson's analysis of the latency stage of development implies that the child is dealing, once again, with the competence/mastery system. Here I would disagree with Erikson.

During the latency years, the child not only learns the skills that will allow him to participate as an adult member of society, but he also learns the "rules of engagement" in a very tough, competitive/territorial world. As he will quickly find out, life is not a "level playing field," and society has rules that heavily favor some groups at the expense of others; this is true not only for our society, but for every society that has ever existed. At home, at the playground, at school, and in the streets, the child learns very specific attitudes about himself and "the other"; the other includes the other sex, other tribes, other races, other ethnic groups, other religions, and other classes. These complex attitudes—all too often blends of contempt, fear, and hatred—are not confined to the schoolyard, and many a parent has had the unhappy surprise of hearing their precious child suddenly begin to sound like a bigot or racist, despite the parents' careful efforts to raise him with a democratic set of values.

The fundamental problem with Erikson's discussion of the latency phase of development stems from his failure to identify correctly the predominant motivational system. As used by Erikson, the term industry connotes that all will go well if the child simply learns what his teachers (as the representatives of society) have to teach (i.e., the competence/mastery system). Unfortunately, this is more wish than reality, even though parents and teachers might like to believe otherwise. During the latency phase of development, it is the competitive/territorial motivational system, not the competence/mastery system, that predominates. More accurately, the child must become competent at mastering the competitive/territorial rules of his society. In our own society, these unwritten rules cover not only such obvious things as race, religion, gender, and sexual orientation, but also more subtle differences such as height, weight, and physical attractiveness. A business leader has commented that if a man had a choice between being six feet tall and going to a lesser business school or being five foot six and going to Harvard Business School, the would-be businessman should choose the height advantage. Today, these societal rules are obviously in the process of change as well as the subject of intense political debate.

During this phase of development, we not only learn attitudes toward groups of people, we begin to learn about ourselves. One of the most important lessons has to do with attitudes toward affects themselves, a phenomenon Tomkins (1980) describes as an "ideo-affective posture" (p. 156). An ideo-affective posture is the direct result of systematic differences in the socialization of affects. Consider the following examples. When a child cries, a parent, following his own ideo-affective beliefs, may elect to convert the distress of the child into a rewarding scene by putting his arms around the child and comforting him. Another parent, following a different set of ideo-affective beliefs, may require the child to stop crying, insisting that the child's distress results from some norm violation and threatening to increase his suffering if he doesn't suppress the response: "If you don't stop crying, I'll give you something to really cry about." As the child internalizes his parent's ideo-affective posture, and also that of other people in his dominance hierarchy, he learns a fundamental attitude toward suffering that will eventually help shape his character structure and color his political attitudes and beliefs. In addition to the reactions to suffering and distress, we also learn very specific attitudes toward unrestrained enthusiasm (a Puritan is someone who lives with the deep fear that, somewhere in the world, a person is really enjoying himself) and rage (it is no accident that the word "mad" means *both* angry and crazy). These ideo-affective attitudes— communicated to us from birth on but consolidated during the latency period through exposure to the ideo-affective postures of other dominant people—play a key role in determining the ease with which the wide range of affective experience can be smoothly integrated into a meaningful whole.

Thus, the latency phase of development presents us with two primary tasks: 1) outwardly, we must come to terms with a society that, despite its democratic trappings, operates by powerful, though sometimes subtle, hierarchical rules; and 2) inwardly, we must come to terms with the full range of powerful and, at times, very painful, affects. The conflict between these two tasks makes the task of integrating them quite difficult.

GENITALITY

In *Three Essays on the Theory of Sexuality,* Freud (1905) sketched in a theory of development based upon the evolution of a sequence of unconscious phantasies. In the last section of this work—"The Transformations of Puberty"—Freud describes the fifth, last, and integrative phase of development: genitality. At the biological level, the onset of puberty allows adolescents to engage in real (as opposed to fantasied) sexual relationships. Psychologically, in Freud's terminology, this provides the possibility that the component instincts combine so that there is "an exact convergence of the two currents directed towards the sexual object and the sexual aim, the affectionate current and the sensual one" (p. 207). In short, physical maturity (puberty) catalyzes the possiblity of combining physical sexuality with love (which has its anlage in the relationship with the mother during the oral phase of development). This theoretical assumption led to Freud's well-known aphorism: "The finding of an object is in fact a refinding of it" (p. 222).

Like Freud, Lichtenberg (1989) and Erikson (1959) see the task of adolescence as consolidating the previous phases of development. In Lichtenberg's work, this goal is not tied to any specific motivational system, but is implicitly interwoven with the need to integrate all of them into a cohesive sense of self. Erikson makes this step explicit, describing the adolescent phase of development as "identity versus identity diffusion." In Erikson's model, the adolescent must synthesize the developmental tasks of the four previous stages into a cohesive whole that creates *"a sense of ego identity"* (p. 89). Interestingly, Erikson's belief that ego identity (using his term) does not occur until adolescence corresponds with Piaget's timing of the shift from "concrete operations" to "formal operations." Piaget and Inhelder (1969) describe the transition from concrete to formal operations:

> The great novelty of this stage [formal operations] is that by means of a differentiation of form and content the subject becomes capable of reasoning correctly about propositions he does not believe, or at least not yet; that is, propositions that he considers pure hypotheses. He becomes capable of drawing the necessary conclusions from truths which are merely possible, which constitutes the beginning of hypothetico-deductive or formal thought [p. 132].

If Piaget's observations are correct, then it would support the hypothesis that the development of an identity is dependent upon the coming on-line of formal thought. Thus, this cognitive development makes possible an affective–symbolic integration, which, as I will argue in the next chapter, forms the basis of the self.

SUMMARY

During each stage of psychosexual development as described by Freud, a different motivational system comes into the foreground. The success or failure of the primary developmental task connected with the motivational system is reflected in a complex background mood. During the oedipal phase of development, the sensual/sexual system comes to the foreground; during latency, the competitive/territorial. Each stage of development emphasizes a different facet of individual experience that must be eventually integrated into the working whole we call the self.

16

Affects and the Self

During the last 20 years, two of the major developments in psycho-analytic theory have centered on an increased interest in affects and the attempt to develop a psychology of the self. The simultaneous emergence of these two issues is not a coincidence; rather, the clarification of the role that affects play in the processing of informa-tion highlights the question of what we mean when we use the word "self." The problem is that, as used in psychology and psychoanalysis today, there are several subtly different usages of the term "self" that overlap and are easily confused. This chapter attempts to clarify some of the meanings of the term "self."

One of the key issues lies in how language affects the organiza-tion and reorganization of experience. One group would conceptual-ize the development of the "sense of self" as a process that begins at birth and continues throughout life; they use the term self as the organizing framework that integrates the various developmental observations about infancy and replaces the ego-id-superego of classical psychoanalysis. For convenience, those holding this view-point might be described as the "self-as-structure" group. The other group reserves the term "self" to describe a *concept* that seems to emerge after the infant begins to use symbols. Implicit in this usage is the belief that the term self is most useful when restricted to human beings, the sole symbol-using animals. However, even with the agreement that the term self is a concept or a protoconcept that the infant develops, its definition has remained vague. Again, for convenience, let us call this the "self-as-concept" group.

THE SELF-AS-STRUCTURE

There is a growing body of literature, which importantly includes the work of Emde (1983) and Stern (1985), that uses the term "self" as the structural framework or scaffolding to organize all developmental observations. Within this definition, the concept of self does not fit into but *supplants* the ego-id-superego model of classical psychoanalytic theories of development. At issue in the debate are not the facts; most observers—perhaps excepting the Kleinians—would be able to agree on a developmental timetable that describes the infant's capacities and would also agree that the capacity to use symbols emerges somewhere during the second year of life. The fundamental disagreement is over the words used to describe the framework that integrates these findings. In contrast to those who use the ego-id-superego model of development, the self-as-structure theorists use the term self as the organizing framework for all developmental observations.

Let us approach the problem developmentally. During the sensorimotor phase of development (prior to the arrival of symbolic functioning), the child must construct a model of reality that serves as the point of departure for all future perceptual, affective, and intellectual development (Piaget and Inhelder, 1969). A central developmental task for the infant, as it is for other mammals, is learning to use his body. In the neurophysiologic model of action constructed by Pribram (1971), this task is accomplished by the construction of an inner schematic model of the body in space, which he calls the "Image-of-Achievement." The Image-of-Achievement is an object (picture) within the organism's perceptual field.[1] Acts (i.e., motor behavior) are accomplished through the process of manipulating the Image-of-Achievement, which is then translated into actions through fast-time calculations by the cerebellum (see Pribram, 1971, ch. 12). These mechanisms allow the baby to get food from the high-chair tray into his mouth, the squirrel to leap from branch to branch without falling, and the hawk to capture its prey in midflight.

---

[1] Pribram's (1971) term the "Image-of-Achievement" connotes a visual image. Obviously, the image is not a picture in the concrete sense, inasmuch as blind infants learn to use their body as well as sighted infants.

The hidden issue is in trying to figure out the boundary between neurophysiological and psychological frames of reference. I suggest that the complex neurophysiologic mechanisms that allow an organism, any organism, to control its body in space are straightforward scientific problems that belong to a different realm of discourse than psychoanalysis. As I attempt to show here, framing these neurophysiological problems in psychoanalytic terms, such as ego or self, is highly misleading.

More than any other single paper, it was Robert Emde's (1983) "The Prerepresentational Self and Its Affective Core" that served as the impetus for using the term self as the organizing framework for all of infant development. A brief examination of how this happened well illustrates the power language has to bewitch us. In the title of the paper, Emde puts forth two separate and distinct concepts: 1) "prerepresentational self"; and 2) "affective core." The second concept, the seemingly simple phrase affective core, contains within it the seed of the solution to understanding affects: affects form the core of a presymbolic information-processing system that is common to all animals. As a consequence of the evocative power of the term affective core, we are prone to accept the other term (prerepresentational self) uncritically. The problem is that Emde is using the term self in a way that is quite different from the way most writers use it. As Emde himself says in the first sentence of the essay, "A 'prerepresentational self' may seem a contradiction in terms" (p. 165), noting that "most developmentalists would agree that organized self-experience, as we usually know it, requires the capacity for 'reflection' [i.e., language], and that awareness of self in this sense emerges in a convincing way during the infant's second year" (p. 166). What Emde does not explain is why he departs from the traditional definition of self and attempts to substitute for it a definition that—as I will attempt to show—is little more than a synonym for biological development.

Emde reaches his conclusion by arguing that the word self should be used as a "process concept": "Once we accept the self as a *process concept*, its developmental aspects *fall into place*" (p. 169). In using the term self as a "process concept," Emde explicitly says that it does not relate to any specific developmental achievement such as "walking, learning to ride a bicycle, *or beginning speech*" (p. 168, emphasis added). The shift in the definition of the term self is accomplished so quickly, it is almost like watching a sleight-of-hand magician. Almost as a throwaway line, Emde describes the acquisition of speech as just another developmental achievement, similar to "learning to ride a bicycle." Thus, in the blink of an eye, the meaning of self shifts from being a concept that the *infant uses* to being a concept that *observers use* to describe the process of biological development.

The definition of self as a virtual synonym for biological development is spelled out in the section of the paper Emde calls "Three Biological Principles" (pp. 169–173). These three biological principles are 1) self-regulation, 2) social fittedness, and 3) affective monitoring. The term "self-regulation" deserves special attention because it is widely used and has acquired a certain cachet within the psychological literature. Emde writes: "*Self-regulation* is the first principle. Modern biology has taught us that self-regulation is basic for all living systems. At the level of physiology, it is built into cardiorespiratory and metabolic systems; were it otherwise, life would not be possible" (p. 169). As used in this sentence, "self-regulation" is nothing more than a restatement of Cannon's (1932) principles of homeostasis, the physiologic processes by which the body attempts to keep the composition of the bloodstream constant. Emde then goes on to say that "self-regulation" applies to behavioral, as well as physiologic systems (pp. 169–170). He concludes that "*self-regulation* is perhaps the most fundamental biological principle of *self*" (p. 170, emphasis added). The problem is that, as used in this sentence, the term self-regulation is used to define the self, making the statement a tautology. If the terms self-regulation and self are subtracted from the subject and predicate of the sentence, then the statement simply says that all living creatures are complexly organized, with the implication (according to Cannon's principles of homeostasis) that feedback loops play an important part in the regulatory process. Unfortunately, when the term "self" is combined with "regulation," the net effect is to blur the distinction between biological development, which is common to all species, and concept formation, which is unique to human beings. As used in the psychological literature today, the important-sounding term self-regulation asserts the accurate, but very obvious, point that all forms of life are complexly organized and regulated.

"Social fittedness" is the second of Emde's "Three Biological Principles" of the prerepresentational self: "*Social fittedness* is the second biological principle underlying the prerepresentational self. More and more we have come to appreciate that the human infant comes to the world preadapted for participating in human interactions. Our biology ensures organized capacities for initiating, maintaining, and terminating such interactions with others" (pp. 170–171). This is certainly an accurate observation about human infants, but it is equally true of all mammals; if an infant is not prewired to interact in a certain way with its mother—whatever that way might be—the species would soon perish. Again, while Emde's observation about basic genetic programming is accurate, it is very difficult to see how it helps clarify the meaning of the term "self."

The third of Emde's "Three Biological Principles" is "affective monitoring." As noted earlier, affects form the core of a presymbolic information-processing system. Consequently the term affective monitoring (or affective core) has a great deal of evocative power because we intuitively sense that it contains the solution to understanding affects. What happens next illustrates how quickly and easily theoretical changes take place: the two terms in the title of Emde's paper combine to become "the affective core of the prerepresentational self." Through the process of condensation, the term "prerepresentational self" becomes shortened to "self." Thus, when we think of Emde's paper, we think of the phrase "the affective core of the self." Almost unnoticed, the term prerepresentational self—a red flag that Emde is using the term self in a new and different way—has disappeared. As we are predisposed to accept this change because of the evocative power of the concept "affective core," we automatically begin to think about a "self" that now has an affective core. (This is an excellent example of the process of concretization.) The net result is to shift the meaning of the term self *from* a concept that the infant uses *to* an organizing concept that functions as the framework on which to integrate all developmental observations. In this way, the term prerepresentational self serves as the hidden bridge that catalyzes a paradigm shift.

The work of Daniel Stern represents the working out of Emde's hypothesis. In his well-known book *The Interpersonal World of the Infant*, Stern (1985) traces the development of the sense of self from the beginnings of life through four stages. The first two months of life are described as the stage of "the sense of an emergent self." From age two to six months, the organism forms "the sense of a core self," which contains four specific capacities: 1) agency; 2) self-coherence; 3) self-affectivity; and 4) self-history (memory) (pp. 76–94). In the third stage (7–15 months), "the sense of a subjective self" emphasizes the central importance of interactive affective communication between infant and caretaker. The fourth stage (15+ months) leads to the formation of "the sense of a verbal self." Thus, Stern has given new names to three specific phases of presymbolic development: 1) the emergent self (0–2 months); 2) the core self (2–6 months); and 3) the subjective self (7–15 months). The net result of the work of Emde and Stern (now elaborated upon by many writers) is to use the term "self" as the conceptual framework for studying the growth and development of the human infant.

As Robert Stolorow (personal communication) has pointed out, Stern's key assumptions are embedded in the term "the sense of self." Stern (1985) himself asks: "A crucial question for this book is, does some kind of preverbal *sense of self* exist before . . . [the development of language and self-reflexive awareness]?" (p. 6, emphasis added). He then outlines the possibilities:

> There are three possibilities. Language and self-reflection could act simply by *revealing* senses of the self that had already existed in the preverbal infant, that is, by making them evident as soon as the child can give an introspective account of inner experiences. Alternatively, language and self-reflection could *transform* or even *create* senses of the self that would only come into existence at the very moment they became the subject matter of self-reflection [p. 6].

The first possibility (reveal) assumes that the sense of self exists prior to the acquisition of language; the second (transform) and third (create) possibilities assume that language catalyzes the emergence of the sense of self. This quotation poses the exact question that needs to be explored; unfortunately, Stern assumes the answer. In the very next paragraph, he says:

> *It is a basic assumption of this book that some senses of the self do exist long prior to self-awareness and language.* These include the senses of agency, of physical cohesion, of continuity in time, of having intentions in mind, and other such experiences we will soon discuss. Self-reflection and language come to work upon these preverbal existential senses of the self and, in so doing, not only reveal their ongoing existence but transform them into new experiences. If we assume that some preverbal senses of the self start to form at birth (if not before), while others require the maturation of later-appearing capacities before they can emerge, then we are freed from the partially semantic task of choosing criteria to decide, a priori, when a sense of self *really* begins [p. 6, emphasis at beginning of quote added].

The bottom line is that Stern simply *assumes* that a sense of self begins at birth "if not before." As he says, this assumption frees him from the difficult task of either defining the term self or answering the question of "when a sense of self *really* begins."

The central problem is that Stern—following Emde's (1983) lead—confuses *biologic capacity* with a sense of self. All sentient species—those species that have the capacity to pay attention (not just mammals, but at least including fish, birds, and reptiles)—have the capacities described by Stern. In other words, Stern's definition of "core self" simply attaches the word "self" as a prefix onto the core capacities that are common to all sentient organisms: 1) motoric control of the body (agency); 2) perceptual discrimination of the organism and its environment (self-coherence); 3) affectivity to process information (self-affectivity); and 4) memory of experience and the ability to learn from it (self-history). There is absolutely no doubt that infants have the abilities enumerated by Stern, but so do all species that have the capacity to pay attention. Are we to think in terms of a dog's "self"? A bird's? A spider's? The phrase sense of self— the key phrase in Stern's book—strongly suggests, rather than describes, something beyond mere biologic capacity. Relabeling these four core capacities as "self-invariants" only confuses the matter. If the term "self" suggests something that human infants possess but that other species do not, then this difference needs to be spelled out.

Many people might think that the difficulties in defining the self are merely semantic or the result of careless thinking. On the contrary, I suggest that the origins are deeper than that, and that our psychoanalytic knowledge may help us in understanding why the problem has persisted so long. Specifically, part of the problem in defining the "self" is secondary to unconscious phantasies evoked by the process of paying attention. As Pribram (1971) has said, the process of paying attention is similar neurophysiologically to the perceptual process of imaging: "To summarize, in real life the perceptual process of Imaging and the cognitive process of recognition cannot easily be separated. We identify, objectify what we sense to be significant at most the moment it is sensed" (p. 326). As Melanie Klein pointed out, every mental process has connected with it an unconscious phantasy of that process (see Isaacs, 1948). Therefore, whenever we think about the process of paying attention, it is easy enough to jump ahead to the next question: *Who* is it that is paying attention? *Who* looks? *Who* listens? *Who* feels hungry? *Who* feels frightened? *Who* manipulates the Image-of-Achievement? *Who?* In his book *The Rediscovery of the Mind,* John Searle (1992) described this process as the Cartesian Theater. Using Cartesian language, this phantasy could be stated as, "I attend. Therefore I am" (Richard Tuch, personal communication).

The concept of the prerepresentational self could more accurately be described as an unconscious phantasy of "the-self-who-pays-attention." This phantasy of someone or something who pays attention has many names: in religious literature, it is often called the soul; for Searle, it is the implied audience watching the Cartesian Theater; to Gilbert Ryle (1949), it was the "ghost in the machine" (p. 20). These phantasies confuse us when we try to think about the mind. Quite simply, it is seven-month-old Johnny, not Johnny's ego or self, who smiles when his mother comes into the room. A great deal of the difficulties and disputes about "the self" is the reification of concretized, unconscious phantasies about the process of attention.

THE SELF-AS-CONCEPT

Most developmentalists, following the lead of Piaget, would agree that "organized self-experience," as it is usually defined, requires the capacity for reflection and that this capacity emerges in a convincing way only during the second year of life (see Emde, 1983, p. 166). The capacity to use symbols—a more precise definition of what we usually call thinking—is manifested not only by the use of speech but also by what is known as *self-recognition*. This developmental milestone has been demonstrated in a series of elegant experiments that involve the infant's looking "at himself" in a mirror. The typical experiment goes something like this: before exposing the infant to a mirror, the mother covertly marks a region of the child's face (the nose or cheek) with a rouge spot; the infant is then placed in front of a mirror and the mother moves aside; task-directed recognition behavior is determined by the infant's looking at his image in the mirror, noticing the spot, and then touching the marked spot or directing a gesture toward it (Schulman and Kaplowitz, 1977; Lewis and Brooks-Gunn, 1979).

The results of these experiments were quite uniform: recognition was not found before 15 months; it occurred in some infants between 15 and 18 months, and in most infants between 18 and 21 months. The conclusion seems inescapable that the infant is beginning to think, "Hey, that's me!" This conclusion is reinforced by the observation that personal pronouns begin to be used at the end of this age period when infants looked at their own pictures (Emde, 1983, p. 166). These experimental studies reinforce what psychoanalytic observers have documented so richly: the last six months of the second year of life usher in the ability to use concepts, which radically alters how the infant functions. This achievement was called willfulness by Freud (1905), autonomy by Erikson (1959), the beginnings of the representational world of self and objects by Sandler and Rosenblatt (1962), and the rapprochement subphase of separation-individuation by Mahler et al. (1975). This important developmental milestone led theorists to use the term self as a shorthand way to describe the specific *concept* that emerges after the infant begins to use symbols and thus to think about "himself." The human ability to process information in two ways, by affect and by symbol, is the experiential substrate that gave rise to what is often referred to as the "divided mind."

We are the only symbol-using animal, which distinguishes us from the rest of the animal kingdom.[2] John Locke's *An Essay Concerning Human Understanding* (1690), which draws the distinction between "a man" and "a person," well illustrates this point. According to Locke, "man" is a living organism whose identity depends upon its biological organization; in contrast, a "person" is

> a thinking intelligent being, that has reason and reflection, and can consider itself as itself, the same thinking thing, in different times and places; which it does only by that consciousness which is inseparable from thinking, and . . . essential to it. . . . When we see, hear, smell, taste, feel, meditate, or will anything, we know that we do so. Thus it is always as to our present sensations and perceptions; and by this everyone is to himself that which he calls *self* [p. 211].

Locke goes on to link the ability to think with consciousness, the self, and the formation of personal identity (pp. 212–213). The distinction that Locke draws between *homo sapiens*, the biological organism, and the *person* who possesses the power to think and reflect (and especially to think about how the mind works), provides the philosophic anlage for the definition of "the self-as-concept."

Much of the work on the self-as-concept in modern psychology began with the famous chapter on the self in William James's monumental two-volume work, *The Principles of Psychology*, which was published a little over a century ago.[3] James (1892) began by distinguishing between "A) the self as known, or the *me*, the 'empirical ego' as it is sometimes called; and . . . B) the self as knower, or the *I*, the 'pure ego' of certain authors" (p. 176). "The empirical self or me" consists of three elements: 1) the material self, which includes the

---

[2] There is some evidence that the higher primates—such as chimpanzees and gorillas—can be taught to use American Sign Language. There is a fierce debate among linguists as to whether this is really using language. In any case, human beings are the only species that, in their natural state, use symbols and language.

[3] However, all quotations from James are from *Psychology: Briefer Course* (1892), an abridgement of *The Principles of Psychology*, which he prepared "to make it more directly available for class-room use" (p. iii).

cravings of the body; 2) the social self, which includes longings for friendship, status, and prestige; and 3) the spiritual self, which includes the pursuit of intellectual, ethical, and religious aspirations. James considered these three aspects of the self—the material, social, and spiritual—as being more amenable to empirical verification than "the sense of personal identity," or what James called "pure ego." "Pure ego" was his way of conceptualizing the sense of continuity and integration of experience.

James found the roots of "the empirical self or me" in possessiveness, that is, in what a person pridefully and importantly calls "his."

> *In its widest possible sense*, however, *a man's Me is the sum total of all that he* CAN *call his*, not only his body and his psychic powers, but his clothes and his house, his wife and children, his ancestors and friends, his reputation and works, his lands and horses, and yacht and bank-account [p. 177].

This includes not only the body (James's "material me") but his relationships and possessions. Few, if any, writers have written more poetically about the importance of relationships than James:

> Our immediate family is a part of ourselves. Our father and mother, our wife and babes, are bone of our bone and flesh of our flesh. When they die, a part of our very selves is gone. If they do anything wrong, it is our shame. If they are insulted, our anger flashes forth as readily as if we stood in their place [p. 178].

James found the origins of selfhood in the kind of objects one *appropriates* and calls one's own (D. Klein, 1970, p. 278). Possessiveness, the sense of ownership, is the essential characteristic of the everyday allusion to the self in such phrases as my wife, my child, my arm, my idea, my doctor, my joke, my country, or my God. The countless uses of the word "my" reflect the wide range of items that come to be incorporated into the self and that people claim as "mine"; thus, "my" reflects not only the possession of land and material goods, but also of feelings, ideas, motives, and purposes.

The problem with grounding the sense of self in possessiveness is that it fails to distinguish human beings as uniquely capable of developing a sense of self. In almost all species at the high end of the phylogenetic scale, the mother takes care of her offspring; they are *her* children. Correspondingly, the babies know that she is *their* mother. As adults, thousands of birds live in pair-bonded relationships, as do some mammalian species, including almost all primates.

Another kind of possessiveness involves territoriality. Wolves manifest this kind of possessiveness; they mark *their* territory with a special scent and will fight to defend it. Given the widespread prevalence of this form of possessiveness throughout the animal kingdom, it is a much too inclusive concept to serve as the ground for "the sense of self." Perhaps more important, in human beings, possessions (and possessiveness) do *not* automatically lead to a solid sense of self.

At this point, it is worthwhile pausing for a moment to consider again how concepts (including the concept of self) interact with affects. The ability of human beings to think and, through the process of thinking, to form intellectual, ethical, and religious ideals and aspirations (what William James called the spiritual self) gives us the power not to be controlled by our affects. By using what we call will power, we can choose not to do what we feel like doing. This does not mean that animals do not make choices; they certainly do, *but the choice is always based on the intensities of two competing affects*. For example, an animal wishing to defend its territory may have to choose whether or not to attack a dangerous adversary (in this case the affect of rage competes with feelings of fear). But what animals do not have is the power to override their affective programming. Hegel said a man becomes truly human when he can ignore his animal nature and act "for glory" (i.e., the pride in living up to one's ideals) (see Fukayama, 1992, pp. 143–152). Thus man has a choice that is not available to the other animals: to decide whether his behavior will be affectively driven or symbolically chosen.[4]

The ability to use symbols does not, however, automatically lead to a sense of self; symbol usage leads to the *possibility* of forming what William James (1892) called "the sense of personal identity" (p. 201). In his emphasis on the importance of an identity, Erikson (1959) appears to represent a continuation of James's ideas. (What Erikson called ego identity seems to me to be a synonym for what James called the sense of personal identity.) In Erikson's model of development, if one fails to achieve a sense of identity, one experiences "*identity diffusion*." As an example of identity diffusion, Erikson refers to Biff in Arthur Miller's *Death of a Salesman:* "I just can't take hold, Mom, I can't take hold of some kind of a life" (p. 91). Although Biff clearly knows who he is and has social relationships

---

[4] I think this is the point that Freud was trying to make through the distinction between "active" and "passive." Animals are always "passive" in that their behavior is always a reaction to their feelings ("reactive" would be a much more phenomenologically descriptive term than "passive").

and intellectual beliefs (James's empirical self), they do not give meaning to his life. He is adrift, lacking the sense of who he is. In Erikson's terms, the failure to consolidate a sense of identity (what Ogden, 1986, will later call a lack of "I-ness") is described as identity diffusion.

In *The Restoration of the Self*, the restoration of which Kohut (1977) speaks is the restoration of this sense of "I-ness." Kohut clearly suggests this definition of self when he says, "I could find no place [within classical psychoanalytic drive theory] for the psycho-logical activities that go by the name of choice, decision, and free will—even though I knew that these were empirically observable phenomena" (p. 244). The words "choice, decision, and free will" suggest, as much as any words can, the concept of I. Kohut himself recognized the ambiguity of the term self:

> In order to describe the restoration of the self, the outlines of a psychology of the self had to be drawn. . . . we must learn to think alternatingly, or even simultaneously, in terms of two theoretical frameworks; that we must, in accordance with a psychological princi-ple of complementarity, recognize that a grasp of the phenomena encountered in our clinical work—and beyond—requires two approaches: a psychology in which the self is seen as the center of the psychological universe, and a psychology in which the self is seen as a content of a mental apparatus [p. xv].

Regrettably, Kohut's clear-cut distinction between traditional meta-psychology and self psychology oversimplifies the issue. Throughout his writing, Freud used the word *Ich*—"I"—for both a mental structure and psychic agency (ego), as well as for the more per-sonal, subjective, experiential term self. As Kernberg (1982) has commented, "Freud never separated what we think of as the metapsychological ego from the experiencing self" (p. 894). At times, the ego was clearly referred to as a structure, eventually leading— by way of Hartmann and Rapaport—to ego psychology. Yet at other times, the word *Ich* is used to designate subjective experience. Perhaps the clearest example is Freud's (1930) statement, "Nor-mally, there is nothing of which we are more certain than the feeling of our self, of our own ego" (p. 65). In this oft-quoted sentence, the terms self and ego are explicitly equated. The ambiguity of the German word *Ich* was certainly compounded by Strachey's decision to translate the word as ego. While ego has a sufficiently impersonal quality that seems appropriate enough for Freud's (1923) structural theory, it seems much less fitting as a translation for the more personal, subjective word self.[5] In any case, issues of translation aside, the real question is how the sense of "I" develops out of the "ego" organization.

Building on the work of Melanie Klein, Ogden (1986) describes this sense of "I-ness" as beginning with the transition from the paranoid–schizoid position into the depressive position (pp. 68–71). I suggest that James, Erikson, Kohut, and Melanie Klein (as interpreted by Ogden) are describing the same developmental step, but using different terms and different theoretical frameworks. The problem is that the ability to use symbols does not, in and of itself, create a sense of self; rather, the ability to use symbols creates the *possibility* of a person having a sense of self. Throughout the course of development, beginning with the use of symbols and continuing throughout life, the meanings attached to "self" acquire broader and deeper resonances. If this developmental process is aborted, the person can be said to lack a sense of self; phenomenologically, this can be manifested by a lack of purpose in life (Biff) or by a clinical depression. In the play *Garden District*, Tennessee Williams put it very well: "[T]he work of a poet is the life of a poet." Properly understood, so it is with us all. The work of a human being *is* the creation of this sense of I-ness.

The sense of "I-ness," the critical ingredient of the self as developed in the work of Kohut and his followers, depends on the differentiation between symbol and symbolized. As Ogden (1986) says:

> At the moment that the infant becomes capable of experiencing himself as the interpreter of his perceptions, the infant as subject is born. . . .
> When the infant becomes an interpreting subject, he can for the first time project that state of mind into his sense of the other and consider the possibility that other people experience feelings and thoughts in much the same way. Awareness of the possibility that another person is a subject as well as an object creates the conditions wherein the infant can feel concern for another person [pp. 72–73].

The key phrase is "the infant becomes capable of experiencing himself as the *interpreter* of his perceptions." As used by Ogden, "to interpret" means to understand, to know, to reflect upon the meaning of the affect.

The knowledge that "other people experience feelings and thoughts in much the same way" as we do dramatically widens our affective

---

[5] See Kernberg's (1982) excellent discussion of these issues.

range. The metamorphosis of grief to sadness and compassion is a good example. It isn't too difficult to know when another person is experiencing grief; the nonverbal communication—posture, gait, facial expression, tone of voice—are easy enough to read. However, if one not only registers the other person's affect, but *understands* what it is like to be that other person, then one begins to feel a sadness, or even compassion, *for him or for her*. In turn, by understanding that another "I" can exist, we also can come to understand that our attacks can do real damage. With this knowledge, a person can become capable of feeling contrition accompanied by the wish to make reparations (Ogden, 1986, pp. 73–74). This knowledge, a combination of affect and understanding, leads to the formation of the self.

ME, MYSELF, AND I

If we listen carefully, ordinary language often reflects subtle distinctions in the functioning of the mind of which we are intuitively aware but that we find difficult to translate into the more exact language of science, philosophy, or psychology. I suggest that part of the difficulty in understanding "the self" is hidden in the multiple uses of the personal pronouns "I," "me," "mine," and "myself." Let us, then, begin with the dictionary definition of "I": "the person speaking or writing. *I* is the nominative case form, *me* the objective, *my* and *mine* the possessive, and *myself* the intensive and reflexive, of the first person singular pronoun." These four different core forms of the personal pronoun "I" are not simply the product of grammatical rules but have their roots in subtly different aspects of mental functioning. These differences are not highlighted but, rather, are obscured when we attempt to translate them into a more scientific language.

As Ogden (1986) said, if we can develop the sense of I-ness in ourselves, we can also begin to recognize the I-ness of the other (pp. 71–76). Martin Buber (1957) defined the relationship between two people with a sense of personal identity as an "I–Thou" relationship. Quite obviously, a person cannot form an I–Thou relationship if he himself lacks a sense of I-ness; in many cases, this lack leads to forming what Buber called an "I–it" or even an "it–it" relationship. Buber's conceptualization of the I–Thou relationship adds an important dimension to the description of I-ness: it involves the recognition of an "I" in the other. The other person is no longer simply an object or a possession. This sense of "I-ness"—I know who I am, where I fit in the world, and where I am going—gives life meaning and represents a specific developmental achievement. In contrast, the distinction between nominative *I* and the possessive *my* or *mine* is much more subtle, leading to a great deal of ambiguity in the definition of the term *self*. In the possessive case, it becomes apparent that one can have a wife or child (my wife, my son), but think of that person as a possession, not a person. One can possess many, many things that are "mine" but still lack the ineffable sense of "I-ness." (This is the fallacy in William James's attempt to ground the self in possessiveness.) As we know, the lack of a sense of I-ness often leads a person to overvalue possessions in the attempt to compensate for this deficit.

Expanding on the distinction made by Buber (1957), one can see that each case of the personal pronoun *I* describes a specific type of relationship:

Pronoun	Case	Type of Relationship
me	objective	it–it (object–object)
I	nominative	I–Thou (subject–subject)
my, mine	possessive	I–it (mine) (subject–object/ possession)
myself	intensive, reflexive	I–Self (subject–internal subject)

In many ways, the word "myself" holds the key to understanding the puzzle of the self. Grammatically, the word "myself" is the intensive or reflexive case form of the personal pronoun "I," but this usage leads to another meaning. In its reflexive form, such as in the sentence, "I hurt myself," there is a partial inward shift in the focus of attention, which, in turn, leads to the use of "myself" as quasi-noun. The dictionary then goes on to explain "in this construction *my* may be considered a possessive pronomial adjective and *self* a noun, and they may be separated; as, *my* own sweet *self*." This evolution of the word "myself" to "my self" suggests an internal relationship between the I that possesses and the self that is possessed. This relationship becomes explicit in the work of Carl Jung (1946), who describes the relationship between the ego (I) and the self. In the paper "The Self," Jung (1948) describes the relationship between the ego and the self; although interlaced with the language of religion, Jung identifies the ego with the "intellect" and the self with "feeling" (p. 31). Thus, Jung was one of the first psychoanalysts to connect the self with what Emde (1983) calls our "affective core."

Within the mainstream of classical psychoanalysis, Winnicott essentially translates Jung's concept of self to describe our affective core into secular terms when he talks about the "True Self." In the short paper "Ego Distortion in Terms of True and False Self," Winnicott (1960a) drew the distinction between the "True Self" and "False Self." Although partially formulated in terms of drive theory (id-demands, id impulse, ego defense), it is quite clear that Winnicott's "True Self" is used to describe what we really feel and that the "False Self" is a symbolic construction designed to prevent someone else from knowing these feelings. (Although contemptuously rejecting what he called "the jargon of Jungian conversation" and specifically rejecting the term "transpersonal," one should note that Winnicott [1960b, p. 159] nonetheless appears to have derived the concept of the True Self from Jung.) This distinction is more or less congruent with ordinary-language usage. For example, when we talk about "being true to ourselves," we usually take it to mean that a person is acting in line with what he feels and is not being guided by careful calculations. For Winnicott (1960a), the results are quite clear: "Only the True Self can be creative and only the True Self can feel real. Whereas a True Self feels real, the existence of a False Self results in a feeling unreal or a sense of futility" (p. 148). These feelings of unreality and futility are the result of being out of contact with our affective core. If we wish to develop a firm "sense of self," then we need to treat our affective core with the same respect that we would treat the other in an I–Thou relationship. The I–Self internalized relationship with our affective life would then parallel the external I–Thou relationship.

THE SELF: AFFECTIVE–SYMBOLIC INTEGRATION

I would strenuously argue that the word self is most usefully defined as a concept that the infant himself develops; the sense of self cannot begin until the infant becomes able to use symbols. Current research indicates—and this finding appears to be amenable to empirical verification—that the ability to use symbols begins somewhere between ten and twelve months and becomes manifest with the advent of spoken language. It is not, however, the mere ability to use symbols (i.e., to think) that creates the sense of self; every human being, save the severely neurologically handicapped, can do this. Nevertheless, a substantial number of people still lack a sense of self. Consequently, it must be that the ability to use symbols creates the *possibility* of developing the sense of self; it does not guarantee it.

What is it, then, that creates the sense of self? Even if we abandon the term self to describe presymbolic functioning (i.e., the "self-as-structure"), we are still left with two meanings of the word self that are diametrically opposed to each other. The first use of the term self is to describe our affective core; this is the self described by Jung as the transpersonal self, Winnicott's True Self, Emde's affective core of the self, and the ordinary-language usage of "being *true* to *oneself*" as a way of expressing the wish to act in harmony with our feelings. The second definition of self would be as the referent for the personal pronoun "I"; this is Freud's usage whereby he equates *Ich* with *Selbst,* and implicitly it is the usage of the term "self" in the self-recognition experiments. These two contradictory usages of the term self strongly suggest that it is the ability to integrate our affects (what we feel) with our thoughts (what we think) that leads to the creation of what most people would call a sense of self.

I suggest that the term self be reserved for a specific concept that emerges as the infant develops the ability to use symbols. If defined in this way, then the term self would apply only to human beings and not to other animals (which is compatible with ordinary English usage). This implies that development has progressed beyond the original organization of perception, sensation, volitional action, affect, and memory, and begins to take place somewhere close to the emergence of spoken language. It also means that the self is a *concept* that the infant uses that is *created* through the lived interaction with another human being and not something he is born with. Some authors—Jung, Winnicott—tend to equate the self with our affective life. Other authors—Freud among them—tend to use the term self as the referent for the personal pronoun "I." I would suggest that we reserve the term self for the personal organization we experience when we are able to effectively integrate our affective experience with what we think in a relatively stable internal relationship. In other words, it is the ability of the individual to create a relationship between his feeling core and his thinking "I" that is at the heart of selfhood. It is the affective–symbolic integration that leads to the creation of the sense of self.

Intermittently throughout this book, I have made several references to the "divided mind." In general, I have argued that it is the experience of conflict between our affective processing system and our later-developed conceptual processing system that constitutes the experiential substrate for theories of the divided mind. Here let me add a surprising corollary, namely, that it is the same substrate (i.e., the fact that our systems for affective and symbolic processing are relatively independent of one another) that also underlies the capacity for selfhood. Put more dramatically still, we can say that the divided mind, that ubiquitous curse of the human condition, is simultaneously the basis for that most valued of human capacities— the true self.

Although the central (i.e., core) neurophysiological control mechanisms that are common to all sentient species form the biologic substrate for the self, the sense of self begins with attempts to translate into conceptual form this experience of oneself as a person (to borrow Locke's distinction between man and person). Inasmuch as all of the infant's presymbolic experience is mediated by affects, it follows that—as Stern (1985) and Demos (1987) point out—the sense of self crystallizes around recurrent affect states. What complicates the situation is that, prior to the acquisition of the ability to use symbols, the infant is subject to behavioral shaping processes that can either facilitate or interfere with his ability to be in contact with his affective life. As Stolorow and Stolorow (1987) point out, this shaping constitutes an important selfobject function on the part of the parents—one that begins even before the "self" has emerged. Among the things that the parents can do before the infant begins to use symbols is to help the child separate and differentiate his affective responses; facilitate the experience of positive affect states such as interest and joy; help the infant master, and thus endure, the potentially disorganizing impact of negative affects such as fear and rage; and protect the child from affective overload, which may be the prelude to a disorganized traumatic state. After the child acquires the ability to use language, the parents can not only help the toddler identify the discrete affect states and put them into words, but also convey to the child that affects, even the painful ones, are not to be avoided, as they are an extremely necessary part of life. A key part of helping the child acquire a sense of self is for the parents to cherish the child's independent mind, even if they strongly disagree with the child. If the parents are good enough at this task, then the various parts coalesce into a cohesive sense of self. As Erikson (1959) points out, this process of integration, which he calls the formation of the sense of identity, continues into adolescence and beyond.

SUMMARY

It is how one uses the capacity for thought in relationship to affects to create meaning that results in the sense of self. The emergence of a sense of self requires the ability to synthesize the various components of the mind—experience, affects, thoughts, hopes, and aspirations—into a cohesive whole. More than any other single factor, it is the capacity to use symbols to blockade affective experience that creates a lost sense of I-ness. Conversely, it is affective–symbolic integration that creates what most people mean by self. Consequently, one of the specific goals of psychoanalysis and of psychodynamically informed psychotherapy is a richly textured affective life both to broaden the patient's affective range and to help him experience these feelings more deeply and with understanding. To paraphrase what Tennessee Williams said: The work of a poet is his life. So it is with us all. To fail in this task is to lose the sense of self.

References

Abelin, E. L. (1971). The role of the father in the separation-individuation process. In: *Separation-Individuation*, ed. J. B. McDevitt & C. F. Settlage. New York: International Universities Press, pp. 229–253.

American Psychiatric Association (1987). *Diagnostic and Statistical Manual of Mental Disorders, Third ed., rev.* (DSM-III-R). Washington, DC: American Psychiatric Association.

Anand, M. (1989). *The Art of Sexual Ecstasy*. Los Angeles: Tarcher.

Arlow, J. (1977). Affects and the psychoanalytic situation. *Internat. J. Psycho-Anal.*, 58:157–170.

Bell, S. (1970). The development of the concept of object as related to infant-mother attachment. *Child Develop.*, 41:291–311.

Berenson, B. (1949). *Sketch for a Self Portrait*. New York: Pantheon.

Bettelheim, B. (1983). *Freud and Man's Soul*. New York: Knopf.

Bower, T. G. R. (1977). *A Primer of Infant Development*. San Francisco: Freeman.

Bowlby, J. (1969). *Attachment, Vol. I*. New York: Basic Books.

Brenner, C. (1974). On the nature and development of affects: A unified theory. *Psychoanal. Quart.*, 43:532–556.

——— (1982). *The Mind in Conflict*. New York: International Universities Press.

Breuer, J. & Freud, S. (1893). On the psychical mechanism of hysterical phenomena: Preliminary communication. *Standard Edition*, 2:1–17. London: Hogarth Press, 1955.

——— & ——— (1895). *Studies on Hysteria. Standard Edition*, 2. London: Hogarth Press, 1955.

251

252   *References*

Broucek, F. (1979). Efficacy in infancy: A review of some experimental studies and their possible implications for clinical theory. *Internat. J. Psycho-Anal.*, 60:311–316.

—— (1982). Shame and its relationship to early narcissistic developments. *Internat. J. Psycho-Anal.*, 63:369–378.

Bruner, J. S. (1964). The course of cognitive growth. In: *Beyond the Information Given*, ed. J. Anglin. New York: Norton, pp. 325–351, 1978.

—— (1966). The growth of representational processes in childhood. In: *Beyond the Information Given*, ed. J. Anglin. New York: Norton, pp. 313–324, 1978.

Buber, M. (1957). *I and Thou* (trans. W. Kaufmann). New York: Charles Scribner's Sons, 1970.

Campos, J. J., Hiatt, S., Ramsey, D., Henderson, C. & Suejda, M. (1978). The emergence of fear on the visual cliff. In: *The Development of Affect,* ed. M. Lewis & L. Rosenblum. New York: Plenum Press, pp. 149–182.

Cannon, W. B. (1932). *Wisdom of the Body.* New York: Norton.

Chomsky, N. (1957). *Syntactic Structures.* The Hague: Mouton.

Clark, E. (1973). What's in a word? On the child's acquisition of semantics in his first language. In: *Cognitive Development and the Acquisition of Language,* ed. T. Moore. New York: Academic Press, pp. 65–110.

Compton, A. (1980). A study of the psychoanalytic formulation of anxiety, III: A preliminary formulation of the anxiety response. *J. Amer. Psychoanal. Assn.*, 28:739–773.

Darwin, C. (1859). *On the Origin of Species.* London: Penguin, 1968.

Davidson, J. & Rees-Mogg, W. (1993). *The Great Reckoning.* New York: Simon & Schuster.

DeCasper, A. J. & Fifer, W. P. (1980). Of human bonding: Newborns prefer their mothers' voices. *Science,* 208:1174–1176.

Demos, E. V. (1987). Affect and the development of the self: A new frontier. In: *Frontiers in Self Psychology: Progress in Self Psychology, Vol. 3,* ed. A. Goldberg. Hillsdale, NJ: The Analytic Press, pp. 27–53.

—— & Kaplan, S. (1986). Motivation and affect reconsidered: Affect biographies of two infants. *Psychoanal. & Contemp. Thought,* 9:147–221.

De Rivera, J. (1977). *A Structural Theory of the Emotions. Psychological Issues,* Monogr. 40. New York: International Universities Press.

Descartes, R. (1641). *Discourse on Method* (trans. J. Veitch). Rutland, VT: Orion/Evergreen Library, 1992.

Diamond, J. (1992). *The Third Chimpanzee.* New York: HarperPerennial.

Emde, R. (1983). The prerepresentational self and its affective core. *The Psychoanalytic Study of the Child,* 38:165–192. New Haven, CT: Yale University Press.

————, Gaensbauer, T. & Harmon, R. (1976). *Emotional Expression in Infancy. Psychological Issues*, Monogr. 37. New York: International Universities Press.

Encyclopedia of Philosophy, The (1967). P. Edwards, editor-in-chief. New York: Macmillan.

Erikson, E. H. (1959). *Identity and the Life Cycle. Psychological Issues*, Monogr. 1. New York: International Universities Press.

Escalona, S. (1963). Patterns of infantile experience and the developmental process. *The Psychoanalytic Study of the Child*, 18:197–244. New York: International Universities Press.

Fraiberg, S. (1969). Libidinal object constancy and mental representation. *The Psychoanalytic Study of the Child*, 24:9–47. New York: International Universities Press.

Freud, A. (1967). Comment on trauma. In: *Psychic Trauma*, ed. S. S. Furst. New York: Basic Books, pp. 235–245.

Freud, E. L., ed. (1960). *The Letters of Sigmund Freud* (trans. T. & J. Stern). New York: Basic Books.

Freud, S. (1894). The neuro-psychoses of defence. *Standard Edition*, 3:41–68. London: Hogarth Press, 1962.

———— (1895a). Project for a scientific psychology. *Standard Edition*, 1:281–397. London: Hogarth Press, 1966.

———— (1895b). On the grounds for detaching a particular syndrome from neurasthenia under the description "anxiety neurosis." *Standard Edition*, 3:85–117. London: Hogarth Press, 1962.

———— (1895c). A reply to criticisms of my paper on anxiety neurosis. *Standard Edition*, 3:119–139. London: Hogarth Press, 1962.

———— (1896). Further remarks on the neuro-psychoses of defence. *Standard Edition*, 3:157–185. London: Hogarth Press, 1962.

———— (1897). Letter to Fliess dated September 21, 1897. *Standard Edition*, 1:259–260. London: Hogarth Press, 1966.

———— (1898). Sexuality in the aetiology of the neuroses. *Standard Edition*, 3:259–285. London: Hogarth Press, 1962.

———— (1900). *The Interpretation of Dreams. Standard Edition*, 4 & 5. London: Hogarth Press, 1953.

———— (1905). *Three Essays on the Theory of Sexuality. Standard Edition*, 7:123–245. London: Hogarth Press, 1953.

———— (1908). Character and anal erotism. *Standard Edition*, 9:167–175. London: Hogarth Press, 1959.

———— (1909). Analysis of a phobia in a five-year-old boy. *Standard Edition*, 10:1–149. London: Hogarth Press, 1955.

———— (1911). Formulations on the two principles of mental functioning. *Standard Edition*, 12:213–226. London: Hogarth Press, 1958.

———— (1912). Recommendations to physicians practicing psychoanalysis. *Standard Edition*, 12:109–120. London: Hogarth Press, 1958.

—— (1914). On narcissism: An Introduction. *Standard Edition*, 14:67–102. London: Hogarth Press, 1957.

—— (1915a). Instincts and their vicissitudes. *Standard Edition*, 14:109–140. London: Hogarth Press, 1957.

—— (1915b). Repression. *Standard Edition*, 14:141–158. London: Hogarth Press, 1957.

—— (1915c). The unconscious. *Standard Edition*, 14:159–215. London: Hogarth Press, 1957.

—— (1915d). Observations on transference-love (Further recommendations on the technique of psycho-analysis III). *Standard Edition*, 12:157–173. London: Hogarth Press, 1958.

—— (1916–1917). *Introductory Lectures on Psycho-Analysis. Standard Edition*, 15 & 16. London: Hogarth Press, 1961 and 1963.

—— (1917a). Mourning and melancholia. *Standard Edition*, 14:237–260. London: Hogarth Press, 1957.

—— (1917b). A difficulty in the path of psycho-analysis. *Standard Edition*, 17:135–144. London: Hogarth Press, 1955.

—— (1920). *Beyond the Pleasure Principle. Standard Edition*, 18:1–64. London: Hogarth Press, 1955.

—— (1921). *Group Psychology and the Analysis of the Ego. Standard Edition*, 18:65–143. London: Hogarth Press, 1955.

—— (1923). *The Ego and the Id. Standard Edition*, 19:1–66. London: Hogarth Press, 1961.

—— (1924a). The economic problem of masochism. *Standard Edition*, 19:155–170. London: Hogarth Press, 1961.

—— (1924b). The dissolution of the Oedipus complex. *Standard Edition*, 19:171–179. London: Hogarth Press, 1961.

—— (1925). Negation. *Standard Edition*, 19:233–239. London: Hogarth Press, 1961.

—— (1926). *Inhibitions, Symptoms and Anxiety. Standard Edition*, 20:75–175. London: Hogarth Press, 1959.

—— (1930). *Civilization and its Discontents. Standard Edition*, 21:57–145. London: Hogarth Press, 1961.

—— (1940a). *An Outline of Psycho-Analysis. Standard Edition*, 23:139–207. London: Hogarth Press, 1964.

—— (1940b). Some elementary lessons in psycho-analysis. *Standard Edition*, 23:279–286. London: Hogarth Press, 1964.

Fukayama, F. (1992). *The End of History and the Last Man*. New York: Macmillan.

Furth, H. (1969). *Piaget and Knowledge*. Englewood Cliffs, NJ: Prentice-Hall.

Gardner, H. (1985). *The Mind's New Science*. New York: Basic Books.

Goethe, J. W. (1790). *Faust* (trans. W. Kaufmann). Garden City, NY: Doubleday/Anchor, 1963.

Goodall, J. (1990). *Through a Window*. Boston: Houghton.

Green, A. (1977). Conceptions of affect. *Internat. J. Psycho-Anal.*, 58:129–156.

Greenacre, P. (1957). The childhood of the artist: Libidinal phase development and giftedness. In: *The Psychoanalytic Study of the Child*, 12:27–72. New York: International Universities Press.

Greenberg, J. & Mitchell, S. (1983). *Object Relations in Psychoanalytic Theory*. Cambridge, MA: Harvard University Press.

Guntrip, H. (1961). *Personality Structure and Human Interaction*. New York: International Universities Press.

Halacy, D. S. (1962). *Computers—The Machines We Think With*. New York: Harper & Row, 1971.

Hampden-Turner, C. (1981). *Maps of the Mind*. New York: Macmillan.

Hartmann, H. (1952). The mutual influences in the development of the ego and the id. In: *Essays on Ego Psychology*. New York: International Universities Press, 1964, pp. 155–182.

——— (1953). Contributions on the metapsychology of schizophrenia. In: *Essays on Ego Psychology*. New York: International Universities Press, 1964, pp. 182–206.

Hendrick, I. (1942). Instinct and the ego during infancy. *Psychoanal. Quart.*, 11:33–58.

——— (1943a). Work and the pleasure principle. *Psychoanal. Quart.*, 12:311–329.

——— (1943b). The discussion of the instinct to master. *Psychoanal. Quart.*, 12:561–565.

Horowitz, M. (1972). Modes of representation of thought. *J. Amer. Psychoanal. Assn.*, 20:793–819.

Huizinga, J. (1938). *Homo Ludens*. Boston: Beacon Press, 1955.

Isaacs, S. (1948). The nature and function of phantasy. *Internat. J. Psycho-Anal.*, 29:73–97.

Izard, C. (1991). *The Psychology of Emotions*. New York: Plenum Press.

——— & Buechler, S. (1980). Aspects of consciousness and personality in terms of differential emotions theory. In: *Theories of Emotion*, ed. R. Plutchik & H. Kellerman. New York: Academic Press, pp. 165–187.

Jacobson, E. (1957). Normal and pathological moods. In: *The Psychoanalytic Study of the Child*, 12:73–113. New York: International Universities Press.

James, W. (1892). *Psychology: Briefer Course*. New York: Henry Holt.

Jonas, H. (1966). *The Phenomenon of Life*. New York: Delta.

Joyce, J. (1922). *Ulysses*. New York: Random House, 1986.

Jung, C. (1946). On the nature of the psyche. In: *The Collected Works of C. G. Jung, Vol. 8,* ed. H. Read, M. Fordham & C. Adler. New York: Pantheon, 1960, pp. 159–234.

——— (1948). The Self. In: *The Collected Works of C. G. Jung, Vol. 9,* Part II, ed. H. Read, M. Fordham & C. Adler. New York: Pantheon, 1959, pp. 23–35.

Kaufmann, W. (1961). *The Faith of a Heretic*. Garden City, NY: Doubleday/New American Library, 1978.

Keller, H. (1902). *The Story of My Life*. Garden City, NY: Doubleday, 1954.

Kernberg, O. (1982). Self, ego, affects, and drives. *J. Amer. Psychoanal. Assn.*, 30:893–917.

Klein, D. B. (1970). *A History of Scientific Psychology*. New York: Basic Books.

Kohut, H. (1977). *The Restoration of the Self*. New York: International Universities Press.

Konner, M. (1982). *The Tangled Wing*. New York: Holt, Rinehart & Winston.

Krystal, H. (1988). *Integration and Self-Healing*. Hillsdale, NJ: The Analytic Press.

Lansky, M. (1992). *Fathers Who Fail*. Hillsdale, NJ: The Analytic Press.

Laplanche, J. & Pontalis, J. D. (1967). *The Language of Psychoanalysis* (trans. D. Nicholson-Smith). New York: Norton.

Lazarus, R., Kanner, A. & Folkman, S. (1980). Emotions: A cognitive-phenomenological analysis. In: *Theories of Emotion*, ed. R. Plutchik & H. Kellerman. New York: Academic Press, pp. 189–217.

Lear, J. (1990). *Love and Its Place in Nature*. New York: Farrar, Straus & Giroux.

Lewis, M. & Brooks-Gunn, J. (1979). *Social Cognition and the Acquisition of Self*. New York: Plenum.

Lichtenberg, J. (1983). *Psychoanalysis and Infant Research*. Hillsdale, NJ: The Analytic Press.

────── (1989). *Psychoanalysis and Motivation*. Hillsdale, NJ: The Analytic Press.

Locke, J. (1690). *An Essay Concerning Human Understanding,* abridged and ed. A. Woozley. London: Collins, 1964.

Lorenz, K. (1966). *On Aggression*. New York: Bantam Books.

MacLean, P. (1949). Psychosomatic disease and the "visceral brain": Recent developments bearing on the Papez theory of emotions. *Psychosom. Med.*, 11:338–353.

────── (1952). Some psychiatric implications of physiological studies on frontotemporal portion of limbic system (visceral brain). *EEG Clin. Neurophysiol.* 4:407–418.

Mahler, M., Pine, F. & Bergman, A. (1975). *The Psychological Birth of the Human Infant*. New York: Basic Books.

Mandler, G. (1980). The generation of emotion: A psychological theory. In: *Theories of Emotion*, ed. R. Plutchik & H. Kellerman. New York: Academic Press, pp. 219–243.

Mason, W. & Kinney, M. (1974). Redirection of filial attachments in rhesus monkeys: Dogs as mother surrogates. *Science*, 183:1209–1211.

Masson, J. M., ed. & trans. (1985). *The Complete Letters of Sigmund Freud to Wilhelm Fliess: 1887–1904*. Cambridge, MA: Belknap Press.

McDevitt, J. B. (1972). Libidinal object constancy: Some developmental considerations. Presented at New York Psychoanalytic Society. New York, January.

Morrison, A. (1989). *Shame: The Underside of Narcissism.* Hillsdale, NJ: The Analytic Press.

Ogden, T. (1986). *The Matrix of the Mind.* Northvale, NJ: Aronson.

O'Neill, E. (1925). *The Great God Brown.* In: *The Plays of Eugene O'Neill,* 3 vols. New York: Random House, 1954.

Panel (1985). A reexamination of the concept of "object" in psychoanalysis (D. A. Goldberg, reporter). *J. Amer. Psychoanal. Assn.,* 33:167–185.

Papousek, H. & Papousek, M. (1975). Cognitive aspects of preverbal social interaction between human infants and adults. Ciba Foundation Symposium. *Parent–Infant Interaction.* New York: Assn. Scientific Pubs.

Parens, H. (1979). *The Development of Aggression in Early Childhood.* New York: Aronson.

Petitto, L. & Marentette, P. (1991). Babbling in the manual mode: Evidence for the ontogeny of language. *Science,* 251:1493–1496.

Piaget, J. & Inhelder, B. (1969). *The Psychology of the Child.* New York: Basic Books.

Piers, G. & Singer, M. (1953). *Shame and Guilt.* Springfield, IL: Chas. C. Thomas.

Plutchik, R. (1980). A general psychoevolutionary theory of emotion. In: *Theories of Emotion,* ed. R. Plutchik & H. Kellerman. New York: Academic Press, pp. 3–33.

——— & Kellerman, H., eds. (1980a). *Theories of Emotion.* New York: Academic Press.

——— & ——— (1980b). Introduction. In: *Theories of Emotion,* ed. R. Plutchik & H. Kellerman. New York: Academic Press, pp. xv–xxi.

Pribram, K. (1971). *Languages of the Brain.* Englewood Cliffs, NJ: Prentice-Hall.

Psychoanalytic Terms and Concepts, ed. B. Moore & B. Fine (1990). New Haven, CT: American Psychoanalytic Assn. & Yale University Press.

Random House Dictionary of the English Language: Unabridged Edition (1966). New York: Random House.

Rangell, L. (1972). Aggression, Oedipus, and historical perspective (presidential address). *Internat. J. Psycho-Anal.,* 53:3–11.

Rapaport, D. (1953). On the psychoanalytic theory of affects. In: *The Collected Papers of David Rapaport,* ed. M. Gill. New York: Basic Books, 1967, pp. 476–512.

Riesmann, D. (1961). *The Lonely Crowd.* New Haven, CT: Yale University Press.

Rorty, R. (1989). *Contingency, Irony, and Solidarity.* Cambridge: Cambridge University Press.

Russell, B. (1945). *A History of Western Philosophy.* New York: Simon & Schuster.

——— & Whitehead, A. (1910). *Principia Mathematica.* Cambridge: Cambridge University Press, 1962.

Ryle, G. (1949). *The Concept of Mind*. New York: Barnes & Noble.

Sackett, G. (1966). Monkeys reared in isolation with pictures as visual impact: Evidence for an innate releasing mechanism. *Science*, 154:1468–1473.

Sacks, O. (1989). *Seeing Voices*. Berkeley: University of California Press.

Sander, L. (1983). Polarity, paradox, and the organizing process in development. In: *Frontiers of Infant Psychiatry*, ed. J. D. Call, E. Galenson & R. Tyson. New York: Basic Books, pp. 315–327.

Sandler, J. & Rosenblatt, B. (1962). The concept of the representational world. *The Psychoanalytic Study of the Child*, 17:128–145. New York: International Universities Press.

Scarr, S. & Salapatek, P. (1970). Patterns of fear development during infancy. *Merrill-Palmer Quart.*, 16:53–90.

Schafer, R. (1964). The clinical analysis of affects. *J. Amer. Psychoanal. Assn.*, 12:275–299.

Schaffer, H. & Callender, W. (1959). Psychological effects of hospitalization in infancy. *Pediatrics*, 24:528–539.

Schimek, J. G. (1975). A critical re-examination of Freud's concept of unconscious mental representation. *Internat. Rev. Psycho-Anal.*, 2:171–187.

Schulman, A. H. & Kaplowitz, C. (1977). Mirror-image response during the first two years of life. *Devel. Psychol.*, 10:133–142.

Searle, J. (1992). *The Rediscovery of the Mind*. Cambridge, MA: MIT Press/Bradford.

Segal, H. (1964). *Introduction to the Work of Melanie Klein*. London: Heinemann/Medical.

Shapiro, D. (1965). *Neurotic Styles*. New York: Basic Books.

Sharpless, E. (1985). Identity formation as reflected in the acquisition of personal pronouns. *J. Amer. Psychoanal. Assn.*, 33:861–865.

Spitz, R. A. (1959). *A Genetic Field Theory of Ego Formation*. New York: International Universities Press.

——— (1965). *The First Year of Life*. New York: International Universities Press.

——— (1967). *No and Yes*. New York: International Universities Press.

——— & Wolf, M. (1946). Anaclitic depression: An inquiry into the genesis of psychiatric conditions in early childhood, II. *The Psychoanalytic Study of the Child*, 2:313–342. New York: International Universities Press.

Sroufe, L. A. (1982). The organization of emotional development. *Psychoanal. Inq.*, 1:575–600.

Stern, D. (1985). *The Interpersonal World of the Infant*. New York: Basic Books.

Stolorow, R. & Atwood, G. (1992). *Contexts of Being*. Hillsdale, NJ: The Analytic Press.

────── & Stolorow, D. (1987). Affects and selfobjects. In: *Psychoanalytic Treatment*, by R. Stolorow, B. Brandchaft & G. Atwood. Hillsdale, NJ: The Analytic Press, pp. 66–87.

Stone, L. (1971). Reflections on the psychoanalytic concept of aggression. *Psychoanal. Quart.*, 40:195–244.

Strachey, J. (1957a). Editor's introduction to "Papers on metapsychology." *Standard Edition*, 14:105–107. London: Hogarth Press.

────── (1957b). Editor's note to "Mourning and melancholia." *Standard Edition*, 14:239–242. London: Hogarth Press.

────── (1959). Editor's introduction to *Inhibitions, Symptoms and Anxiety*. *Standard Edition*, 20:77–86. London: Hogarth Press.

────── (1962a). The emergence of Freud's fundamental hypotheses. *Standard Edition*, 3:62–68. London: Hogarth Press.

────── (1962b). The term *"Angst"* and its English translation. *Standard Edition*, 3:116–117. London: Hogarth Press.

────── (1966a). Notes on some technical terms whose translation calls for comment. *Standard Edition*, 1:xxiii–xxvi. London: Hogarth Press.

────── (1966b). Editor's introduction to the "Project for a scientific psychology." *Standard Edition*, 1:283–293. London: Hogarth Press.

Taylor, C. (1984). Philosophy and its history. In: *Philosophy in History*, ed. R. Rorty, J. B. Schneewind & Q. Skinner. Cambridge: Cambridge University Press.

Tomkins, S. (1962). *Affect, Imagery, Consciousness, Vol. I*. New York: Springer.

────── (1963). *Affect, Imagery, Consciousness, Vol. II*. New York: Springer.

────── (1980). Affect as amplification: Some modifications in theory. In: *Theories of Emotion*, ed. R. Plutchik & H. Kellerman. New York: Academic Press, pp. 141–164.

Vygotsky, L. S. (1934). *Thought and Language* (trans. anon.). Cambridge, MA: MIT Press, 1989.

Watson, J. S. (1972). Smiling, cooing, and ". . . the game." *Merrill-Palmer Quart.*, 18:323–340.

Webster's Deluxe Unabridged Dictionary (1979). New York: Simon & Schuster.

White, R. (1959). Motivation reconsidered: The concept of competence. *Psychol. Rev.*, 66:297–333.

Winnicott, D. W. (1960a). Ego distortion in terms of true and false self. In: *The Maturational Processes and the Facilitating Environment*. New York: International Universities Press, 1965, pp. 140–152.

────── (1960b). Counter-transference. In: *The Maturational Processes and the Facilitating Environment*. New York: International Universities Press, 1965, pp. 158–165.

Wittgenstein, L. (1945). *Philosophical Investigations* (trans. G. E. M. Anscombe). Oxford: Basil Blackwell, 1953.

Wolff, P. (1960). *The Developmental Psychologies of Jean Piaget and Psychoanalysis. Psychological Issues*, Monogr. 5. New York: International Universities Press.

———— (1966). *The Causes, Controls, and Organization of Behavior in the Neonate. Psychological Issues*, Monogr. 17. New York: International Universities Press.

Zetzel, E. R. (1965). Depression and the incapacity to bear it. In: *Drives, Affects, and Behavior, Vol. 2,* ed. M. Schur. New York: International Universities Press, pp. 243–274.

Index

261